Barclay on the Lectionary
Mark: Year B

THE NEW DAILY STUDY BIBLE

The Gospel of Matthew Vol. 1
The Gospel of Matthew Vol. 2
The Gospel of Mark
The Gospel of Luke
The Gospel of John Vol. 1
The Gospel of John Vol. 2
The Acts of the Apostles
The Letter to the Romans
The Letters to the Corinthians
The Letters to the Galatians and the Ephesians
The Letters to the Philippians, Colossians and Thessalonians
The Letters to Timothy, Titus and Philemon
The Letter to the Hebrews
The Letters of James and Peter
The Letters of John and Jude
The Revelation of John Vol. 1
The Revelation of John Vol. 2

Barclay on the Lectionary

Mark: Year B

William Barclay

SAINT ANDREW PRESS

Edinburgh

First published in 2014 by
SAINT ANDREW PRESS
121 George Street
Edinburgh EH2 4YN

ISBN 978 0 86153 797 6

British Library Cataloguing in Publication Date
A catalogue record for this book is available from the British Library.

It is the publisher's policy to only use papers that are natural and recy-
clable and that have been manufactured from timber grown in renew-
able, properly managed forests. All of the manufacturing processes of the
papers are expected to conform to the environmental regulations of the
country of origin.

Typeset by Manila Typesetting Company
Printed in the United Kingdom by
CPI Group (UK) Ltd, Croydon

Contents

Publisher's Introduction — ix

The First Sunday of Advent — 1
The Second Sunday of Advent — 7
The Third Sunday of Advent — 13
The Fourth Sunday of Advent — 17
The First Sunday of Christmas — 22
The Second Sunday of Christmas — 26
The First Sunday of Epiphany (The Baptism of Christ) — 32
The Second Sunday of Epiphany — 36
The Third Sunday of Epiphany — 42
The Fourth Sunday of Epiphany — 48
The Sunday between 3 and 9 February — 54
The Sunday between 10 and 16 February — 60
The Sunday between 17 and 23 February — 65
The Second Sunday before Lent — 70
The Sunday next before Lent — 75
The First Sunday of Lent — 80
The Second Sunday of Lent — 85
The Third Sunday of Lent — 90
The Fourth Sunday of Lent — 96
The Fifth Sunday of Lent — 101
Palm Sunday — 105

Easter Day   110
The Second Sunday of Easter   115
The Third Sunday of Easter   121
The Fourth Sunday of Easter   126
The Fifth Sunday of Easter   131
The Sixth Sunday of Easter   137
The Seventh Sunday of Easter   143
Pentecost   148
Trinity Sunday   153
The Sunday between 29 May and 4 June   159
The Sunday between 5 and 11 June   165
The Sunday between 12 and 18 June   172
The Sunday between 19 and 25 June   177
The Sunday between 26 June and 2 July   182
The Sunday between 3 and 9 July   187
The Sunday between 10 and 16 July   193
The Sunday between 17 and 23 July   198
The Sunday between 24 and 30 July   203
The Sunday between 31 July and 6 August   209
The Sunday between 7 and 13 August   215
The Sunday between 14 and 20 August   221
The Sunday between 21 and 27 August   226
The Sunday between 28 August and 3 September   231
The Sunday between 4 and 10 September   237
The Sunday between 11 and 17 September   243
The Sunday between 18 and 24 September   248
The Sunday between 25 September and 1 October   253
The Sunday between 2 and 8 October   258
The Sunday between 9 and 15 October   263
The Sunday between 16 and 22 October   269

The Sunday between 23 and 29 October   275

The Last Sunday after Trinity (Bible Sunday)   281

The Fourth Sunday before Advent   286

The Third Sunday before Advent   292

The Second Sunday before Advent   297

The Sunday next before Advent   303

Publisher's Introduction

William Barclay was a biblical scholar who possessed a remarkable gift of communication. His belief that the results of biblical scholarship should not be the preserve of academics but should be made available and accessible to the ordinary reader resulted in the now famous series of commentaries, *The Daily Study Bible*.

Those commentaries are full of colourful stories and numerous quotations from poetry and hymnody which bring the text alive, but Barclay was not afraid to challenge the reader by going straightforwardly and fascinatingly into more academic topics. His talent for enthralling communication enabled him to delve in a highly accessible way into the root of language and explain the meaning of the original Greek words or explore the complex background of Judaism and the Roman world.

William Barclay was Professor of Biblical Criticism, but he was also a minister of the Church of Scotland and he makes it very clear in his Introduction to the series that the primary aim of *The Daily Study Bible* series has never been academic. He explains that the aim 'could be summed up in the famous words of Richard of Chichester's prayer – to enable men and women to know Jesus Christ more clearly, to love him more dearly, and to follow him more nearly'.

It is therefore appropriate that William Barclay's commentary, now taken from *The New Daily Study Bible* (revised in c. 2001), should be set alongside the readings from the Common Worship Lectionary, offering readers a chance to engage with Barclay's unique guide to reading the scriptures in a new pattern of daily readings.

The readings in *Barclay on the Lectionary* are those chosen for the Principal Sunday services and, as the Lectionary follows a three-year cycle, with concentration each year on the readings in one particular Gospel, readers have the opportunity to follow a single narrative throughout the year. In this volume, *Barclay on the Lectionary* follows Year B – the Gospel of Mark. In other volumes, Year A (the Gospel of Matthew) and Year C (the Gospel of Luke – to be published in 2015) are followed. In each volume, some readings from John's Gospel are also included.

As you read, you may develop a wish to engage further with Barclay's writing. It should be remembered that when Barclay wrote he was not following any lectionary but working his way through each book of the New Testament in sequence. So, in a few cases, you will find that his commentary is relatively brief and, in many more instances it has been necessary to edit texts to accommodate a more uniform length for each day's selection. However, those who wish to see the full commentary (which often includes more examples and stories used as illustration or further examination of a particular passage) and take exploration further can turn to the full text in *The New Daily Study Bible* series.

In bringing together commentary and lectionary in this way, it is hoped that new readers will discover William Barclay's special ways of drawing meaning from the biblical text, and that those already familiar with his work will find new inspiration for their Bible reading, so fulfilling his own expressed prayer that 'God will continue to use *The Daily Study Bible* to enable men and women better to understand his word'.

The First Sunday of Advent
The Necessity of Thanksgiving *and* His Coming Again
1 Corinthians 1:3–9

In this passage of thanksgiving, three things stand out.

(1) There is the promise which came true. When Paul preached Christianity to the Corinthians, he told them that Christ could do certain things for them, and now he proudly claims that all that he pledged that Christ could do has come true. A missionary told one of the ancient Scottish kings: 'If you will accept Christ, you will find wonder upon wonder – and every one of them true.' In the last analysis, we cannot argue anyone into Christianity; we can only say: 'Try it and see what happens,' in the certainty that, if that challenge is taken up, the claims we make for it will all come true.

(2) There is the gift which has been given. Paul here uses a favourite word of his. It is *charisma*, which means a gift freely given to someone, a gift which was not deserved and which could never have been earned by that individual's own efforts. This gift of God, as Paul saw it, comes in two ways.

(a) Salvation is the *charisma* of God. To enter into a right relationship with God is something which we could never achieve ourselves. It is an unearned gift, coming from the sheer generosity of the love of God (cf. Romans 6:23).

(b) It gives to each of us whatever special gifts we may possess and whatever special equipment we may have for life (1 Corinthians 12:4–10; 1 Timothy 4:14; 1 Peter 4:10). If we have the gift of speech or the gift of healing, if we have the gift of music or of any art, if we have the gift to use our hands creatively, all these are gifts from God. If we fully realized that, it would bring a new atmosphere and character into life.

Such skills as we possess are not our own achievement; they are gifts from God, and, therefore, they are held in trust. They are to be used not as *we* want to use them but as *God* wants us to use them; not for our profit or prestige but for the glory of God and the good of all.

(3) There is the ultimate end. In the Old Testament, the phrase *the day* of *the Lord* keeps recurring. It was the day when the Jews expected God to break directly into history, the day when the old world would be wiped out and the new world born, the day when everyone would be judged. The Christians took over this idea, only they took *the day of the Lord* in the sense of *the day of the Lord Jesus*, and regarded it as the day on which Jesus would come back in all his power and glory.

That indeed would be a day of judgement. Caedmon, the eighth-century English saint and poet, drew a picture in one of his poems about the day of judgement. He imagined the cross set in the centre of the world; and from the cross there streamed a strange light which had a penetrating X-ray quality about it and stripped the disguises from things and showed them as they were. It is Paul's belief that, when the ultimate judgement comes, those who are in Christ can meet even that unafraid, because they will be clothed not in their own merits but in the merits of Christ so that no one will be able to impeach them.

Mark 13:24–37

Here Jesus unmistakably speaks of his coming again. But – and this is important – he clothes the idea in three pictures which are part and parcel of the apparatus connected with the day of the Lord.

The Jews never doubted that they were the chosen people, and they never doubted that one day they would occupy the place in the world which the chosen people, as they saw it, deserved and were bound to have in the end. They had long since abandoned the idea that they could ever win that place by human means, and they were confident that in the end God would directly intervene in history and win it for them. The day of God's intervention was *the day of the Lord*. Before that day of the Lord, there would be a time of terror and trouble when the world would be shaken to its foundations and judgement would come. But it would be followed by the new world and the new age and the new glory.

In one sense, this idea is the product of unconquerable optimism. The Jews were quite certain that God would break in. In another sense, it was the product of bleak *pessimism*, because it was based on the idea that this world was so utterly bad that only its complete destruction and the emergence of a new world would suffice. They did not look for reformation. They looked for a re-creating of the entire scheme of things.

(1) The day of the Lord was to be preceded by the darkening of sun and moon. The Old Testament itself is full of that (Amos 8:9; Joel 2:10, 3:15; Ezekiel 32:7–8; Isaiah 13:10, 34:4); again the popular literature of Jesus' day is full of it, too.

> And the sun shall suddenly begin to shine at night,
> And the moon during the day,
> . . .
> and the stars shall fall. (4 Ezra [2 Esdras] 5:4–5)

Second Baruch 32:1 speaks of 'the time in which the mighty one is to shake the whole creation'. The Assumption of Moses foresees a time when:

> The horns of the sun shall be broken and he shall be turned into darkness,
> And the moon shall not give her light, and be turned wholly into blood,
> And the circle of the stars shall be disturbed. (10:5)

It is clear that Jesus is using the popular language which everyone knew.

(2) It was a regular part of the imagery that the Jews were to be gathered back to Palestine from the four corners of the earth. The Old Testament itself is full of that idea (Isaiah 27:13, 35:8–10; Micah 7:12; Zechariah 10:6–11); once more the popular literature loves the idea:

> Blow ye in Zion on the trumpet to summon the saints,
> Cause ye to be heard in Jerusalem the voice of him that bringeth good tidings,
> For God hath had pity on Israel in visiting them.
> Stand on the height, O Jerusalem, and behold thy children,
> From the East and the West gathered together by the Lord.
> (Psalms of Solomon 11:1–3)

> The Lord will gather you together in faith through His tender mercy, and for the sake of Abraham and Isaac and Jacob.
> (The Testament of Asher 7:7)

Jesus was working with the only ideas that people knew. But he knew, as they knew, that these things were only pictures, for no one could really tell what would happen when God broke in.

There are three special things to note about verses 28–37.

(1) It is sometimes held that when Jesus said that these things were to happen within this generation he was in error. But Jesus was right, for this sentence does not refer to the second coming. It could not when the next sentence says he does not know when that day will be. It refers to Jesus' prophecies about the fall of Jerusalem and the destruction of the Temple, and they were abundantly fulfilled.

(2) Jesus says that he does not know the day or the hour when he will come again. There were things which even he left without questioning in the hand of God. There can be no greater warning and rebuke to those who work out dates and timetables as to when he will come again. Surely it is nothing less than blasphemy for us to inquire into that of which our Lord consented to be ignorant.

(3) Jesus draws a practical conclusion. We are like those who know that their master will come, but who do not know when. We live in the shadow of eternity. That is no reason for fearful and hysterical expectation. But it means that day by day our work must be completed. It means that we must so live that it does not matter when he comes. It gives us the great task of making every day fit for him to see and being at any moment ready to meet him face to face. All life becomes a preparation to meet the King.

Chapter 13 of Mark's Gospel is a difficult chapter, but in the end it has permanent truth to tell us. It tells us that only God's people can see into the secrets of history. Jesus saw the fate of Jerusalem although others were blind to it. Leaders of real stature must be men and women of God. To guide any country its leaders must be themselves God-guided. Only those who know God can enter into something of the plan of God.

It tells us two things about the doctrine of the second coming. (a) It tells us that it contains a fact we forget or disregard at our peril. (b) It tells us that the imagery in which it is clothed is the imagery of Jesus' own time, and that to speculate on it is useless, when Jesus himself was content not to know. The one thing of which we can be sure is that history is going somewhere; there is a consummation to come.

It tells us that of all things to forget God and to become immersed in material concerns is most foolish. The truly wise never forget that they must be ready when the summons comes. For those who live in that memory, the end will not be terror, but eternal joy.

(For discussion of verses 1–8 and the prophecies about Jerusalem, see The Second Sunday before Advent, pp. 299–302.)

The Second Sunday of Advent
The Mercy of God's Delay *and*
The Beginning of the Story

2 Peter 3:8–15a

Here we find three great truths which can nourish the mind and bring rest to the heart.

(1) Time is not the same to God as it is to us. As the psalmist had it: 'For a thousand years in your sight are like yesterday when it is past, or like a watch in the night' (Psalm 90:4). When we think of the world's hundreds of thousands of years of existence, it is easy to feel dwarfed into insignificance; when we think of the slowness of human progress, it is easy to become discouraged into pessimism. There is comfort in the thought of a God who has all eternity to work in. It is only against the background of eternity that things appear in their true proportions and assume their real value.

(2) We can also see from this passage that time is always to be regarded as an opportunity. As Peter saw it, the years God gave the world were a further opportunity for men and women to repent and turn to him. Every day which comes to us is a gift of mercy. It is an opportunity to develop ourselves, to render some service to our neighbours, to take one step nearer to God.

(3) There is another echo of a truth which so often lies in the background of New Testament thought. God, says Peter, does not want anyone to perish. God, says Paul, has shut them all up together in unbelief, that he might have mercy on all (Romans 11:32). Timothy, in a tremendous phrase, speaks of God who desires everyone to be saved (1 Timothy 2:4).

Time after time, we see in Scripture the glint of the larger hope. We are not forbidden to believe that somehow and at some time the God who loves the world will bring the whole world to himself.

It is always the case that we have to speak and think in the terms which we know. That is what Peter is doing here. He is speaking of the New Testament teaching of the second coming of Jesus Christ, but he is describing it in terms of the Old Testament teaching of the day of the Lord.

The day of the Lord is a concept which runs all through the prophetic books of the Old Testament. The Jews saw time in terms of two ages – *this present age*, which is wholly bad and beyond remedy, and *the age to come*, which is the golden age of God. The change from one to the other could not come about by human effort but by the direct intervention of God. The Jews called the time of that intervention the day of the Lord. It was to come without warning. It was to be a time when the universe was shaken to its foundations. It was to be a time when the judgement and obliteration of sinners would come to pass, and therefore it would be a time of terror. 'See, the day of the Lord comes, cruel, with wrath and fierce anger, to make the earth a desolation, and to destroy its sinners from it' (Isaiah 13:9). 'For the day of the Lord is coming, it is near – a day of darkness and gloom, a day of clouds and thick darkness' (Joel 2:1–2). 'I will make the heavens tremble, and the earth will be shaken out of its place, at the wrath of the Lord of hosts on the day of his fierce anger' (Isaiah 13:10–13).

Peter's picture here of the second coming of Jesus is drawn in terms of the Old Testament picture of the day of the Lord. We need not take these pictures absolutely literally. It is enough to note that Peter sees the second coming as a time of terror for those who are the enemies of Christ.

The whole concept of the second coming is full of difficulties. But this is certain – there comes a day when God breaks into every life, for there comes a day when we must die; and for that day we must be prepared. We may say what we will about the coming of Christ as a future event; we may feel it is a doctrine we have to lay aside; but we cannot escape from the certainty of the entry of God into our own experience.

There is in this passage yet another great concept. Peter speaks of Christians as not only eagerly awaiting the coming of Christ but as actually hastening it on. The New Testament tells us certain ways in which this may be done.

(1) It may be done by *prayer*. Jesus taught us to pray: 'Your kingdom come' (Matthew 6:10). The earnest prayer of the Christian heart hastens the coming of the King. If in no other way, it does so in this – that those who pray open their own hearts for the entry of the King.

(2) It may be done by *preaching*. Matthew tells us that Jesus said: 'And this good news of the kingdom will be proclaimed throughout the world, as a testimony to all the nations; and then the end will come' (Matthew 24:14). Everyone must be given the chance to know and to love Jesus Christ before the end of creation is reached. The missionary activity of the Church is the hastening of the coming of the King.

(3) It may be done by *penitence* and *obedience*. Of all things, this would be nearest to Peter's mind and heart. The Rabbis had a saying: 'If Israel would perfectly keep the law for one day, the Messiah would come.' In true penitence and in real obedience, men and women open their own hearts to the coming of the King and bring nearer that coming throughout the world. We do well to remember that our coldness of heart and our disobedience delay the coming of the King.

Mark 1:1–8

Mark starts the story of Jesus a long way back. It did not begin with Jesus' birth; it did not even begin with John the Baptizer in the wilderness; it began with the dreams of the prophets long ago; that is to say, it began long, long ago in the mind of God.

The Stoics were strong believers in the ordered plan of God. 'The things of God', said Marcus Aurelius, 'are full of foresight. All things flow from heaven.' There are things we may well learn here.

(1) It has been said that 'the thoughts of youth are long, long thoughts', and so are the thoughts of God. God is characteristically a God who is working his purposes out. History is not a random kaleidoscope of disconnected events; it is a process directed by the God who sees the end in the beginning.

(2) We are within that process, and because of that we can either help or hinder it. In one sense it is as great an honour to help in some great process as it is a privilege to see the ultimate goal. Life would be very different if, instead of yearning for some distant and at present unattainable goal, we did all that we could to bring that goal nearer. The goal will never be reached unless there are those who labour to make it possible.

The prophetic quotation which Mark uses is suggestive. *I send my messenger before you and he will prepare your road for you.* This is from Malachi 3:1. In its original context it is a threat. In Malachi's day the priests were failing in their duty. The offerings were blemished and shoddy second-bests; the service of the Temple was a weariness to them. The messenger was *to cleanse and purify* the worship of the Temple before the Anointed One of God emerged upon the earth. So then the coming of Christ was a *purification of life*. And the world needed that purification.

John came announcing a *baptism of repentance*. Jews were familiar with ritual washings. Leviticus 11–15 details them. Symbolic washing and purifying was woven into the very fabric of Jewish ritual. Gentiles were necessarily unclean for they had never kept any part of the Jewish law. Therefore, when a Gentile became a *proselyte*, that is a convert to the Jewish faith, he had to undergo three things. First, he had to undergo *circumcision*, for that was the mark of the covenant people; second, *sacrifice* had to be made for him, for he stood in need of atonement and only blood could atone for sin; third, he had to undergo *baptism*, which symbolized cleansing from all the pollution of his past life. Naturally, therefore, the baptism was not a mere sprinkling with water, but a bath in which the whole body was bathed. Jews knew baptism; but the amazing thing about John's baptism was that he, a Jew, was asking Jews to submit to that which only a Gentile was supposed to need. John had made the tremendous discovery that to be a Jew in the racial sense was not to be a member of God's chosen people; a Jew might be in exactly the same position as a Gentile; not the Jewish life, but the cleansed life belonged to God.

It is clear that the ministry of John was mightily effective, for they flocked out to listen to him and to submit to his baptism.

(1) His message was effective because he told people what in their heart of hearts they knew and brought them what in the depths of their souls they were waiting for.

(a) When John summoned men and women to repentance he was confronting them with a decision that they knew in their heart of hearts they ought to make. Long ago Plato said that education did not consist in telling people new things but in extracting from their memories what they already knew. No message is so effective as that which speaks to a person's own conscience, and that message becomes well-nigh irresistible when it is spoken by someone who obviously has the right to speak.

(b) The people of Israel were well aware that for 300 years the voice of prophecy had been silent. They were waiting for some authentic word from God. And in John they heard it. In every walk of life the expert is recognizable. We recognize at once a doctor who has real skill. We recognize at once speakers who know their subject. John had come from God, and to hear him was to know it.

(2) His message was effective because he was completely humble. His own verdict on himself was that he was not fit for the duty of

a slave. Sandals were composed simply of leather soles fastened to the foot by straps passing through the toes. The roads were unsurfaced. In dry weather they were dust-heaps; in wet weather rivers of mud. To remove the sandals was the work and office of a slave. John asked nothing for himself but everything for the Christ whom he proclaimed. The man's obvious self-forgottenness, his patent yieldedness, his complete self-effacement, his utter lostness in his message compelled people to listen.

(3) His message was effective because he pointed to something and someone beyond himself. He told men and women that his baptism drenched them in water, but one was coming who would drench them in the Holy Spirit; and while water could cleanse the body, the Holy Spirit could cleanse a person's life and self and heart. John's one aim was not to occupy the centre of the stage himself, but to try to connect men and women with the one who was greater and stronger than he; and they listened to him because he pointed, not to himself, but to the one whom we all need.

The Third Sunday of Advent
Advice to a Church *and* The Witness of John

1 Thessalonians 5:16–24

Paul ends this letter with a chain of jewels of good advice. He sets them out in the most concise way; but every one is of such value that every Christian should ponder it. Verses 16–18 give us three marks of a genuine church.

(1) It is *a happy church*. There is in it that atmosphere of joy which makes its members feel that they are bathed in sunshine. True Christianity is exhilarating, not depressing.

(2) It is *a praying church*. Maybe our church's prayers would be more effective if we remembered that 'they pray best together who also pray alone'.

(3) It is *a thankful church*. There is always something for which to give thanks; even on the darkest day, there are blessings to count. We must remember that, if we face the sun, the shadows will fall behind us; but, if we turn our backs on the sun, all the shadows will be in front.

In verses 19–20, Paul warns the Thessalonians not to despise spiritual gifts. The prophets were really the equivalent of our modern preachers. It was they who brought the message of God to the congregation. Paul is really saying: 'If people have anything to say, don't stop them saying it.'

Verses 21–2 describe the constant duty of Christians. They must use Christ as the standard by which to test all things, and even when it is hard they must keep on doing the fine thing and hold themselves apart from every kind of evil. When a church lives up to

Paul's advice, it will indeed shine like a light in a dark place; it will have joy within itself and power to win others.

Finally, Paul commends his friends to God in body, soul and spirit.

John 1:6–8, 19–28

The deputation which came to interview John could think of three things that John might claim to be.

(1) They asked him if he was the Messiah. The Jews were waiting, and are waiting to this day, for the Messiah. There was no one idea of the Messiah. Some people expected one who would bring peace over all the earth. Some expected one who would bring in the reign of righteousness. Most expected one who would be a great national champion to lead the armies of the Jews as conquerors over all the world. Some expected a supernatural figure straight from God. Still more expected a prince to rise from David's line. Frequently, messianic pretenders arose and caused rebellions. The time of Jesus was an excited age. It was natural to ask John if he claimed to be the Messiah. John completely rejected that claim; but he rejected it with a certain hint. In the Greek, the word *I* is stressed by its position. It is as if John said: '*I* am not the Messiah; but, if you only knew, the Messiah is here.'

(2) They asked him if he was Elijah. It was the Jewish belief that, before the Messiah came, Elijah would return to herald his coming and to prepare the world to receive him. Particularly, Elijah was to come to arrange all disputes. He would settle what things and what people were clean and unclean; he would bring together again families which were estranged. So much did the Jews believe this that the traditional law said that money and property whose owners were disputed, or anything found whose owner was unknown, must wait 'until Elijah comes'. This belief, that Elijah would come

before the Messiah, goes back to Malachi 4:5. It was even believed that Elijah would anoint the Messiah to his kingly office, as all kings were anointed, and that he would raise the dead to share in the new kingdom; but John denied that any such honour was his.

(3) They asked him if he was the expected and promised prophet. It was sometimes believed that Isaiah and, especially, Jeremiah would return at the coming of the Messiah. But this is really a reference to the assurance which Moses gave to the people in Deuteronomy 18:15: 'The Lord your God will raise up for you a prophet like me from among your own people; you shall heed such a prophet.' That was a promise that no Jew ever forgot. They waited and longed for the emergence of the prophet who would be the greatest of all prophets, *the Prophet par excellence*. But once again John denied that this honour was his.

So they asked him who he was; his answer was that he was nothing but a voice bidding men and women prepare the way for the King. The quotation is from Isaiah 40:3. All the gospels cite it (Mark 1:3; Matthew 3:3; Luke 3:4). The idea behind it is this. The roads of Palestine were mere tracks. When a king was about to visit a province, when a conqueror was about to travel through his domains, the roads were smoothed and straightened out and put in order. What John was saying was: 'I am nobody; I am only a voice telling you to get ready for the coming of the King, for he is on the way.' John was what every true preacher and teacher ought to be – only a voice, a pointer to the King. The last thing that he wanted anyone to do was to look at him; he wanted people to forget him and see only the King.

But the Pharisees were puzzled about one thing – what right had John to baptize? If he had been the Messiah, or even Elijah or the prophet, he might have baptized. Ezekiel had said: 'I will sprinkle clean water upon you, and you shall be clean' (Ezekiel 36:25). Zechariah had said: 'On that day a fountain shall be opened for the house of David and the inhabitants of Jerusalem, to cleanse them from sin and impurity' (Zechariah 13:1). But why should John baptize?

What made the matter still more strange was this. This kind of baptism was not for Israelites at all. It was *proselytes*, incomers from other faiths, who were baptized. Israelites were never baptized; they were God's already and did not need to be washed. But *Gentiles* had to be washed in baptism. John was making Israelites do what only Gentiles had to do. He was suggesting that *the chosen people had to be cleansed*. That was indeed precisely what John believed. But he did not answer directly.

He said: 'I am baptizing only with water; but there is one among you – you don't recognize him – and I am not worthy to untie the straps of his shoes.' John could not have cited a more menial office. To untie the straps of sandals was slaves' work. There was a Rabbinic saying which said that a disciple might do for his master anything that a servant did, *except* only to untie his sandals. That was too menial a service for even a disciple to render. So John said: 'One is coming whose slave I am not fit to be.' We are to understand that by this time the baptism of Jesus had taken place at which John had recognized Jesus. So here John is saying again: 'The King is coming. And, for his coming, you need to be cleansed as much as any Gentile. Prepare yourself for the entry into history of the King.'

John's function was to be only the preparer of the way. Any greatness he had came from the greatness of the one whose coming he foretold. He is the great example of a man prepared to obliterate himself in order that Jesus Christ may be seen. He was only, as he saw it, a signpost pointing to Christ. God give *us* grace to forget ourselves and to remember only Christ.

The Fourth Sunday of Advent
The End is Praise *and* God's Message to Mary

Romans 16:25–27

The letter to the Romans comes to an end with a doxology which is also a summary of the gospel which Paul preached and loved.

(1) It is a gospel which makes men and women able to stand firm. God said to Ezekiel: 'Stand up on your feet, and I will speak with you' (Ezekiel 2:1). The gospel is a power which enables us to stand firm and upright against the shocks of the world and the assaults of temptation. A journalist relates a great incident of the Spanish Civil War. There was a little garrison that was surrounded. The end was near, and some wished to surrender and so to save their lives; but others wished to fight on. The matter was settled when one brave man declared: 'It is better to die upon our feet than to live upon our knees.' Life can be difficult; sometimes people are beaten to their knees by the battering that it gives to them. Life can be dangerous; sometimes people are liable to fall in the slippery places of temptation. The gospel is God's power to save – that power which keeps people upright on their feet, even when life is at its worst and its most threatening.

(2) It is a gospel which Paul preached and which was offered by Jesus Christ. That is to say, the gospel takes its source in Christ and is transmitted by men and women. Without Jesus Christ, there can be no gospel at all; but, without people to transmit it, others can never hear of it. The Christian duty is that, when anyone is found by Christ, that person should immediately go and find others for him. After Andrew was found by Jesus, John says of him:

'He first found his brother Simon and said to him, "We have found the Messiah"' (John 1:41).

Here is the Christian privilege and the Christian duty. The Christian privilege is to take hold of the good news for ourselves; the Christian duty is to transmit that good news to others. A famous story tells how Jesus, after the cross and the resurrection, returned to his glory, still bearing the marks of his sufferings. One of the angels said to him: 'You must have suffered terribly for men and women down there.' 'I did,' said Jesus. 'Do they all know about what you did for them?' asked the angel. 'No,' said Jesus, 'not yet. Only a few know about it so far.' 'And,' said the angel, 'what have you done that they should all know?' 'Well,' said Jesus, 'I asked Peter and James and John to make it their business to tell others, and the others still others, until the furthest person on the widest circle has heard the story.' The angel looked doubtful, for he knew well what poor creatures human beings were. 'Yes,' he said, 'but what if Peter and James and John forget? What if they grow weary of the telling? What if, way ahead in the twenty-first century, people fail to tell the story of your love for them? What then? Haven't you made any other plans?' Back came the answer of Jesus: 'I haven't made any other plans. *I'm counting on them.*' Jesus died to give us the gospel; and now he is counting on us to transmit it to all the world.

(3) It is a gospel which is the fulfilment of history. It is something which was there from all ages and which at the coming of Christ was revealed to the world. With the coming of Jesus, something unique happened: Eternity invaded time, and God emerged on earth. His coming was the event to which all history was working up and the event from which all subsequent history flows. After the coming of Christ, the world could never be the same again. It was the central fact of history, so that we date time in terms of before and after Christ's birth. It is as if, with his coming, life and the world began all over again.

(4) It is a gospel which is meant for *all* and which was *always* meant for all. It is not a gospel which was meant for the Jews only; its going out to the Gentiles was not an afterthought. The prophets, perhaps scarcely knowing what they were saying, had their hints and forecasts of a time when all people of all nations would know God. That time is not yet; but it is the dream of God that some day the knowledge of him will cover the earth as the waters cover the sea, and it is our glory that we can help make God's dream come true.

(5) It is a gospel which issues in an obedient world, a world where God is King. But that obedience is not founded on submission to an iron law, which breaks those who oppose it; it is an obedience founded on faith, on a surrender which is the result of love. For Paul, Christians are not people who have surrendered to a power that cannot be resisted and from which there is no escape; they are men and women who have fallen in love with the God who is the lover of human souls and whose love stands forever fully displayed in Jesus Christ. And so, the long argument of the letter to the Romans comes to an end in a song of praise.

Luke 1.26–38

Mary was betrothed to Joseph. Betrothal lasted for a year and was quite as binding as marriage. It could be dissolved only by divorce. Should the man to whom a girl was betrothed die, in the eyes of the law she was a widow. In the law there occurs the strange-sounding phrase, 'a virgin who is a widow'.

In this passage we are face to face with one of the great controversial doctrines of the Christian faith – the virgin birth. The Church does not insist that we believe in this doctrine. Let us look at the reasons for and against believing in it, and then we may make our own decision. There are two great reasons for accepting it.

(1) The literal meaning of this passage, and still more of Matthew 1:18–25, clearly is that Jesus was to be born of Mary without a human father.

(2) It is natural to argue that if Jesus was, as we believe, a very special person, he would have a special entry into the world.

Now let us look at the things which may make us wonder if the story of the virgin birth is to be taken as literally as all that.

(1) The genealogies of Jesus both in Luke and in Matthew (Luke 3:23–38; Matthew 1:1–17) trace the genealogy of Jesus through *Joseph*, which is strange if Joseph was not his real father.

(2) When Mary was looking for Jesus on the occasion that he lingered behind in the Temple, she said, 'Your father and I have been searching for you in great anxiety' (Luke 2:48). The name *father* is definitely given by Mary to Joseph.

(3) Repeatedly Jesus is referred to as Joseph's son (Matthew 13:55; John 6:42).

(4) The rest of the New Testament knows nothing of the virgin birth. True, in Galatians 4:4 Paul speaks of Jesus as 'born of woman'. But this is the natural phrase for any human being (cf. Job 14:1, 15:14, 25:4).

But let us ask, 'If we do not take the story of the virgin birth literally, how did it arise?' The Jews had a saying that in the birth of *every* child there are three partners – the father, the mother and the Spirit of God. They believed that no child could ever be born without the Spirit. And it may well be that the New Testament stories of the birth of Jesus are lovely, poetical ways of saying that, even if he had a human father, the Holy Spirit of God was operative in his birth in a unique way.

In this matter we may make our own decision. It may be that we will desire to cling to the literal doctrine of the virgin birth; it may be that we will prefer to think of it as a beautiful way of stressing the presence of the Spirit of God in family life.

Mary's submission is a very lovely thing. 'Whatever God says, I accept.' Mary had learned to forget the world's commonest prayer – 'Your will be *changed*' – and to pray the world's greatest prayer – 'Your will be *done*.'

The First Sunday of Christmas
The Days of Childhood *and* Shepherds and Angels

Galatians 4:4–7

In verses 1–3 Paul has explained the situation of men and women before the coming of Christ. In the ancient world, the process of growing up was much more clearly defined than it is today.

(1) In the Jewish world, on the first Sabbath after a boy had passed his 12th birthday, his father took him to the synagogue, where he became *a son of the law*. At that point, the father said a blessing: 'Blessed are you, O God, who has taken from me the responsibility for this boy.' The boy prayed a prayer in which he said: 'O my God and God of my fathers! On this solemn and sacred day, which marks my passage from boyhood to manhood, I humbly raise my eyes to you, and declare, with sincerity and truth, that henceforth I will keep your commandments, and undertake and bear the responsibility of my actions towards you.' There was a clear dividing line in the boy's life; almost overnight he became a man.

(2) In Greece, a boy was under his father's care from the age of 7 until he was 18. He then became what was called an *ephebos*, which may be translated as *cadet*, and for two years he was under the direction of the state. The Athenians were divided into ten *phratriai*, or *clans*. Before a boy became an *ephebos*, at a festival called the *Apatouria*, he was received into the clan; and in a ceremonial act his long hair was cut off and offered to the gods. Once again, growing up was quite a distinct process.

(3) Under Roman law, the year at which a boy grew up was not definitely fixed, but it was always between the ages of 14 and 17.

At a sacred festival in the family called the *Liberalia*, he took off the *toga praetexta*, which was a toga with a narrow purple band at the foot of it, and put on the *toga virilis*, which was a plain toga worn by adults. He was then escorted by his friends and relatives down to the forum and formally introduced to public life. It was essentially a religious ceremony. Once again, there was a quite definite day on which the boy attained manhood. There was a Roman custom that, on the day a boy or girl grew up, they offered their toys to Apollo to show that they had put away childish things.

When a boy was an *infant* in the eyes of the law, he might be the owner of a vast property, but he could take no legal decision; he was not in control of his own life; everything was done and directed for him; and, therefore, for all practical purposes he had no more freedom than if he were a slave; but, when he became a man, he entered into his full inheritance.

So – Paul argues – in the childhood of the world, the law was in control. But the law was only elementary knowledge. To describe it, Paul uses the word *stoicheia*. A *stoicheion* was originally a line of things; for instance, it can mean a line of soldiers. But it came to mean any elementary knowledge, like the teaching of the alphabet to children.

It has another meaning which some would see here – the elements of which the world is composed, and, in particular, the stars. The ancient world was haunted by a belief in astrology. If an individual was born under a certain star, that person's fate, they believed, was settled. People lived under the tyranny of the stars and longed for release. Some scholars think that Paul is saying that at one time the Galatians had been tyrannized by their belief in the evil and threatening influence of the stars. But the whole passage seems to make it necessary to take *stoicheia* in the sense of basic knowledge.

Paul says that when the Galatians – and indeed all men and women – were mere children, they were under the tyranny of the law; then, when everything was ready, Christ came and released them from that tyranny. So, now they are no longer slaves of the law; they have become heirs and have entered into their inheritance. The childhood which belonged to the law should be past; the freedom of adulthood has come.

The proof that we are God's children comes from the instinctive cry of the heart. In our deepest need, we cry: 'Father!' to God. Paul uses the double phrase, 'Abba! Father!' *Abba* is the Aramaic word for *father*. It must have often been on Jesus' lips, and its sound was so sacred that the original language was retained. This instinctive cry of the heart Paul believes to be the work of the Holy Spirit. If our hearts cry out in this way, we know that we are God's children, and all the inheritance of grace is ours.

For Paul, those who governed their lives by slavery to the law were still children; those who had learned the way of grace had become mature in the Christian faith.

Luke 2:15–21

It is a wonderful thing that the story should tell that the first announcement of God came to some shepherds. Shepherds were despised by the orthodox good people of the day. They were quite unable to keep the details of the ceremonial law; they could not observe all the meticulous hand-washings and rules and regulations. Their flocks made constant demands on them; and so the orthodox looked down on them. It was to simple men of the fields that God's message first came. But these were in all likelihood very special shepherds.

In the Temple, morning and evening, an unblemished lamb was offered as a sacrifice to God. To see that the supply of perfect offerings was always available the Temple authorities had their own private sheep flocks; and we know that these flocks were pastured near

Bethlehem. It is most likely that these shepherds were in charge of the flocks from which the Temple offerings were chosen. It is a lovely thought that the shepherds who looked after the Temple lambs were the first to see the Lamb of God who takes away the sin of the world.

When a boy was born, it was usual for the local musicians to congregate at the house to greet him with simple music. Jesus was born in a stable in Bethlehem and therefore that ceremony could not be carried out. It is lovely to think that, in delivering the message to the shepherds, the minstrelsy of heaven took the place of the minstrelsy of earth, and angels sang the songs for Jesus that the earthly singers could not sing.

This reading shows all too clearly the rough simplicity of the birth of the Son of God. We might have expected that, if he had to be born into this world at all, it would be in a palace or a mansion. There was a European monarch who worried his court by often disappearing and walking incognito among his people. When he was asked not to do so for security's sake, he answered, 'I cannot rule my people unless I know how they live.' It is the great thought of the Christian faith that we have a God who knows the life we live because he too lived it and claimed no special advantage over ordinary people.

Finally, in this passage we see Jesus undergoing the ancient ceremony which every Jewish boy had to undergo. Every Jewish boy was circumcised on the eighth day after his birth. So sacred was that ceremony that it could be carried out even on a Sabbath when the law forbade almost every other act which was not absolutely essential; and it was on that day that a boy received his name.

The Second Sunday of Christmas
The Plan of God *and*
The Inexhaustible Fullness

Ephesians 1:3–14

In the Greek, the long passage from verses 3–14 is one sentence. It is so long and complicated because it represents not so much a reasoned statement as a lyrical song of praise. Paul's mind goes on and on, not because he is thinking in logical stages, but because gift after gift and wonder after wonder from God pass before his eyes.

In verses 3–4 Paul is thinking of Christians as the chosen people of God, and his mind runs along three lines.

(1) He thinks of *the fact of God's choice*. Paul never thought of himself as having chosen to do God's work. He always thought of God as having chosen him. Jesus said to his disciples: 'You did not choose me but I chose you' (John 15:16). Here precisely lies the wonder. It would not be so wonderful that we should choose God; the wonder is that God should choose us.

(2) Paul thinks of *the generosity of God's choice*. God chose us to bless us with the blessings which are to be found only in heaven. There are certain things which we can discover for ourselves; but there are others which are beyond us. People can acquire certain skills, can reach certain positions, can amass a certain amount of this world's goods by their own means; but by themselves they can never achieve goodness or peace of mind. God chose us to give us those things which he alone can give.

(3) Paul thinks of *the purpose of God's choice*. God chose us that we should be *holy* and *blameless*. Here are two great words. Holy is the Greek word *hagios*, which always has in it the idea of *difference* and of *separation*. A temple is *holy* because it is different from other buildings; priests are *holy* because they are different from ordinary men and women; God is supremely holy because he is different from us; the Sabbath is *holy* because it is different from other days. So, God chose Christians that they should be *different* from other people.

Here is the challenge that the modern Church has been very slow to face. In the early Church, Christians never had any doubt that they must be different from the world; they, in fact, knew that they must be so different that the probability was that the world would kill them and the certainty was that the world would hate them. But the tendency in the modern Church has been to play down the difference between the Church and the world. It must always be remembered that this difference on which Christ insists is not one which takes us *out* of the world; it makes us different *within* the world. It is the simple fact of the matter that if enough Christians became *hagios*, different, they would revolutionize society.

The Greek word translated *blameless* is a sacrificial word. Under Jewish law, before an animal could be offered as a sacrifice, it had to be inspected; and, if any blemish was found, it had to be rejected as unfit for an offering to God. Only the best was fit to offer to God. *Blameless* thinks of the whole person as an offering to God. It thinks of taking every part of our life, work, pleasure, sport, home life and personal relationships, and making them all fit to be offered to God. This word does not mean that Christians must be respectable; it means that they must banish contentment with everything that is second best; it means that the Christian standard is nothing less than perfection.

In verses 5–6 Paul speaks to us of the plan of God. One of the pictures that he uses more than once to illustrate what God does for us is that of adoption (cf. Romans 8:23; Galatians 4:5). God adopted us into his family as his children.

In the ancient world, where Roman law prevailed, this would be an even more meaningful picture than it is to us. For there, the family was based on what was called the *patria potestas*, the father's power. A father had absolute power over his children as long as he and they lived. He could sell his children as slaves or even kill them. The Roman historian Dio Cassius tells us that 'the law of the Romans gives a father absolute authority over his son, and that for the son's whole life.'

Under Roman law, children could not possess anything; and any inheritance willed to them, or any gifts given to them, became the property of their father. It did not matter how old a son was, or to what honours and responsibility he had risen; he was absolutely in his father's power.

In circumstances like that, it is obvious that adoption was a very serious step. It was, however, not uncommon, for children were often adopted to ensure that some family line should not die out. The ritual of adoption must have been very impressive. It was carried out by a symbolic sale after which the adopting father had to go to the *praetor*, one of the principal Roman magistrates, and plead the case for the adoption. Only after all this had been gone through was the adoption complete, the person who had been adopted had all the rights of a legitimate son in his new family and lost absolutely all rights in his old family. In the eyes of the law, he was a new person. So new was he that even all debts and obligations connected with his previous family were abolished as if they had never existed.

That is what Paul says that God has done for us. We were absolutely in the power of sin and of the world; God, through Jesus, took us out of that power into his; and that adoption wipes out the past and makes us new.

(For the discussion of verses 9–10, see The Sunday between 10 and 16 July, pp. 193–197.)

John 1:10–18

In the final verses of this passage John says three great things about Jesus.

(1) On his fullness we all have drawn. The word that John uses for *fullness* is a great word; it is *plērōma*, and it means the sum total of all that is in God. It is a word which Paul uses often. In Colossians 1:19, he says that all *plērōma* dwelt in Christ. In Colossians 2:9, he says that in Christ there dwelt the *plērōma* of deity in a bodily form. He meant that in Jesus there dwelt the totality of the wisdom, the power and the love of God. Just because of that, Jesus is inexhaustible. We can go to Jesus with any need and find that need supplied.

We can go to Jesus with any ideal and find that ideal realized. In Jesus, the person who is in love with beauty will find the supreme beauty. In Jesus, the person to whom life is the search for knowledge will find the supreme revelation. In Jesus, the person who needs courage will find the pattern and the secret of being brave. In Jesus, the person who feels unable to cope with life will find the Master of life and the power to live. In Jesus, the person who is conscious of sin will find the forgiveness for that sin and the strength to be good. In Jesus, the *plērōma*, the fullness of God, all that is in God, what the scholar B. F. Westcott called 'the spring of divine life', becomes available to everyone.

(2) From him we have received grace upon grace. Literally the Greek means *grace instead of grace*. What does that strange phrase mean?

(a) It may mean that in Christ we have found one wonder leading to another. When a missionary came to one of the ancient Scottish kings, the king asked him what he might expect if he became a Christian. The missionary answered: 'You will find wonder upon wonder and every one of them true.' Sometimes when we travel a very lovely road, vista after vista opens to us. At every view we think that nothing could be lovelier, and then we turn another corner and an even greater loveliness opens before us. When we embark on the study of some great subject, like music or poetry or art, we never get to the end of it. Always there are fresh experiences of beauty waiting for us. It is so with Christ.

The more we know of him, the more wonderful he becomes. The longer we live with him, the more loveliness we discover. The more we think about him and with him, the wider the horizon of truth becomes. This phrase may be John's way of expressing the limitlessness of Christ. It may be his way of saying that those who keep company with Christ will find new wonders dawning upon their souls and enlightening their minds and capturing their hearts every day.

(b) It may be that we ought to take this expression quite literally. In Christ, we find *grace instead of grace*. The different ages and the different situations in life demand a different kind of grace. We need one grace in the days of prosperity and another in the days of adversity. We need one grace in the sunlit days of youth and another when the shadows of age begin to lengthen. The Church needs one grace in the days of persecution and another when the days of acceptance have come. We need one grace when we feel that we are on top of things and another when we are depressed and discouraged and near to despair. We need one grace to bear our own burdens and another to bear one another's burdens. We need one grace when we are sure of things and another when there seems nothing certain left in the world. The grace of God is never a static but always a dynamic thing. It never fails to meet the situation. One need invades life and one grace comes with it. That need passes and another need assaults us and with it another grace comes.

All through life we are constantly receiving grace instead of grace, for the grace of Christ is triumphantly adequate to deal with any situation.

(3) The law was given by Moses, but grace and truth came through Jesus Christ. In the old way, life was governed by law. People had to do a thing whether they liked it or not, and whether they knew the reason for it or not; but with the coming of Jesus we no longer seek to obey the law of God like slaves; we seek to answer the love of God like sons and daughters. It is through Jesus Christ that God the law-giver has become God the Father, that God the judge has become God the lover of human souls.

The First Sunday of Epiphany (The Baptism of Christ)
Incomplete Christianity *and* The Day of Decision

Acts 19:1–7

In Ephesus, Paul met some men whose Christianity was not yet complete. They had received the baptism of John, but they did not even know of the Holy Spirit in the Christian sense of the term. What was the difference between the baptism of John and baptism in the name of Jesus? The accounts of the preaching of John (Matthew 3:7–12; Luke 3:3–11) reveal one fundamental difference between it and the preaching of Jesus. The preaching of John was a threat; the preaching of Jesus was good news. John's preaching was a stage on the way. He himself knew that he only pointed to one still to come (Matthew 3:11; Luke 3:16).

John's preaching was a necessary stage, because there are two stages in the religious life. First, there is the stage in which we awaken to our own inadequacy and the fact that we are deserving of condemnation at the hand of God. That stage is closely linked to an endeavour to do better that inevitably fails because we try in our own strength. Second, there is the stage when we come to see that through the grace of Jesus Christ our condemnation may be taken away. Closely linked with that stage is the time when we find that all our efforts to do better are strengthened by the work of the Holy Spirit, through whom we can do what we could never do on our own.

These Christians knew the condemnation and the moral duty of being better; but the grace of Christ and the help of the Holy Spirit they did not know. Their faith was incomplete. Their religion was inevitably a matter of struggle and had not reached the stage of being an experience of peace. The incident shows us one great truth – that without the Holy Spirit there can be no such thing as complete Christianity. Even when we see the error of our ways and repent and determine to change them, we can never make the change without the help which only the spirit can give.

Mark 1:4–11

To any thinking person the baptism of Jesus presents a problem. John's baptism was a baptism of repentance, meant for those who were sorry for their sins and who wished to express their determination to have done with them. What had such a baptism to do with Jesus? Was he not the sinless one, and was not such a baptism unnecessary and quite irrelevant as far as he was concerned? For Jesus the baptism was four things.

(1) It was the moment of *decision*. For thirty years he had stayed in Nazareth. Faithfully he had done his day's work and discharged his duties to his home. For a long time he must have been conscious that the time for him to go out had to come. He must have waited for a sign. The emergence of John was that sign. This, he saw, was the moment when he had to launch out upon his task. In every life there come moments of decision which may be accepted or rejected. To accept them is to succeed; to reject them, or to shirk them, is to fail.

To each of us there comes the unreturning decisive moment. As Shakespeare expressed it in the words of Brutus:

There is a tide in the affairs of men,
Which, taken at the flood, leads on to fortune;
Omitted, all the voyage of their lives
Is bound in shallows and in miseries.
The undecided life is the wasted life, the frustrated life,
The discontented life and often the tragic life.

As John Oxenham saw it when he wrote 'The Ways':

To every man there openeth
A way and ways and a way;
The high soul treads the high way,
And the low soul gropes the low,
And in between on the misty flats,
The rest drift to and fro.

The drifting life can never be the happy life. Jesus knew when John emerged that the moment of decision had come. Nazareth was peaceful and home was sweet, but he answered the summons and the challenge of God.

(2) It was the moment of *identification*. It is true that Jesus did not need to repent from sin; but here was a movement of the people back to God; and with that Godward movement he was determined to identify himself. It is possible to possess ease and comfort and wealth and still to identify with a movement to bring better things to the downtrodden and the poor and the ill-housed and the overworked and the underpaid. The really great identification is when people identify with a movement, not for their own sake, but for the sake of others.

In John Bunyan's dream, Christian came in his journeying with Interpreter to the Palace which was heavily guarded and required a battle to seek an entry. At the door there sat the man with the ink horn taking the names of those who would dare the assault.

All were hanging back, then Christian saw 'a man of a very stout countenance come up to the man that sat there to write, saying, "Set down my name, sir"'. When great things are afoot the Christian is bound to say, 'Set down my name, sir,' for that is what Jesus did when he came to be baptized.

(3) It was the moment of *approval*. No one lightly leaves home and sets out on an unknown way. He or she must be very sure that the decision is right. Jesus had decided on his course of action, and now he was looking for the seal of the approval of God. In the time of Jesus, the Jews spoke of what they called the *Bath Qol*, which means *the daughter of a voice*. By this time they believed in a series of heavens, in the highest of which sat God in the light to which no one could approach. There were rare times when the heavens opened and God spoke; but, to them, God was so distant that it was only the faraway echo of his voice that they heard. To Jesus the voice came directly. As Mark tells the story, this was a personal experience which Jesus had and not in any sense a demonstration to the crowd. The voice did not say, 'This is my Son, the Beloved,' as Matthew has it (Matthew 3:17). It said, 'You are my beloved Son,' speaking directly to Jesus. At the baptism Jesus submitted his decision to God and that decision was unmistakably approved.

(4) It was the moment of *equipment*. At that time the Holy Spirit descended upon him. There is a certain symbolism here. The Spirit descended as a dove might descend. The simile is not chosen by accident. The dove is the symbol of *gentleness*. Both Matthew and Luke tell us of the preaching of John (Matthew 3:7–12; Luke 3:7–13). John's was a message of the axe laid to the root of the tree, of the terrible sifting, of the consuming fire. It was a message of doom and not of good news. But from the very beginning the picture of the Spirit likened to a dove is a picture of gentleness. He will conquer, but the conquest will be the conquest of love.

The Second Sunday of Epiphany
The Lion of Judah and the Root of David *and* The Surrender of Nathanael

Revelation 5:1–10

John has been weeping because there is no one to whom God may reveal his secrets. One of the elders, acting as the messenger of Christ, comes to him, saying: 'Do not weep.' The elder then tells John that Jesus Christ has won such a victory that he is able to open the book and to loosen the seals. That means three things. It means that, because of his victory over death and all the powers of evil and because of his complete obedience to God, he is able to *know* God's secrets; he is able to *reveal* God's secrets; and it is his privilege and duty to *control* the things which shall be. Because of what Jesus did, he is the Lord of truth and of history. He is called by two great titles.

(1) He is the *Lion of Judah*. This title goes back to Jacob's final blessing of his sons before his death. In that blessing, he calls Judah 'a lion's whelp' (Genesis 49:9). If Judah himself is a lion's whelp, it is fitting to call the greatest member of the tribe of Judah the *Lion of Judah*. In the books written between the Testaments, this became a messianic title. One such book, 2 Esdras, speaks of the figure of a lion and says: 'This is the anointed one, that is, the Messiah' (2 Esdras [4 Ezra] 12:32). The lion's strength and its undoubted place as king of beasts make him a fitting emblem of the all-powerful Messiah whom the Jews awaited.

(2) He is the *Root of David*. This title goes back to Isaiah's prophecy that there will come forth a shoot from the stump of Jesse and a root of Jesse who shall be a signal to the people (Isaiah 11:1, 11:10).

Jesse was the father of David, and this means that Jesus Christ was the Son of David, the promised Messiah.

So, here we have two great titles which are particularly Jewish. They have their origin in the pictures of the coming Messiah; and they lay it down that Jesus Christ triumphantly performed the work of the Messiah and is, therefore, able to know and to reveal the secrets of God, and to preside over the working out of his purposes in the events of history.

At the end of this passage, the praise offered to the Lamb by the four living creatures and the elders is given because he died. In this song, the results of the death of Jesus Christ are summed up.

(1) It was a *sacrificial* death. That is to say, it was a death with purpose in it. It was not an accident of history; it was not even the tragic death of a good and heroic man in the cause of righteousness and of God; it was a sacrificial death. The object of sacrifice is to restore the lost relationship between God and humanity; and it was for that purpose, *and with that result*, that Jesus Christ died.

(2) The death of Jesus Christ was a death which brought freedom. From beginning to end, the New Testament is full of the idea of the liberation achieved by him for all people. He gave his life as a ransom for many (Mark 10:45). He gave himself as a ransom for all (1 Timothy 2:6). He redeemed us from – literally *bought us out from* – the curse of the law (Galatians 3:13). We are bought with a price (1 Corinthians 6:20, 7:23). The New Testament consistently declares that it cost the death of Jesus Christ to rescue us from the dilemma and the slavery into which sin had brought us. The New Testament has no 'official' theory of how that effect was achieved; but of the effect itself it is in no doubt whatever.

(3) The death of Jesus Christ was *universal* in its benefits. It was for men and women of every race. There was a time when the Jews could hold that God cared only for them and wished for nothing but the destruction of other peoples. But in Jesus Christ we meet

a God who loves *the world*. The death of Christ was for all people, and therefore it is the task of the Church to tell everyone about it.

(4) The death of Jesus Christ was a death which was of *benefit*. He did not die for nothing. In this song, three aspects of the work of Christ are singled out.

(a) He made us *royal*. He opened to men and women the royalty of the children of God. Human beings have always been God's children by creation; but now there is a new relationship of grace open to all.

(b) He made us *priests*. In the ancient world, only the priest had the right of approach to God. When ordinary Jews entered the Temple, they could make their way through the Court of the Gentiles, through the Court of the Women, into the Court of the Israelites; but into the Court of the Priests they could not go. It was a case of so far and no further. But Jesus Christ opened the way to God for all people. We all become priests in the sense that we have the right of access to God.

(c) He gave us *triumph*. His people shall reign upon the earth. This is not political triumph or material lordship. It is the secret of victorious living under any circumstances. 'In the world you face persecution. But take courage; I have conquered the world!' (John 16:33). In Christ, there is victory over self, victory over circumstance and victory over sin. When we think of what the death and life of Jesus Christ have done for us, it is no wonder that the living creatures and the elders burst into praise of him.

John 1:43–51

At this point in the story, Jesus left the south and went north to Galilee. There he found and called Philip. Philip, like Andrew, could not keep the good news to himself. So he went and found his friend Nathanael. He told him that he believed that he had discovered the long-promised Messiah in Jesus, the man from Nazareth. Nathanael was contemptuous. There was nothing in the Old Testament which foretold that God's chosen one should come from Nazareth. Nazareth was a quite undistinguished place. Nathanael himself came from Cana, another Galilaean town, and, in country places, jealousy between town and town, and rivalry between village and village, is notorious. Nathanael's reaction was to declare that Nazareth was not the kind of place that anything good was likely to come out of. Philip was wise. He did not argue. He said simply: 'Come and see!'

Not very many people have ever been argued into Christianity. Often our arguments do more harm than good. The only way to convince people of the supremacy of Christ is to confront them with Christ. On the whole, it is true to say that it is not argumentative and philosophical preaching and teaching which have won men and women for Christ; it is the presentation of the story of the cross. The best argument is to say to people: 'Come and see!' Of course, we have to know Christ ourselves before we can invite others to come to him. The true evangelist must personally have met Christ first.

So Nathanael came; and Jesus could see into his heart. 'Here', said Jesus, 'is a genuine Israelite, a man in whose heart there is no guile.' That was a tribute that any devout Israelite would recognize. 'Happy are those', said the psalmist, 'to whom the Lord imputes no iniquity, and in whose spirit there is no deceit' (Psalm 32:2). 'He had done no violence,' said the prophet of the Servant of the Lord, 'and there was no deceit in his mouth' (Isaiah 53:9).

Nathanael was surprised that anyone could give a verdict like that on so short an acquaintance, and he demanded how Jesus could possibly know him. Jesus told him that he had already seen him under the fig tree. What is the significance of that? To the Jews, the fig tree always stood for peace. Their idea of peace was when they could be undisturbed under their own vines and their own fig trees (cf. 1 Kings 4:25; Micah 4:4). Further, the fig tree was leafy and shady and it was the custom to sit and meditate under the roof of its branches. No doubt that was what Nathanael had been doing; and no doubt as he sat under the fig tree he had prayed for the day when God's chosen one should come. No doubt he had been meditating on the promises of God. And now he felt that Jesus had seen into the very depths of his heart.

It was not so much that Jesus had seen him under the fig tree that surprised Nathanael; it was the fact that Jesus had read the thoughts of his inmost heart. Nathanael said to himself: 'Here is the man who understands my dreams! Here is the man who knows my prayers! Here is the man who has seen into my most intimate and secret longings, longings which I have never even dared put into words! Here is the man who can translate the inarticulate sigh of my soul! This must be God's promised Anointed One and no other.' Nathanael capitulated forever to the man who read and understood and satisfied his heart.

It may be that Jesus smiled. He quoted the old story of Jacob at Bethel who had seen the golden ladder leading up to heaven (Genesis 28:12–13). It was as if Jesus said: 'Nathanael, I can do far more than read your heart. I can be for you and for everyone the way, the ladder that leads to heaven.' It is through Jesus and Jesus alone that human souls can mount the ladder which leads to heaven.

But who was Nathanael? In the Fourth Gospel, he is one of the first group of disciples; in the other three gospels, he never appears at all.

It has been suggested that Nathanael is not a real figure at all, but an ideal figure standing for all the true Israelites who burst the bonds of national pride and prejudice and gave themselves to Jesus Christ.

There is a simpler explanation. *Nathanael* was brought to Jesus by *Philip*. *Nathanael's* name is never mentioned in the other three gospels; and in the Fourth Gospel *Bartholomew's* name is never mentioned. Now, in the list of the disciples in Matthew 10:3 and Mark 3:18, *Philip* and *Bartholomew* come together, as if it was natural and inevitable to connect them. Moreover, *Bartholomew* is really a second name. It means *Son of Tholmai* or *Ptolemy*. *Bartholomew* must have had another name, a first name; and it is at least possible that *Bartholomew* and *Nathanael* are the same person under different names. That certainly fits the facts.

Whatever else, it is true that *Nathanael* stands for the Israelite whose heart was cleansed of pride and prejudice and who saw in Jesus the one who satisfied the longing of his waiting, seeking heart.

The Third Sunday of Epiphany
The Almighty and His Kingdom *and*
The New Exhilaration
Revelation 19:6–10

This passage begins with the shout of praise by the host of the redeemed. John goes out of his way to heap up similes to describe its sound. It was like 'the din of a vast concourse, the roar of a cataract, the roll of thunder'. Here John finds his inspiration in the words of Scripture. In his mind are two things. First, he is remembering Psalm 97:1: 'The Lord is King! Let the earth rejoice.' Second, he says: 'Let us rejoice and exult.' There is only one other place in the New Testament where these two verbs come together – in Jesus Christ's promise to the persecuted: '*Rejoice* and *be glad*, for your reward is great in heaven' (Matthew 5:12). It is as if the multitude of the redeemed sent up their shout of praise because the promise of Christ to his persecuted ones had come abundantly true.

Next comes the marriage of the Lamb to his bride. That picture stands for the final union between Jesus Christ and his Church. R. H. Charles expresses it well when he says that the marriage symbolism 'denotes the intimate and indissoluble communion of Christ with the community which he has purchased with his own blood' – a communion which is 'first reached in fullness by the host of the martyrs'.

The thought of the relationship between God and his people as a marriage goes far back into the Old Testament. Again and again, the prophets thought of Israel as the chosen bride of God. 'I will take you for my wife forever,' Hosea hears God say, 'I will take you for my wife in righteousness' (Hosea 2:19–20). 'For your Maker is your husband, the Lord of hosts is his name,' says Isaiah (Isaiah 54:5). Jeremiah hears God say and appeal: 'Return, O faithless children . . . for I am your master' (Jeremiah 3:14). Ezekiel works out the whole picture most fully in Chapter 16.

The marriage symbolism runs all through the gospels. We read of the marriage feast (Matthew 22:2); of the bride-chamber and the wedding garment (Matthew 22:10–11); of the wedding guests (Mark 2:19); of the bridegroom (Mark 2:19; Matthew 25:1); of the friends of the bridegroom (John 3:29). And Paul speaks of himself as promising the Church in marriage to Christ like a pure virgin (2 Corinthians 11:2). For him, the relationship of Christ to his Church is the great model of the relationship of husband and wife (Ephesians 5:21–33).

This may seem to us a strange metaphor. But it contains certain great truths. In any real marriage, there must be four things which must also be in the relationship between the Christian and Christ.

(1) There is *love*. A loveless marriage is a contradiction in terms. (2) There is *intimate communion*, so intimate that husband and wife become one flesh. The relationship of the Christian and Christ must be the closest in all life. (3) There is *joy*. There is nothing like the joy of loving and of being loved. If Christianity does not bring joy, it does not bring anything. (4) There is *fidelity*. No marriage can last without fidelity; and Christians must be as faithful to Jesus Christ as Jesus Christ is to them.

This passage calls God by a certain name and says that he has entered into his kingdom. It calls God the *Almighty*. The word is *pantokratōr*, literally the one who controls all things. The significant thing about this great word is that it occurs ten times in the New Testament.

Once it is in an Old Testament quotation in 2 Corinthians 6:18; the other nine times are all in Revelation (1:8, 4:8, 11:17, 15:3, 16:7, 16:14, 19:6, 19:15, 21:22). In other words, this is the characteristic title for God in Revelation. There was never a time in history in which such forces were drawn up against the Church as when Revelation was written. There was never a time when Christians were called upon to undergo such suffering and to accept so continually the prospect of a cruel death. And yet, in such times, John calls God *pantokratōr*.

Here is faith and confidence; and the whole point of this passage is that that faith and confidence are vindicated. The Church, the bride of Christ, is clothed in fine linen, pure and shining. There is a contrast with the scarlet and gold of the great whore. The white linen represents the good deeds of God's dedicated people; that is to say, it is character which forms the robe in which the bride of Christ is dressed.

The Jews had the idea that, when the Messiah came, God's people would, as it were, be entertained by God to a great messianic banquet. Isaiah speaks of God preparing for his people 'a feast of rich food, a feast of well-aged wines, of rich food filled with marrow, of well-aged wines strained clear' (Isaiah 25:6). Jesus speaks of many coming from the east and the west and sitting down with the patriarchs in the kingdom of heaven (Matthew 8:11). The word used for sitting down is the word for reclining at a meal. The picture is of everyone *sitting down* at the messianic banquet of God. At the Last Supper, Jesus said that he would not again drink of the cup until he drank it new in his Father's kingdom (Matthew 26:29). That was Jesus looking forward to the great messianic banquet.

It may well be that the idea of the marriage feast of the Lamb came from that old Jewish idea, for that indeed would be the true messianic banquet. It is a simple picture, not to be taken with crude literalness, but simply saying very beautifully that in his kingdom everyone will enjoy the generosity of God.

John 2:1–11

When we look for the meaning of this story, we must remember that John was writing out of a double background. He was a Jew and he was writing for Jews; but his great object was to write the story of Jesus in such a way that it would come home also to the Greeks.

Let us look at it first of all from the *Jewish* point of view. We must always remember that beneath John's simple stories there is a deeper meaning which is open only to those who have eyes to see. In all his gospel, John never wrote an unnecessary or an insignificant detail. Everything means something, and everything points beyond.

There were six stone water pots; and at the command of Jesus, the water in them turned to wine. According to the Jews, *seven* is the number which is complete and perfect; and *six* is the number which is unfinished and imperfect. The six stone water pots stand for all the imperfections of the Jewish law. Jesus came to do away with the imperfections of the law and to put in their place the new wine of the gospel of his grace. Jesus turned the imperfection of the law into the perfection of grace.

There is another thing to note in this connection. There were six water pots; each held between twenty and thirty gallons of water; Jesus turned the water into wine. That would give anything up to 180 gallons of wine. Simply to state that fact is to show that John did not mean the story to be taken with crude literalness. What John did mean to say is that when the grace of Jesus comes to men and women there is enough and to spare for all. No wedding party on earth could drink 180 gallons of wine. No need on earth can exhaust the grace of Christ; there is a glorious superabundance in it. John is telling us that in Jesus the imperfections have become perfection, and the grace has become illimitable, sufficient and more than sufficient for every need.

Let us look at it now from the Greek point of view. It so happens that the Greeks actually possessed stories like this. Dionysos was the Greek god of wine. Pausanias was a Greek who wrote a description of his country and of its ancient ceremonies. In his description of

Elis, he describes an old ceremony and belief: 'Between the market place and the Menius is an old theatre and a sanctuary of Dionysos; the image is by Praxiteles. No god is more revered by the Eleans than Dionysos is, and they say that he attends their festival of the Thyia. The place where they hold the festival called the Thyia is about a mile from the city. Three empty kettles are taken into the building and deposited there by the priests in the presence of the citizens and of any strangers who may happen to be staying in the country. On the doors of the buildings the priests, and all who choose to do so, put their seals. Next day they are free to examine the seals, and on entering the building they find the kettles full of wine. I was not there myself at the time of the festival, but the most respectable men of Elis, and strangers too, swore that the facts were as I have said.'

So the Greeks, too, had their stories like this; and it is as if John said to them: 'You have your stories and your legends about your gods. They are only stories and you know that they are not really true. But Jesus has come to do what you have always dreamed that your gods could do. He has come to make the things you longed for come true.'

To the Jews, John said: 'Jesus has come to turn the imperfection of the law into the perfection of grace.' To the Greeks, he said: 'Jesus has come really and truly to do the things you only dreamed the gods could do.'

Now we can see what John is teaching us. Every story tells us not of something Jesus did once and never again, but of something which he is forever doing. John tells us not of things that Jesus once did in Palestine, but of things that he still does today. And what John wants us to see here is not that Jesus once on a day turned some water pots of water into wine; he wants us to see that whenever Jesus comes into a person's life, there comes a new quality which is like turning water into wine. Without Jesus, life is dull and stale and flat; when Jesus comes into it, life becomes vivid and sparkling and exciting. Without Jesus, life is drab and uninteresting; with him it is thrilling and exhilarating.

When the missionary doctor Sir Wilfred Grenfell was appealing for volunteers for his work in Labrador, he said that he could not promise them much money, but he could promise them the time of their lives. That is what Jesus promises us. John was writing seventy years after Jesus was crucified. For seventy years he had thought and meditated and remembered, until he saw meanings and significances that he had not seen at the time. When John told this story, he was remembering what life with Jesus was like; and he said, 'Wherever Jesus went and whenever he came into life, it was like water turning into wine.' This story is John saying to *us*: 'If you want the new exhilaration, become a follower of Jesus Christ, and there will come a change in your life which will be like water turning into wine.'

The Fourth Sunday of Epiphany
The Hatred of the Dragon *and* The First Victory Over the Powers of Evil

Revelation 12:1–5a

John saw an amazing vision, like a dramatic scene in the sky, whose details he draws from many sources. The woman is clothed with the sun; the moon is her footstool; and she has a crown of twelve stars. The psalmist says of God that he wraps himself in light as with a garment (Psalm 104:2). In the Song of Solomon, the poet describes his loved one as being fair as the moon and clear as the sun (Song of Solomon 6:10). So John got part of his picture from the Old Testament. But he added something which the people of Asia Minor would also recognize as part of the old Babylonian picture of the divine. They frequently depicted their goddesses as crowned with the twelve signs of the zodiac; and this is also in John's mind. It is as if he took all the signs of divinity and beauty which he could find and added them together.

This woman is in labour, giving birth to a child who is undoubtedly the Messiah, Christ (cf. verse 5, where he is said to be destined to rule the nations with a rod of iron – a quotation from Psalm 2:9, and an accepted description of the Messiah). So, the woman is the mother of the Messiah.

(1) If the woman is the 'mother' of the Messiah, an obvious suggestion is that she should be identified with Mary; but she is so clearly a superhuman figure that she can hardly be identified with any single human being.

(2) The persecution of the woman by the dragon suggests that she might be identified with the Christian Church. The objection

to that suggestion is that the Christian Church could hardly be called the mother of the Messiah.

(3) In the Old Testament, the chosen people, the ideal Israel, the community of the people of God, is often called the bride of God. 'Your Maker is your husband' (Isaiah 54:5). It is Jeremiah's sad complaint that Israel has played the whore in disloyalty to God (Jeremiah 3:6–10). Hosea hears God say: 'I will take you for my wife for ever' (Hosea 2:19). In Revelation itself, we hear of the marriage feast of the Lamb and the bride of the Lamb (Revelation 19:7, 21:9). 'I promised you in marriage to one husband,' writes Paul to the Corinthian church, 'to present you as a chaste virgin to Christ' (2 Corinthians 11:2).

This will give us a line of approach. It was from the chosen people that Jesus Christ came in his human lineage. The woman stands for the ideal community of the chosen ones of God. Out of that community Christ came, and it was that community which underwent such terrible suffering at the hands of the hostile world. We may indeed call this the Church, if we remember that the Church is the community of God's people in *every* age.

From this picture, we learn three great things about this community of God. First, it was out of it that Christ came; and out of it Christ has still to come for those who have never known him. Second, there are forces of evil, spiritual and human, which are set on the destruction of the community of God. Third, however strong the opposition against it and however terrible its sufferings, the community of God is under the protection of God and, therefore, it can never be ultimately destroyed.

Here we have the picture of the great, flame-coloured dragon. In the past history of the tradition of the antichrist, the people of the middle east regarded creation in the light of the struggle between the dragon of chaos and the creating God of order. In the Temple of Marduk – the creating god – in Babylon, there was a great image of a 'red-gleaming serpent' who stood for the defeated dragon of chaos. There can be little doubt that that is where John got his picture. This dragon appears in many forms in the Old Testament.

It appears as *Rahab*. 'Was it not you who cut Rahab in pieces, who pierced the dragon?' (Isaiah 51:9). It appears as the *leviathan*. 'You broke the heads of the dragons in the waters. You crushed the heads of Leviathan' (Psalm 74:13–14). In the day of the Lord, God with his cruel and great and strong sword will punish the leviathan (Isaiah 27:1). It appears in the dramatic picture of the *behemoth* in Job 40:15–24. The dragon which is the arch-enemy of God is a common and terrible figure in the thought of the middle east. It is the connection of the dragon and the sea which explains the rivers of water which the dragon pours out to overcome the woman (verse 15).

The dragon has seven heads and ten horns. This signifies its mighty power. It has seven royal diadems. This signifies its complete power over the kingdoms of this world as opposed to the kingdom of God. The image of the dragon sweeping the stars from the sky with its tail comes from the picture in Daniel of the little horn which cast the stars to the ground and trampled on them (Daniel 8:10). The picture of the dragon waiting to devour the child comes from Jeremiah, in which it is said of Nebuchadnezzar that 'he has swallowed me like a monster' (Jeremiah 51:34).

This picture illustrates the symbolism of an eternal truth about the human situation. In the human situation, as Christian history sees it, there are two figures who occupy the centre of the scene. There is humanity, men and women, fallen and always under the attack of the powers of evil but always struggling towards the birth of a higher life. And there is the power of evil, always watching for its opportunity to frustrate every attempt to achieve higher things. That struggle had its culmination on the cross.

Mark 1:21–28

This is the point at which Jesus deliberately launches his campaign.

The synagogue was primarily *a teaching institution*. The synagogue service consisted of only three things – prayer, the reading of God's word and the exposition of it. The law laid it down that wherever there were ten Jewish families there must be a synagogue, and, therefore, wherever there was a colony of Jews, there was a synagogue. If a man had a message from God to give, the natural place to which he would turn would be the place where God's people met together. That is precisely what Jesus did. He began his campaign in the synagogue.

When the people met at the synagogue service it was open to the ruler to call on any competent person to give the address and the exposition. There was no professional ministry whatsoever. That is why Jesus was able to open his campaign in the synagogues. He was known to be a man with a message; and for that very reason the synagogue of every community provided him with a pulpit from which to instruct and to appeal to the people.

The scribes, who were the experts in the law, had three duties.

(1) They set themselves, out of the great moral principles of the Torah, to extract rules and regulations for every possible situation in life. (2) It was their task to transmit and to teach this law and its developments. These deduced and extracted rules and regulations were never written down; they are known *as the oral law*. Although never written down, they were considered to be even *more* binding than the written law. From generation to generation of scribes, they were taught and committed to memory.

(3) They had the duty of giving judgement in individual cases; and, in the nature of things, practically every individual case must have produced a new law.

When Jesus taught in the synagogue, the whole method and atmosphere of his teaching was like a new revelation. He taught with *personal authority*. No scribe ever gave a decision on his own. He would always begin, 'There is a teaching that . . .' and would then quote all his authorities. If he made a statement, he would buttress it with this, that and the next quotation from the great legal masters of the past. The last thing he ever gave was an independent judgement. How different was Jesus! When he spoke, he spoke as if he needed no authority beyond himself. He spoke with utter independence. He cited no authorities and quoted no experts. He spoke with the finality of the voice of God. To the people, it was like a breeze from heaven to hear someone speak like that. The terrific, positive certainty of Jesus was the very antithesis of the careful quotations of the scribes. The note of personal authority rang out – and that is a note which captures everyone's attention.

If Jesus' words had amazed the people in the synagogue, his deeds left them thunderstruck. In the synagogue, there was a man in the grip of an unclean spirit. He created a disturbance, and Jesus healed him.

All through the gospels, we keep meeting people who had unclean spirits and who were possessed by demons or devils. What lies behind this?

The Jews, and indeed the whole ancient world, believed strongly in demons and devils. Where did these demons come from? There were three answers to that question. (a) Some believed that they were as old as creation itself. (b) Some believed that they were the spirits of the wicked who had died and were still carrying on their malignant work. (c) Most people connected the demons with the old story in Genesis 6:1–8 (cf. 2 Peter 2:4–5). The Jews elaborated the story in this way. There were two angels who forsook God and came to this earth because they were attracted by the beauty of mortal women. One of them returned to God; the other remained on earth and gratified his lust; and the demons are the children that he fathered and their children. The word used for the demons meant *one who does harm*. So the demons were malignant beings intermediate between God and human beings and who were out to work harm.

There were many exorcists who claimed to be able to cast out demons. But there was this difference – the ordinary Jewish and pagan exorcist used elaborate incantations and spells and magical rites. Jesus with one word of clear, simple, brief authority exorcised the demon. No one had ever seen anything like this before. The power was not in the spell, the formula, the incantation, the elaborate rite; the power was in Jesus, and people were astonished.

This is a subject on which we cannot dogmatize. We may take three different positions. (1) We may relegate the whole matter of demon-possession to the sphere of primitive thought and say that it was a way of accounting for things in the days before more was known about the human body or the working of the mind. (2) We may accept the fact of demon possession as being true in New Testament times and as being still true today. (3) If we accept the first position, we have to explain the attitude and actions of Jesus. Either he knew no more on this matter than the people of his day – and that is a thing we can easily accept, for Jesus was not a scientist and did not come to teach science. Or he knew perfectly well that he could never cure the person in trouble unless he assumed the reality of the disease. It was real to the person concerned and had to be treated as such or it could never be cured. In the end we come to the conclusion that there are some answers we do not know.

The Sunday between 3 and 9 February

The Privilege and the Task *and*
The Beginning of the Crowds

1 Corinthians 9:16–23

In this passage, there is a kind of outline of Paul's whole conception of his ministry.

(1) He regarded it as *a privilege*. The one thing he will not do is take money for working for Christ. When a certain famous American professor retired from his academic chair, he made a speech in which he thanked his university for paying him a salary for so many years for doing work which he would gladly have paid to do. This does not mean that people must always work for nothing. There are certain obligations that must be fulfilled which cannot be fulfilled for nothing; but it does mean that people should never work primarily for money. They should regard work not as a career of accumulation but as an opportunity for service. They must see themselves as having a primary duty not to help themselves but to take up the privilege of serving others for God's sake.

(2) He regarded it as *a duty*. Paul's point of view was that, if he had chosen to be a preacher of the gospel, he might quite legitimately have demanded payment for his work; but he had not chosen the work, it had chosen him. He could no more stop doing it than he could stop breathing, and there could, therefore, be no question of payment.

Ramon Lull, the great thirteenth-century Spanish saint and mystic, tells how he became a missionary of Christ. He had been living a carefree and pleasure-loving life. Then one day, when he was alone, Christ came carrying his cross and saying to him: 'Carry this for me.' But he refused. Again, when he was in the silence of a vast cathedral, Christ came and asked him to carry his cross; and again he refused. In a lonely moment, Christ came a third time, and this time, said Ramon Lull, 'He took his cross and with a look he left it lying in my hands. What could I do but take it up and carry it on?' Paul would have said: 'What can I do but tell men and women the good news of Christ?'

(3) In spite of the fact that he would take no payment, Paul knew that every day he received *a great reward*. He had the satisfaction of bringing the gospel freely to all who would receive it. It is always true that the real reward of any task is not the financial payment but the satisfaction of a job well done. That is why the biggest thing in life is to choose not the job with the biggest pay but the one in which we will find the greatest satisfaction.

The German physician and theologian Albert Schweitzer describes the kind of moment which brought him the greatest happiness. Someone suffering intensely is brought into his hospital. He soothes the man by telling him that he will put him to sleep and will operate on him and all will be well. After the operation, he sits beside the patient waiting for him to regain consciousness. Slowly, the patient opens his eyes and then whispers in sheer wonderment: 'I have no more pain.' That was it. There was no material reward there, but a satisfaction as deep as the depths of the heart itself. To have mended one shattered life, to have restored one wanderer to the right way, to have healed one broken heart, to have brought one individual to Christ is not a thing whose reward can be measured in financial terms; but its joy is beyond all measurement.

(4) Finally, Paul speaks about *the method of his ministry*, which was to become all things to all people. This is not a case of being hypocritically one thing to one person and another to another. It is a matter of being able to get along with someone. Those who can never see anything but their own point of view and who never

make any attempt to understand the mind and heart of others will never make pastors or evangelists or even succeed as friends.

James Boswell speaks of 'the art of accommodating oneself to others'. That was an art which the famed eighteenth-century man of letters Dr Johnson possessed in a supreme degree; for not only was he a great talker, he was also a great listener with a supreme ability to get along with other people. A friend said of him that he had the art of 'leading people to talk on their favourite subjects, and on what they knew best'. The Irish essayist Robert Lynd speaks of Johnson's 'readiness to throw himself into the interests of other people. He was a man who would have enjoyed discussing the manufacture of spectacles with a spectacle-maker, law with a lawyer, pigs with a pig-breeder, diseases with a doctor, or ships with a ship-builder. He knew that in conversation it is only more blessed to give than to receive.'

We can never achieve any kind of success in evangelism or friendship without speaking the same language and thinking the same thoughts as the other person. Someone once described teaching, medicine and the ministry as 'the three patronizing professions'. As long as we patronize people and make no effort to understand them, we can never get anywhere with them. Paul, the supreme missionary, who won more people for Christ than anyone else, saw how essential it was to become all things to all people. One of our greatest necessities is to learn the art of getting along with people; and so often the trouble is that we do not even try.

Mark 1:29–39

In the synagogue, Jesus had spoken and acted in the most amazing way. The synagogue service ended and Jesus went with his friends to Peter's house. The things that Jesus had done in Capernaum could not be concealed. The emergence of so great a new power and authority was not something which could be kept secret. So the evening found Peter's house besieged with crowds seeking Jesus' healing touch. They waited until evening because the law forbade the carrying of any burden through a town on the Sabbath day (cf. Jeremiah 17:24). So the people of Capernaum waited until the sun had set and the stars were out and then they came, carrying their sick, to Jesus; and he healed them.

The people flocked to Jesus because they recognized in him a man *who could do things*. There were plenty who could talk and expound and lecture and preach; but here was one who dealt not only in words but also in actions. The person people want is the effective person. Jesus could, and can, produce results. But there is the beginning of tragedy here. The crowds came, but they came *because they wanted something out of Jesus*. They did not come because they loved him or because they had caught a glimpse of some new vision; in the last analysis they wanted to use him. That is what nearly everyone wants to do with God and his Son. For one prayer that goes up to God in days of prosperity, 10,000 go up in time of adversity. Many who have never prayed when the sun was shining begin to pray when the cold winds come.

Religion is for many a crisis affair. It is only when they have got life into a mess, or when life deals them some knock-out blow, that they begin to remember God. We must all go to Jesus, for he alone can give us the things we need for life; but if that going and these gifts do not produce in us an answering love and gratitude there is something tragically wrong. God is not someone to be used in the day of misfortune; he is someone to be loved and remembered every day of our lives.

Simply to read the record of the things that happened at Capernaum is to see that Jesus was left with no time alone. Now Jesus knew well that he could not live without God; that if he was going to be forever giving out, he must be at least sometimes taking in, that if he was going to spend himself for others, he must constantly summon spiritual reinforcements to his aid. He knew that he could not live without prayer. Not to pray is to be guilty of the incredible folly of ignoring the possibility of adding God to our resources. In prayer we give the perfect mind of God an opportunity to feed our mental powers. Jesus knew this; he knew that if he was to meet people he must first meet God. If prayer was necessary for Jesus, how much more must it be necessary for us?

Even there they sought him out. There was no way in which Jesus could shut the door. A great doctor has said that the duty of medicine is 'sometimes to heal, often to afford relief, and always to bring consolation'. That duty was always upon Jesus. It is human nature to try to put up the barriers and to have time and peace to oneself; that is what Jesus never did. Conscious as he was of his own weariness and exhaustion, he was still more conscious of the insistent cry of human need. So when they came for him he rose from his knees to meet the challenge of his task. Prayer will never do our work for us; what it will do is to strengthen us for work which must be done. Jesus set out on a preaching tour of the synagogues of Galilee. As he went he *preached* and he *healed*. There were three pairs of things which Jesus never separated.

(1) He never separated *words and actions*. He never thought that a work was done when that work was stated; he never believed that his duty was completed when he had exhorted people to God and to goodness. Always the statement and the exhortation were put into action. The American Baptist, Harry Emerson Fosdick, tells of a student who bought the best possible books and the best possible equipment and got a special study chair with a special bookrest to make study easy, and then sat down in the chair – and went to sleep. The person who deals in words with no actions to follow is very like that.

(2) He never separated *soul and body*. There have been types of Christianity which spoke as if the body did not matter. But human beings are *both* soul and body. And the task of Christianity is to

redeem the whole person and not just a part. Missionaries do not only take the Bible; they take education and medicine; they take the school and the hospital. It is quite wrong to talk about the *social gospel* as if it were an extra, or an option, or even a separate part of the Christian message. The Christian message is one, and it preaches and works for the good of the body as well as the good of the soul.

(3) Jesus never separated *earth and heaven*. There are those who are so concerned with heaven that they forget all about earth and so become impractical visionaries. There are those who are so concerned with earth that they forget about heaven and limit good to material good. The dream of Jesus was a time when God's will would be done on earth as it is in heaven (Matthew 6:10), and earth and heaven be one.

The Sunday between 10 and 16 February
A Real Fight *and* The Leper is Cleansed

1 Corinthians 9:24–27

Here Paul insists to those Corinthians who want to take the easy way that no one will ever get anywhere without the sternest self-discipline. Paul was always fascinated by the picture of the athlete. An athlete must train with intensity in order to win the contest; and Corinth knew how thrilling contests could be, for at Corinth the Isthmian Games, second only to the Olympic Games, were held. Furthermore, the athlete undergoes this self-discipline and this training to win a crown of laurel leaves that within days will be a withered wreath. How much more should Christians discipline themselves to win the crown which is eternal life?

In this passage, Paul sets out a kind of brief philosophy of life.

(1) Life is a battle. As the American philosopher William James put it, 'If this life be not a real fight, in which something is eternally gained for the universe by success, it is not better than a game of private theatricals from which one may withdraw at will. But it *feels* like a fight – as if there were something really wild in the universe which we, with all our idealities and faithfulnesses, are needed to redeem.' As Samuel Taylor Coleridge had it, 'So far from the world being a goddess in petticoats, it is rather a devil in a strait waistcoat.' A flabby soldier cannot win battles; a slack trainer cannot win races. We must regard ourselves always as being engaged upon a campaign, and as pressing onwards to a goal.

(2) To win the fight and to be victorious in the race demands discipline. We have to discipline our bodies; it is one of the neglected

facts of the spiritual life that very often spiritual depression springs from simply being physically unfit. If we are going to do our best work in any aspect of life, we must bring to it bodies that are as fit as we can make them. We have to discipline our minds; it is one of the tragedies of life that many may refuse to think until they become incapable of thinking. We can never solve problems by refusing to see them or by running away from them. We must discipline our souls; we can do so by facing life's sorrows with calm endurance, its temptations with the strength God gives, and its disappointments with courage.

(3) We need to know our goal. A distressing thing is the obvious aimlessness of the lives of so many people; they are drifting anywhere instead of going somewhere. The Dutch novelist Maarten Maartens has a parable: 'There was a man once, a satirist. In the natural course of time his friends slew him, and he died. And the people came and stood round about his corpse. "He treated the whole round world as his football," they said indignantly, "and he kicked it." The dead man opened one eye. "But," he said, "*always towards the goal*."' Someone once drew a cartoon showing two men on Mars looking down at the people in this world scurrying here, there and everywhere. One said to the other: 'What are they doing?' The other replied: 'They are going.' 'But', said the first, 'where are they going?' 'Oh,' said the other, 'they are not going anywhere; they are just going.' And to go just anywhere is the certain way to arrive nowhere.

(4) We need to know the worth of our goal. The great appeal of Jesus was rarely based on penalty and punishment. It was based on the declaration: 'Look what you are missing if you do not take my way.' The goal is *life*, and surely it is worth anything to win that.

(5) We cannot save others unless we take control of ourselves. Sigmund Freud once said: 'Psychoanalysis is learnt first of all on oneself, through the study of one's own personality.' The Greeks declared that the first rule of life is: 'Know thyself.' Certainly, we

cannot serve others until we have taken charge of ourselves; we cannot teach what we do not know; we cannot bring others to Christ until we ourselves have found him.

Mark 1:40–45

In the New Testament there is no disease regarded with more terror and pity than leprosy. There are three kinds of leprosy.

(1) There is *nodular* or *tubercular leprosy*. It begins with an unaccountable lethargy and pains in the joints. Then there appear on the body, especially on the back, symmetrical discoloured patches. On them little nodules form, at first pink, then turning brown. The skin is thickened. The nodules gather specially in the folds of the cheek, the nose, the lips and the forehead. The whole appearance of the face is changed. The nodules grow larger and larger; they ulcerate and from them comes a foul discharge. The eyebrows fall out; the eyes become staring; the voice becomes hoarse and the breath wheezes because of the ulceration of the vocal chords. The hands and the feet also ulcerate. Slowly the sufferer becomes a mass of ulcerated growths. The average course of the disease is nine years, and it ends in mental decay, coma and ultimately death. Those suffering from this type of leprosy become utterly repulsive both to themselves and to others.

(2) There is *anaesthetic leprosy*. The initial stages are the same; but the nerve trunks also are affected. The infected area loses all sensation. This may happen without those who suffer from the disease knowing that it has happened; and they may not realize that it has happened until they suffer some burning or scalding and find that there is no feeling whatsoever where pain ought to be. As the disease develops, the injury to the nerves causes discoloured patches and blisters. The muscles waste away; the tendons contract until the hands become like claws. There is always disfigurement of the

fingernails. There ensues chronic ulceration of the feet and of the hands and then the progressive loss of fingers and of toes. The duration of the disease is anything from twenty to thirty years. It is a kind of terrible progressive death of the body.

(3) The third kind of leprosy is a type – the commonest of all – where nodular and anaesthetic leprosy are mixed. That is leprosy proper, and there is no doubt that there were many lepers like that in Palestine in the time of Jesus. From the description in Leviticus 13 it is quite clear that in New Testament times the term *leprosy* was also used to cover other skin diseases. It seems to have been used to include *psoriasis*, a disease which covers the body with white scales, and which would give rise to the phrase 'a leper as white as snow'. It seems also to have included ring-worm, which is still very common in the middle east. The Hebrew word used in Leviticus for leprosy seems to have covered any kind of creeping skin disease. Primitive medical knowledge meant that diagnosis did not distinguish between the different kinds of skin disease and included both the deadly and incurable and the non-fatal and comparatively harmless under the one inclusive title.

Any such skin disease rendered the sufferers unclean. They were banished from the fellowship of others; they must dwell alone outside the camp; they must go with rent clothes, bared heads and a covering upon their upper lips, and as they went they must give warning of their polluted presence with the cry, 'Unclean, unclean!' Lepers had not only to bear the physical pain of their disease, they had to bear the mental anguish and the heartbreak of being completely banished from human society and totally shunned.

If ever a leper was cured – and real leprosy was incurable, so it is some of the other skin diseases which must be referred to – he had to undergo a complicated ceremony of restoration (see Leviticus 14). He was examined by the priest. Two birds were taken and one was killed over running water. In addition, there were taken cedar, crimson yarn and hyssop. These things and the living bird were dipped in the blood of the dead bird and then the live bird was allowed to go free. The man washed himself and his clothes and shaved himself. Seven days then elapsed and he was re-examined. He had then to shave his hair, his head, his eyebrows. Certain sacrifices were made – two male lambs without blemish and one ewe lamb; a measure of fine flour mixed with oil and one log (a liquid measure) of oil. The amounts were less for the poor. The restored sufferer was touched on the tip of the right ear, the right thumb and the right big toe with blood and oil. He was given a final examination and, if clear of the disease, he was allowed to go with a certificate that he was clean.

Here is one of the most revealing pictures of Jesus.

(1) He did not drive away a man who had broken the law. The leper had no right to have spoken to him at all, but Jesus met the desperation of human need with an understanding compassion.

(2) Jesus stretched out his hand and touched him. He touched the man who was unclean. To Jesus he was not unclean; he was simply a human soul in desperate need.

(3) Having cleansed him, Jesus sent him to fulfil the prescribed ritual. He fulfilled the human law and human righteousness. He did not recklessly defy the conventions, but, when need be, submitted to them.

Here we see compassion, power and wisdom all at work together.

The Sunday between 17 and 23 February

God's Yes in Jesus Christ *and* A Faith that Would not be Denied

2 Corinthians 1:18–22

At first sight, this is a difficult passage. Behind it lies an accusation and slander against Paul. Paul had said that he would visit the Corinthians, but the situation had become so bitter that he postponed his visit in order not to give them pain (verse 23). His enemies had promptly accused him of being the kind of man who made frivolous promises with a fickle intention and who could not be pinned down to a definite yes or no. That was bad enough; but they went on to argue: 'If we cannot trust Paul's everyday promises, how can we trust the things he told us about God?' Paul's answer is that we can rely on God and that there is no wavering in Jesus between yes and no.

Then he summarizes the matter in a vivid phrase: 'Jesus is the yes to every promise of God.' He means this: had Jesus never come, we might have doubted the tremendous promises of God, and might have argued that they were too good to be true. But a God who loves us so much that he gave us his Son is quite certain to fulfil every promise that he ever made. He is the personal guarantee of God that the greatest and the least of his promises are all true.

Although the Corinthians were slandering Paul, there remains this salutary truth: the trustworthiness of the messenger affects the trustworthiness of the message. Preaching is always 'truth through personality'. And if people cannot trust the preacher, they are not likely to trust the preacher's message. Among the Jewish regulations regarding the conduct and character of a teacher, it is laid down that he must never promise anything to a class which he cannot or will not do. This would be to accustom the class to falsehood. Here is a warning that promises should never be given lightly, for they may well be broken just as lightly. Before we make a promise, we should count the cost of keeping it and make sure that we are able and willing to pay that price.

Paul goes on to say two great things.

(1) It is through Jesus that we say 'Amen' to the promises of God. We finish our prayers by saying: 'Through Jesus Christ our Lord. Amen.' When we have read Scripture, we frequently conclude it by saying: 'Amen.' *Amen* means *So let it be*, and the great truth is that it is not just a formality and a bit of ritual; it is the word that expresses our sure belief that, because Jesus came, we can offer our prayers with every confidence to God and can appropriate with confidence all his great promises, because Jesus is the guarantee, the unbreakable yes of God, that our prayers will be heard and that all the great promises are true.

(2) Finally, Paul speaks about what the Authorized Version calls the *earnest* of the Spirit. The Greek word is *arrabon*. An *arrabon* was the first instalment of a payment, paid as a guarantee that the rest was sure to follow. It is a common word in Greek legal documents. A woman selling a cow receives 1,000 drachmae as *arrabon* that the rest of the purchase price will be paid. Some dancing girls being engaged for a village festival receive an agreed amount as *arrabon*, which will be included in the final payment, but which is a present guarantee that the contract will be honoured and the full money paid. A certain man writes to his master that he has paid Lampon, the mouse-catcher, an *arrabon* of eight drachmae so that he will start work and catch the mice while they are still pregnant. It was the first instalment and the guarantee that the rest would be paid.

Everyone knew this word. It is the same idea as is in the Scots word *arles*, which was a token payment made when someone was employed or a house was bought, and a guarantee that the full contract would be honoured. When Paul speaks of the Holy Spirit as an *arrabon* given to us by God, he means that the kind of life we live by the help of the Holy Spirit is the first instalment of the life of heaven and the guarantee that the fullness of that life will some day open upon us. The gift of the Holy Spirit is God's token and pledge of still greater things to come.

Mark 2:1–12

Jesus had returned to Capernaum. The news of his coming immediately spread abroad. In no time, a crowd had filled the house to capacity and jammed the pavement round the door; and they were all eagerly listening to what Jesus had to say. Into this crowd came four men carrying on a stretcher a friend of theirs who was paralysed. They could not get through the crowd at all, but they were men of resource. They dug out the filling between two of the roof beams and let their friend down directly at Jesus' feet. When Jesus saw this faith that laughed at barriers, he must have smiled an understanding smile. He looked at the man, 'Child,' he said, 'your sins are forgiven.'

It may seem an odd way to begin a cure. But in Palestine, in the time of Jesus, it was natural and inevitable. The Jews integrally connected sin and suffering and any Jew would have agreed that forgiveness of sins was a prior condition of cure.

It may well be, however, that there is more than this in this story. The Jews made this connection between illness and sin, and it may well be that, in this case, *the man's conscience agreed*. And it may well be that that consciousness of sin had actually produced the paralysis. The power of the mind, especially the subconscious mind, over the body is an amazing thing.

The man in this story may well have been paralysed because consciously or unconsciously his conscience agreed that he was a sinner, and the thought of being a sinner brought the illness which he believed was the inevitable consequence of sin. The first thing that Jesus said to him was, 'Child, God is not angry with you. It's all right.' It was like speaking to a frightened child in the dark. The burden of the terror of God and estrangement from God rolled from his heart, and that very fact made the cure all but complete.

It is a lovely story because the first thing that Jesus does for every one of us is to say, 'Child, God is not angry with you. Come home, and don't be afraid.'

Because Jesus had drawn such crowds, he had also attracted the notice of the official leaders of the Jews. The Sanhedrin was their supreme court. One of its great functions was to be the guardian of orthodoxy, and especially to deal with anyone who was a false prophet. It seems that it had sent out a kind of scouting party to check up on Jesus; and they were there in Capernaum. No doubt they had taken up a prominent place in the front of the crowd and were sitting there critically watching everything that was going on.

When they heard Jesus say to the man that his sins were forgiven, it came as a shattering shock. It was an essential of Judaism that only God could forgive sins. For any human being to claim to do so was to insult God; that was blasphemy, and the penalty for blasphemy was death by stoning (Leviticus 24:16). At the moment they were not ready to launch their attack in public, but it was not difficult for Jesus to see how their minds were working. So he determined to fling down a challenge and to meet them on their own ground.

It was their own firm belief that sin and sickness were indissolubly linked together. Those who were sick had sinned. So Jesus asked them: 'Is it easier to say to this man, "Your sins are forgiven," or to say, "Get up and walk"?' Any charlatan could say, 'Your sins are forgiven.' There was no possibility of ever demonstrating whether his words were effective or not. But to say, 'Get up and walk' was to say something whose effectiveness would either be proved or disproved there and then. So Jesus said in effect: 'You say that I have no right to forgive sins? You hold as a matter of belief that if this man is ill he is a sinner and he cannot be cured till he is forgiven? Very well, then, watch this!' So Jesus spoke the word and the man was cured.

The experts in the law were caught at their own game. On their own stated beliefs the man could not be cured, unless he was forgiven. He *was* cured, therefore he *was* forgiven. Therefore, Jesus' claim to forgive sin *must* be true. Jesus must have left a completely baffled set of legal experts; and, worse, he must have left them in a baffled rage.

For all that, it is an extremely difficult incident. What does it mean that Jesus can forgive sin? There are three possible ways of looking at this.

(1) We could take it that Jesus was *conveying* God's forgiveness to the man, that he was assuring the man of God's forgiveness, conveying to him something which God had already given him.

(2) We could take it that Jesus was acting as God's representative. We could take it that God delegated to Jesus his powers and privileges, and that the word Jesus spoke was none other than the word of God.

(3) We could take it in still another way. The whole essence of Jesus' life is that in him we see clearly displayed the attitude of God to men and women. Now that attitude was not the perceived attitude of stern, severe, austere justice, not an attitude of continual demand. It was an attitude of perfect love, of a heart yearning with love and eager to forgive. Jesus literally brought men and women God's forgiveness upon earth. Without him, they would never have even remotely known about it. 'I tell you,' he said to the man, 'and I tell you here and now, upon earth, you are a forgiven man.' Jesus showed perfectly the attitude of God to all people. He could say, 'I forgive,' because in him God was saying, 'I forgive.'

The Second Sunday before Lent
What Jesus Christ is to Creation *and*
The Creator of All Things

Colossians 1:15–20

In this letter Paul goes out of his way to respond to the heresy known as Gnosticism. The Gnostics argued that God was spirit, then he was altogether good and could not possibly work with this evil matter. Therefore God was *not* the creator of the world. He put out a series of emanations, each of which was a little more distant from God, until at the end of the series there was an emanation so distant that it could handle matter; and it was this emanation which created the world. Since each emanation was more distant from God, it was also more ignorant of him. As the series went on, that ignorance turned to hostility. So the emanations most distant from God were both ignorant of him and hostile to him. It followed that he who created the world was both completely ignorant of, and at the same time utterly hostile to, the true God.

Paul's aim is to stress the part that Christ played in creation. It is his teaching that God's agent in creation is the Son; and in this passage he has four things to say about the Son in regard to creation.

(1) He is the first-born of all creation (Colossians 1:15). We must be very careful to attach the right meaning to this phrase. As it stands in English, it might well mean that the Son was the first person to be created; but in Hebrew and Greek thought the word *first-born* (*prōtotokos*) has only very indirectly a time significance. There are two things to note.

First-born is very commonly a title of *honour*. Israel, for instance, as a nation is the first-born son of God (Exodus 4:22). The meaning is that the nation of Israel is the most favoured child of God. Second, we must note that *first-born* is a title of the Messiah. In Psalm 89:27, as the Jews themselves interpreted it, the promise regarding the Messiah is: 'I will make him the firstborn, the highest of the kings of the earth.' Clearly, *first-born* is not used in a time sense at all, but in the sense of special honour. So, when Paul says of the Son that he is the *first-born* of all creation, he means that the highest honour which creation holds belongs to him. If we wish to keep the time sense and the honour sense combined, we may translate the phrase as 'He was brought to birth before all creation.'

(2) It was by the Son that all things were created (verse 16). This is true of things in heaven and things in earth, of things seen and unseen. The Jews themselves, and even more the Gnostics, had a highly developed system of angels. With the Gnostics, that was only to be expected with their long series of intermediaries between human beings and God. Thrones, lordships, powers and authorities were different grades of angels having their places in different spheres of the seven heavens. Paul dismisses them all with complete indifference. He is in effect saying to the Gnostics: 'You give a great place in your thinking to angels. You rate Jesus Christ merely as one of them. But, far from that, he created them.' Paul lays it down that the agent of God in creation is no inferior, ignorant and hostile secondary god, but the Son himself.

(3) It was for the Son that all things were created (verse 17). The Son is not only the agent of creation, he is also the goal of creation. That is to say, creation was created to be his, and in its worship and its love he might find his honour and his joy.

(4) Paul uses the strange phrase: 'In him, all things hold together.' This means not only that the Son is the agent of creation in the beginning and the goal of creation in the end; but also, between the beginning and the end, during time as we know it, it is he who holds the world together. That is to say, all the laws which govern and sustain order and not chaos in the universe are an expression

of the mind of the Son. The law of gravity and the rest, the laws by which the universe hangs together, are not only scientific laws but also divine.

So, the Son is the beginning of creation, and the end of creation, and the power who holds creation together, the creator, the sustainer and the final goal of the world.

John 1:1–14

It may seem strange to us that John so stresses the way in which the world was created; and it may seem strange that he so definitely connects Jesus with the work of creation. But he had to do this because of a certain tendency in the thought of his day.

In the time of John, there was a kind of heresy called *Gnosticism*. Its characteristic was that it was an intellectual and philosophical approach to Christianity. To the Gnostics, the simple beliefs of the ordinary Christian were not enough. They tried to construct a philosophic system out of Christianity. They were troubled about the existence of sin and evil and sorrow and suffering in this world, so they worked out a theory to explain it. The theory was this.

In the beginning, two things existed – the one was God and the other was matter. Matter was always there and was the raw material out of which the world was made. The Gnostics held that this original matter was flawed and imperfect. We might put it that the world got off to a bad start. It was made of material which had the seeds of corruption in it.

As we saw when looking at Colossians (p. 70), the Gnostics went further. God, they said, is pure spirit, and pure spirit can never touch matter at all, still less matter which is imperfect. Therefore it was not possible for God to carry out the work of creation himself. So he put out from himself a series of emanations. Each emanation was further and further away from God; and, as the emanations got further and further away from him, they knew less and less about him. About half-way down the series, there was an emanation which knew nothing at all about God. Beyond that stage, the emanations began to be not only ignorant of but actually hostile to God. Finally in the series, there was an emanation which was so distant from God that it was totally ignorant of him and totally hostile to him – and that emanation was the power which created the world, because it was so distant from God that it was possible for it to touch this flawed and evil matter. The creator god was utterly divorced from and utterly at enmity with the real God.

The Gnostics took one step further. They identified the creator god with the God of the Old Testament; and they held that the God of the Old Testament was quite different from, quite ignorant of and quite hostile to the God and Father of Jesus Christ.

In the time of John, this kind of belief was widespread. It was believed that the world was evil and that an evil God had created it. It is to combat this teaching that John here lays down two basic Christian truths. In point of fact, the connection of Jesus with creation is repeatedly laid down in the New Testament, just because of this background of thought which divorced God from the world in which we live. In Colossians 1:16, Paul writes: 'For in him all things in heaven and on earth were created . . . all things have been created through him and for him.' In 1 Corinthians 8:6, he writes of the Lord Jesus Christ 'through whom are all things'. The writer to the Hebrews speaks of the one who was the Son, 'through whom he also created the worlds' (Hebrews 1:2). John and the other New Testament writers who spoke like this were stressing two great truths.

(1) Christianity has always believed in what is called *creation out of nothing*. We do not believe that in his creation of the world God had to work with alien and evil matter. We do not believe that the world began with an essential flaw in it. We do not believe that the world began with God and something else. It is our belief that behind everything there is God and God alone.

(2) Christianity has always believed that this is *God's world*. So far from being so detached from the world that he could have nothing to do with it, God is intimately involved in it. The Gnostics tried to put the blame for the evil of the world on the shoulders of its creator. Christianity believes that what is wrong with the world is due to human sin. But even though sin has injured the world and kept it from being what it might have been, we can never despise the world, because it is essentially God's. If we believe this, it gives us a new sense of the value of the world and a new sense of responsibility to it.

There is a story of a child from the back streets of a great city who was taken for a day in the country. When she saw the bluebells in the woods, she asked: 'Do you think God would mind if I picked some of his flowers?' This is God's world; because of that, nothing is out of his control; and because of that, we must use all things in the awareness that they belong to God. Christians do not belittle the world by thinking that it was created by an ignorant and hostile god; they glorify it by remembering that everywhere God is behind it and in it. They believe that the Christ who re-creates the world was the co-worker of God when the world was first created, and that, in the act of redemption, God is seeking to win back that which was always his own.

The Sunday next before Lent
The Blinded Eye *and* The Glory
of the Mountain Top

2 Corinthians 4:3–6

Paul here speaks about those who have refused to accept the gospel. In spite of the fact that he has proclaimed the gospel in such a way that anyone with any kind of conscience at all is bound to acknowledge its claim and its appeal, some remain deaf to its appeal and blind to its glory. What about them?

Paul says something very difficult about them. He says that the god of this world has blinded their minds so that they cannot believe. All through the Bible, the writers are conscious that in this world there is a power of evil. Sometimes that power is called Satan, sometimes the devil. Three times, the Gospel according to John makes Jesus speak of *the ruler of this world* and of his defeat (John 12:31, 14:30, 16:11). In Ephesians 2:2, Paul speaks of the *ruler of the power of the air*, and here he speaks of *the god of this world*. Even in the Lord's Prayer, there is a reference to this malign power, for it is most probable that the correct translation of Matthew 6:13 is: 'Deliver us from *the evil one*.' Behind this idea, as it emerges in the New Testament, there are certain influences.

(a) The Persian faith called Zoroastrianism sees the whole universe as a battle ground between the god of the light and the god of the dark, between Ormuzd and Ahriman. That which settles human destiny is the side chosen in this cosmic conflict. When the Jews were conquered and ruled by the Persians, they came into contact with that idea, and it undoubtedly coloured their thinking.

(b) Fundamental to Judaism is the belief in the two ages – the present age and the age to come. By the time of the Christian era, the Jews had come to think of the present age as incurably bad and destined for total destruction when the age to come dawned. It could indeed be said that the present age was under the power of the god of this world and at enmity with the true God.

(c) It has to be remembered that this idea of an evil and a hostile power is not so much a theological idea as a fact of experience. If we regard it in a theological way, we are up against serious difficulties. Where did that evil power come from in a universe created by God? What is its ultimate end? But, if we regard it as a matter of experience, we all know how real the evil of the world is. The writer Robert Louis Stevenson once said: 'You know the Caledonian Railway Station in Edinburgh? One cold, east windy morning I met Satan there.' Everyone knows the kind of experience of which Stevenson speaks. However difficult the idea of a power of evil may be theologically or philosophically, it is one which experience understands only too well. Those who cannot accept the good news of Christ are those who have given themselves over to the evil of the world to such a degree that they can no longer hear God's invitation. It is not that God has abandoned them; by their own conduct they have shut themselves off from him.

Finally, Paul has something to say about Jesus. The great thought that he drives home here is that in Jesus Christ we see what God is like. 'Whoever has seen me', said Jesus, 'has seen the Father' (John 14:9). When Paul preached, he did not say: 'Look at me!' He said: 'Look at Jesus Christ! And there you will see the glory of God which came to earth in a form that everyone can understand.'

Mark 9:2–9

We are face to face with an incident in the life of Jesus that is cloaked in mystery. We can only try to understand. Mark says that this happened six days after the incidents near Caesarea Philippi. Luke says that it happened eight days afterwards. There is no discrepancy here. They both mean what we might express by saying, 'about a week afterwards'. Both the eastern and the western Churches hold their remembrance of the transfiguration on 6th August. It does not matter whether or not that is the actual date, but it is a time we do well to remember.

Tradition says that the transfiguration took place on the top of Mount Tabor. The eastern Church actually calls the Festival of the Transfiguration the *Taborion*. It may be that the choice is based on the mention of Mount Tabor in Psalm 89:12, but it is unfortunate. Tabor is in the *south* of Galilee and Caesarea Philippi is away to the north. Tabor is no more than 1,000 feet high, and, in the time of Jesus, there was a fortress on the top. It is much more likely that this event took place amid the eternal snows of Mount Hermon, which is 9,200 feet high and much nearer Caesarea Philippi and where the solitude would be much more complete.

What happened we cannot tell. We can only bow in reverence as we try to understand. Mark tells us that the garments of Jesus became radiant. The word he uses (*stilbein*) is the word used for the glistening gleam of burnished brass or gold or of polished steel or of the golden glare of the sunlight. When the incident came to an end, a cloud overshadowed them.

In Jewish thought, the presence of God is regularly connected with the cloud. It was in the cloud that Moses met God. It was in the cloud that God came to the Tabernacle. It was the cloud which filled the Temple when it was dedicated after Solomon had built it. And it was the dream of the Jews that when the Messiah came the cloud of God's presence would return to the Temple (Exodus 16:10, 19:9, 33:9; 1 Kings 8:10; 2 Maccabees 2:8). The descent of the cloud is a way of saying that the Messiah had come, and any Jew would understand it like that.

The transfiguration has a double significance.

(1) It did something very precious for Jesus. Jesus had to take his own decisions. He had taken the decision to go to Jerusalem, and that was the decision to face and accept the cross. Obviously he had to be absolutely sure that was right before he could go on. On the mountain top, he received a double approval of his decision.

(a) Moses and Elijah met with him. Now Moses was the *supreme law-giver* of Israel. To him the nation owed the laws of God. Elijah was *the first and the greatest of the prophets*. People always looked back to him as the prophet who brought to them the very voice of God. When these two great figures met with Jesus, it meant that the greatest of the law-givers and the greatest of the prophets said to him, 'Go on!' It meant that they saw in Jesus the consummation of all that they had dreamed of in the past. It meant that they saw in him all that history had longed for and hoped for and looked forward to. It is as if at that moment Jesus was assured that he was on the right way because all history had been leading up to the cross.

(b) God spoke with Jesus. As always, Jesus did not consult his own wishes. He went to God and said, 'What will you have me do?' He put all his plans and intentions before God. And God said to him, 'You are acting as my own beloved Son should act and must act. Go on!' On the mountain of the transfiguration, Jesus was assured that he had not chosen the wrong way. He saw not only the inevitability but the essential rightness of the cross.

(2) It did something very precious for the disciples.

(a) They had been shattered by Jesus' statement that he was going to Jerusalem to die. That seemed to them the complete negation of all that they understood of the Messiah. They were still bewildered and uncomprehending. Things were happening which not only baffled their minds but were also breaking their hearts. What they saw on the mountain of the transfiguration would give them something to hold on to, even when they could not understand.

Cross or no cross, they had heard God's voice acknowledge Jesus as his Son.

(b) It made them in a special sense witnesses of the glory of Christ. A witness has been defined as someone who first *sees* and then *shows*. This time on the mountain had shown them the glory of Christ, and now they had the story of this glory to hide in their hearts and to tell to others, not at the moment, but when the time came.

The First Sunday of Lent
Christian Baptism *and*
The Testing Time

1 Peter 3:18–22

Peter has been speaking about the wicked who were disobedient and corrupt in the days of Noah; they were ultimately destroyed. But, in the destruction by the flood, eight people – Noah and his wife, his sons Shem, Ham and Japheth, and their wives – were brought to safety in the ark. Immediately, the idea of being *brought to safety through the water* turns Peter's thoughts to Christian baptism, which is also a bringing to safety through the water. What Peter literally says is that baptism is an *antitype* of Noah and his people in the ark.

This word introduces us to a special way of looking at the Old Testament. There are two closely connected words. There is *tupos*, type, which means a seal, and there is *antitupos*, antitype, which means the *impression of the seal*. Clearly, between the seal and its impression there is the closest possible correspondence. So there are people and events and customs in the Old Testament which are types, and which find their antitypes in the New Testament. The Old Testament event or person is like the seal; the New Testament event or person is like the impression; the two answer to each other. We might put it that the Old Testament event symbolically represents and foreshadows the New Testament event. The science of finding types and antitypes in the Old and the New Testaments is very highly developed. But, to take very simple and obvious examples, the Passover lamb and the scapegoat, that bore the sins of the people, are types of Jesus; and the work of the high priest in making sacrifice for the sins of the people is a type of his saving work.

Here, Peter sees the bringing of Noah and his family safely through the waters as a type of baptism.

In this passage, Peter has three great things to say about baptism. It must be remembered that at this stage of the Church's history we are still dealing with adult baptism, the baptism of people who had come straight from the worship of Greek and Roman gods into Christianity and who were taking upon themselves a new way of life.

(1) Baptism is not merely a physical cleansing; it is a spiritual cleansing of the whole heart and soul and life. Its effect must be on an individual's very soul and on that person's whole life.

(2) Peter calls baptism *the pledge of a good conscience to God* (verse 21). The word Peter uses for *pledge* is the technical Greek word for the question-and-answer clause found in a business contract and which made that contract binding. The question was: 'Do you accept the terms of this contract, and bind yourself to observe them?' And the answer, before witnesses, was: 'Yes.' Without that question and answer, the contract was not valid.

Peter is, in effect, saying that in baptism God said to those coming direct from the old religion: 'Do you accept the terms of my service? Do you accept its privileges and promises, and do you undertake its responsibilities and its demands?' And, in the act of being baptized, each individual answered: 'Yes.'

We use the word *sacrament*. *Sacrament* is derived from the Latin *sacramentum*, which means *a soldier's oath of loyalty* on entering the army. Here, we have basically the same picture. We cannot easily apply this question and answer to infant baptism, unless it is to the parents; but, as we have said, baptism in the very early Church was of adult men and women coming spontaneously from worshipping the ancestral gods into the Church. The modern parallel is entering full membership of the Church. When we enter into Church membership, God asks us: 'Do you accept the conditions of my service, with all privileges and all its responsibilities, with all its promises and all its demands?' and we answer: 'Yes.' All new members should have a clear understanding of what they are doing when they take upon themselves membership of the Church.

(3) The whole idea and effectiveness of baptism is dependent on the resurrection of Jesus Christ. It is the grace of the risen Lord which cleanses us; it is to the risen, living Lord that we pledge ourselves; it is to the risen, living Lord that we look for strength to keep the promise that we have made. Once again, where infant baptism is the practice, we must take these great ideas and apply them to the time when we enter upon full membership of the Church.

Mark 1:9–15

No sooner was the glory of the hour of the baptism (verses 9–11) over than there came the battle of the temptations. One thing stands out here in such a vivid way that we cannot miss it. It was the *Spirit* who thrust Jesus out into the wilderness for the testing time. The very Spirit who came upon him at his baptism now drove him out for his test.

In this life it is impossible to escape the assault of temptation; but one thing is sure – temptations are not sent to us to make us fall; they are sent to strengthen the nerve and the sinew of our minds and hearts and souls. They are not meant for our ruin, but for our good. They are meant to enable us to prove ourselves and to emerge the stronger for the fight.

Forty days is a phrase which is not to be taken literally. It is the regular Hebrew phrase for a considerable time. Moses was said to be on the mountain with God for forty days (Exodus 24:18); it was for forty days that Elijah went in the strength of the meal the angel gave him (1 Kings 19:8). Just as we use the phrase *ten days or so, so forty days* simply means a fair length of time.

It was Satan who tempted Jesus. The development of the conception of *Satan* is very interesting. The word Satan in Hebrew simply means an *adversary*; and in the Old Testament it is so used of ordinary human adversaries and opponents again and again. The angel of the Lord is the satan who stands in Balaam's way (Numbers 22:22); Solomon declares that God has given him such peace and prosperity that he has no *satan* left to oppose him (1 Kings 5:4). The word began by meaning an *adversary* in the widest sense of the term.

But it begins to mean *one who pleads a case against a person*. It is in this sense that it is used in the first chapter of Job. In that chapter, Satan is no less than one of the sons of God (Job 1:6); but his particular task was to consider human beings (Job 1:7) and to search for some case that could be pleaded against them in the presence of God. He was the accuser of men and women before God. The word is so used in Job 2:2 and Zechariah 3:2. The task of Satan was to say everything that could be said against anyone.

The other title of Satan is the *devil*; the word *devil* comes from the Greek *diabolos*, which literally means *a slanderer*. It is a small step from the thought of one who searches for everything that can be said against an individual to the thought of one who deliberately and maliciously slanders all human beings in the presence of God. But in the Old Testament, Satan is still an emissary of God and not yet the malignant, supreme enemy of God. He is the *adversary of human beings*.

Through their captivity, the Jews learned something of Persian thought which is based on the conception that in this universe there are two powers, a power of the light and a power of the dark, Ormuzd and Ahriman; the whole universe is a battle ground between them, and people must choose one side or the other in that cosmic conflict. In this world there is God and *God's Adversary*. It was almost inevitable that Satan should come to be regarded as *The Adversary par excellence* – the essence of everything that is against God.

When we turn to the New Testament we find that it is the devil or Satan who is behind human disease and suffering (Luke 13:16); it is Satan who seduces Judas (Luke 22:3); it is the devil whom we must fight (1 Peter 5:8–9; James 4:7); it is the devil who is destined for final destruction (Matthew 25:41). Satan is the power which is against God.

Here we have the whole essence of the temptation story. Jesus had to decide how he was to do his work. He was conscious of a tremendous task and he was also conscious of tremendous powers. God was saying to him, 'Take my love to men and women; love them till you die for them; conquer them by this unconquerable love even if you finish up upon a cross.' Satan was saying to Jesus, 'Use your power to blast men and women; obliterate your enemies; win the world by might and power and bloodshed.' God said to Jesus, 'Set up a reign of love.' Satan said to Jesus, 'Set up a dictatorship of force.' Jesus had to choose that day between the way of God and the way of the Adversary of God.

The Second Sunday of Lent
Believing in the God Who Makes the Impossible Possible *and* The Tempter Speaks in the Voice of a Friend

Romans 4:13–25

To Abraham, God made a very great and wonderful promise. He promised that he would become a great nation, and that in him all families of the earth would be blessed (Genesis 12:2–3). In truth, the earth would be given to him as his inheritance. Now, that promise came to Abraham because of the faith that he showed towards God. It did not come because he piled up merit by doing works of the law. It was the outgoing of God's generous grace in answer to Abraham's absolute faith. The promise, as Paul saw it, was dependent on two things and two things only – the free grace of God and the perfect faith of Abraham.

Paul sets before the Romans two ways. The one is a way in which men and women seek a right relationship with God through their own efforts. It is doomed to failure. The other is a way in which men and women enter by faith into a relationship with God, which by God's grace already exists for them to come into in trust.

In verses 18–25 Paul's thoughts turn to an outstanding example of Abraham's willingness to take God at his word. The promise that all families of the earth would be blessed in his descendants was given to Abraham when he was an old man. His wife, Sarah, had always been childless; and now, when he was 100 years old and she was 90 (Genesis 17:17), there came the promise that a son would be born to them. It seemed, on the face of it, beyond all belief and beyond all hope of fulfilment, for he was long past the age of fathering a child, and she was long past child-bearing age. Yet, once again, Abraham took God at his word, and once again it was this faith that was 'accounted to him as righteousness'.

It was this willingness to take God at his word which put Abraham into a right relationship with him. Now, the Jewish Rabbis had a saying to which Paul here refers. They said: 'What is written of Abraham is written also of his children.' They meant that any promise that God made to Abraham also extends to his children. Therefore, if Abraham's willingness to take God at his word brought him into a right relationship with God, so it will be the same for us. It is not works of the law, it is this trusting faith which establishes the relationship between God and his people which ought to exist.

The essence of Abraham's faith in this case was that he believed that God could make the impossible possible. As long as we believe that everything depends on our efforts, we are bound to be pessimists, for experience has taught the grim lesson that our own efforts can achieve very little. When we realize that it is not our own efforts but God's grace and power which matter, then we become optimists, because we are bound to believe that with God nothing is impossible.

It is told that, once, Saint Teresa of Avila set out to build a convent with only a few coins as her complete resources. Someone said to her: 'Not even Saint Teresa can accomplish much with so little.' 'True,' she answered, 'but Saint Teresa and a few coins *and God* can do anything.' We may well hesitate to attempt a great task by ourselves; there is no need to hesitate in attempting anything with God. Ann Hunter Small, the great missionary teacher, tells how her father, himself a missionary, used to say: 'Oh! the wickedness as well as the stupidity of the croakers [prophets of doom]!' And she herself had a favourite saying: 'A church which is alive dares to do anything.' That daring only becomes possible to the individual and to the church that takes God at his word.

Mark 8:31–38

When Jesus connected Messiahship with suffering and death, he was making statements that were to the disciples both incredible and incomprehensible. All their lives they had thought of the Messiah in terms of irresistible conquest, and they were now being presented with an idea which staggered them. That is why Peter protested so violently. To him the whole thing was impossible.

Why did Jesus rebuke Peter so sternly? Because he was putting into words the very temptations which were assailing Jesus. Jesus did not want to die. He knew that he had powers which he could use for conquest. At this moment, he was refighting the battle of temptations in the wilderness. This was the devil tempting him again to fall down and worship him, to take his way instead of God's way.

It is a strange thing, and sometimes a terrible thing, that the tempter sometimes speaks to us in the voice of a well-meaning friend. We may have decided on a course which is the right course but which will inevitably bring trouble, loss, unpopularity, sacrifice. And some well-meaning friend tries with the best intentions in the world to stop us. I knew a man who decided to take a course which would almost inevitably land him in trouble. A friend came to him and tried to dissuade him. 'Remember', said the friend, 'that you have a wife and a family. You can't do this.' It is quite possible for our friends to love us so much that they want us to avoid trouble and to play safe.

The tempter can make no more terrible attack than in the voice of those who love us and who think they seek only our good. That is what happened to Jesus that day; that is why he answered so sternly. Not even the pleading voice of love must silence for us the imperious voice of God.

Jesus never sought to lure anyone to him by the offer of an easy way; he sought to challenge men and women, to waken the boldness and moral courage in their souls, by the offer of a way than which none could be higher and harder. He came not to make life easy but to challenge people to greatness.

But Jesus never called on anyone to do or face anything which he was not prepared to do and face himself. That indeed is the characteristic of the leader whom people will follow. Jesus was not the kind of leader who sat remote and played with people's lives like expendable pawns. What he demanded that they should face, he, too, was ready to face. Jesus had a right to call on us to take up a cross, for he himself first bore one.

Jesus said of those who would be his disciples, 'Let them deny themselves.' We will understand the meaning of this demand best if we take it very simply and literally. 'Let them say no to self.' If we would follow Jesus Christ we must say no to ourselves and yes to Christ. We must say no to our own natural love of ease and comfort. We must say no to every course of action based on self-seeking and self-will. We must say no to the instincts and the desires which prompt us to touch and taste and handle the forbidden things. We must unhesitatingly say yes to the voice and the command of Jesus Christ. We must be able to say with Paul, 'It is no longer I who live, but it is Christ who lives in me' (Galatians 2:20). We live no longer to follow our own will, but to follow the will of Christ, and in that service we find perfect freedom.

There are certain things which are lost by being kept and saved by being used. Any individual talent is like that. If it is used, it will develop into something still greater. If someone refuses to use it, in the end that talent will be lost. Supremely so, life is like that. History is full of examples of men and women who, by throwing away their lives, gained life eternal.

God gave us life to spend and not to keep. If we live carefully, always thinking first of our own profit, ease, comfort and security, if our sole aim is to make life as long and as trouble-free as possible, if we will make no effort except for ourselves, we are losing life all the time. But if we spend life for others, if we forget health and time and wealth and comfort in our desire to do something for Jesus and for those for whom Jesus died, we are winning life all the time.

The very essence of life is in risking life and spending life, not in saving it and hoarding it. True, it is the way of weariness, of exhaustion, of giving to the uttermost – but it is better any day to burn out than to rust out, for that is the way to happiness and the way to God.

The Third Sunday of Lent
A Stumbling-block to the Jews and Foolishness to the Greeks *and* The New Temple

1 Corinthians 1:18–25

Both to cultured Greeks and to pious Jews, the story that Christianity had to tell sounded like the sheerest folly. Paul begins by making free use of two quotations from Isaiah (29:14, 33:18) to show how mere human wisdom is bound to fail. He cites the undeniable fact that, for all its wisdom, the world had never found God and was still blindly and gropingly seeking him. That very search was designed by God to show men and women their own helplessness and so to prepare the way for the acceptance of the one who is the one true way.

What, then, was this Christian message? If we study the four great sermons in the Book of Acts (2:14–39, 3:12–26, 4:8–12, 10:36–43), we find that there are certain constant elements in the Christian preaching. (1) There is the claim that the great promised time of God has come. (2) There is a summary of the life, death and resurrection of Jesus. (3) There is a claim that all this was the fulfilment of prophecy. (4) There is the assertion that Jesus will come again. (5) There is an urgent invitation to men and women to repent and receive the promised gift of the Holy Spirit.

(1) To the *Jews*, that message was a stumbling-block. There were two reasons.

(a) To them, it was incredible that someone who had ended life upon a cross could possibly be God's chosen one. They pointed to their own law which unmistakably said: 'Anyone hung on a tree is under God's curse' (Deuteronomy 21:23). To a Jew, the fact of the crucifixion, so far from proving that Jesus was the Son of God, disproved it finally. The cross, to the Jews, was and is an insuperable barrier to belief in Jesus.

(b) The Jews sought for signs. When the golden age of God came, they looked for startling happenings. This very time during which Paul was writing produced a crop of false Messiahs, and all of them had tricked and deceived the people into accepting them by the promise of wonders. In AD 45, a man called Theudas had emerged. He had persuaded thousands of people to abandon their homes and follow him out to the Jordan, by promising that, at his word of command, the Jordan would divide and he would lead them across without getting their feet wet. That was the kind of thing that the Jews were looking for. In Jesus, they saw one who was meek and lowly, one who deliberately avoided the spectacular, one who served and who ended on a cross – and it seemed to them an impossible picture of the chosen one of God.

(2) To the *Greeks*, the message was foolishness. Again, there were two reasons.

(a) In Greek thought, the first characteristic of God was *apatheia*. That word means more than *apathy*; it means *total inability to feel*. The Greeks argued that, if God can feel joy or sorrow or anger or grief, it means that some human being has for that moment influenced God and is therefore greater than God. So, they went on to argue, it follows that God must be incapable of all feeling, so that none may ever affect him. A God who suffered was to the Greeks a contradiction in terms.

They went further. Plutarch, the great historian and philosopher, declared that it was an insult to God to involve him in human affairs. God, of necessity, was utterly detached. The very idea of *incarnation*, of God becoming a man, was revolting to the Greek mind. St Augustine, who was a very great scholar long before he became a Christian, could say that, in the Greek philosophers, he found a parallel to almost all the teaching of Christianity; but one thing, he said, he never found: 'The Word became flesh and dwelt among us.' To any thinking Greek, the incarnation was a total impossibility. It was incredible that one who had suffered as Jesus had suffered could possibly be the Son of God.

(b) The Greeks sought wisdom. Originally, the Greek word *sophist* meant a *wise man* in the good sense; but it came to mean a man with a clever mind and cunning tongue, a mental acrobat, a man who with glittering and persuasive rhetoric could make the worse appear the better reason. It meant a man who would spend endless hours discussing hair-splitting trifles and who had no real interest in solutions. The first-century writer Dio Chrysostom describes the Greek wise men: 'They croak like frogs in a marsh; they are the most wretched of men, because, though ignorant, they think themselves wise; they are like peacocks, showing off their reputation and the number of their pupils as peacocks do their tails.'

It is impossible to exaggerate the almost fantastic mastery that the silver-tongued rhetorician held in Greece. They thought not of what they were saying, but of how they were saying it. Their thought might be poisonous as long as it was enveloped in honeyed words. The Greeks were intoxicated with fine words; and, to them, a Christian preacher with a blunt message seemed a crude and uncultured figure, to be laughed at and ridiculed rather than to be listened to and respected.

It looked as if the Christian message had little chance of success against the background of Jewish or Greek life; but, as Paul said, 'What looks like God's foolishness is wiser than human wisdom; and what looks like God's weakness is stronger than human strength.'

John 2:13–22

It was quite certain that an act like the cleansing of the Temple would produce an immediate reaction in those who saw it happening. It was not the kind of thing that anyone could look at with complete indifference. It was much too staggering for that.

In verses 17–22 we have two reactions. First, there is the reaction of the disciples, which was to remember the words of Psalm 69:9. The point is that this Psalm was taken to refer to the Messiah. When the Messiah came, he would be burned up with a zeal for the house of God. When this verse leapt into their minds, it meant the conviction that Jesus was the Messiah seized the minds of the disciples even more deeply and more definitely. This action befitted none but the Messiah, and they were surer than ever that Jesus was in fact the Anointed One of God.

Second, there is the reaction of the Jews, a very natural one. They asked what right Jesus had to act like that and demanded that he should at once prove his credentials by some sign. The point is this. They acknowledged the act of Jesus to be that of one who thereby claimed to be the Messiah. It was always expected that when the Messiah came he would confirm his claims by doing amazing things. False Messiahs did in fact arise and promise to cleave the waters of Jordan in two or make the walls of the city collapse at a word. The popular idea of the Messiah was connected with wonders. So the Jews said: 'By this act of yours you have publicly claimed to be the Messiah. Now show us some wonder which will prove your claim.'

We must remember that verses 21 and 22 are John's interpretation written long afterwards. He was inevitably reading into the passage ideas which were the product of seventy years of thinking about and experience of the risen Christ. But what did Jesus originally say and what did he originally mean?

There is no possible doubt that Jesus spoke words which were very like these, words which could be maliciously twisted into a destructive claim. When Jesus was on trial, the false witness borne against him was: 'This fellow said, "I am able to destroy the temple of God and to build it in three days"' (Matthew 26:61).

First, Jesus certainly never said he would destroy the material Temple and then rebuild it. Jesus in fact looked for the end of the Temple. He said to the woman of Samaria that the day was coming when God would be worshipped neither in Mount Gerizim, nor in Jerusalem, but in spirit and in truth (John 4:21). Second, the cleansing of the Temple was a dramatic way of showing that the whole Temple worship with its ritual and its sacrifice was irrelevant and could do nothing to lead people to God. It is clear that Jesus did expect that the Temple would pass away; that he had come to render its worship unnecessary and obsolete; and that therefore he would never suggest that he would rebuild it.

If we turn to Mark's Gospel, we find the little extra suggestive and illuminating phrase there. As Mark relates the charge against Jesus, it ran: 'I will destroy this temple that is made with hands, and in three days I will build another, *not made with hands'* (Mark 14:58). What Jesus really meant was that his coming had put an end to this way of worshipping God that was made and arranged according to human design and had put in its place a spiritual worship; that he put an end to all this business of animal sacrifice and priestly ritual and put in its place a direct approach to the Spirit of God which did not need an elaborately built Temple and a ritual of incense and sacrifice offered by human hands. The threat of Jesus was: 'Your Temple worship, your elaborate ritual and your lavish animal sacrifices are at an end, because I have come.' The promise of Jesus was: 'I will give you a way to come to God without all this human elaboration and human ritual. I have come to destroy this Temple in Jerusalem and to make the whole earth the Temple where it is possible to know the presence of the living God.' Jesus shattered the Jews by telling them that all its magnificence and splendour and all the money and skill that had been lavished on it were completely irrelevant; that he had come to show people a way to come to God without any Temple at all.

That must be what Jesus actually said; but in the years to come John saw far more than that in Jesus' saying. He saw in it nothing less than a prophecy of the resurrection; *and John was right.* He was right because the whole round earth could never become the temple of the living God until Jesus was released from the body and was everywhere present; and until he was with men and women everywhere, even to the end of the world.

It is the presence of the living, risen Christ which makes the whole world into the Temple of God. So John says that when they remembered, they saw in this a promise of the resurrection. They did not see that at the time; they could not; it was only their own experience of the living Christ which one day showed them the true depth of what Jesus said.

We have here the tremendous truth that our contact with God, our entry into his presence and our approach to him are not dependent on anything that human hands can build or human minds devise. In the street, in the home, at business, on the hills, on the open road or in church, we have our inner temple, the presence of the risen Christ forever with us throughout all the world.

The Fourth Sunday of Lent
The Work of Christ *and* Love and Judgement

Ephesians 2:1–10

Paul begins by saying that, as we are, we are dead in sins and trespasses; he then goes on to say that God in his love and mercy has made us alive in Jesus Christ.

(1) Sin kills innocence. Not even Jesus can give back lost innocence, for not even Jesus can put back the clock; but what he can do is take away the sense of guilt which the lost innocence necessarily brings with it.

The first thing sin does is create a feeling of estrangement between us and God. Whenever people realize that they have sinned, they are weighed down by the feeling that they dare not approach God. When Isaiah received his vision of God, his first reaction was to say: 'Woe is me! I am lost, for I am a man of unclean lips, and I live among a people of unclean lips' (Isaiah 6:5). When Peter realized who Jesus was, his first reaction was: 'Go away from me, Lord, for I am a sinful man!' (Luke 5:8).

Jesus begins by taking that sense of estrangement away. He came to tell us that, no matter what we are like, the door is open to the presence of God. He came to take away the sense of estrangement and of guilt, by telling us that God wants us just as we are.

(2) Sin killed the ideals by which people live. Jesus reawakens the ideal in our hearts.

The story is told of an engineer in a river ferryboat in America. His boat was old and he did not worry overmuch about it; the engines were grimy and ill-cared for. This engineer was completely converted to Christianity. The first thing he did was to go back to his ferryboat and polish his engines until every part of the machinery shone like a mirror. One of the regular passengers commented on the change. 'What have you been up to?' he asked the engineer. 'What set you cleaning and polishing these old engines of yours?' 'Sir,' answered the engineer, 'I've got a glory.' That is what Christ does for people. He gives them a glory.

(3) Greater than anything else, Jesus Christ revives and restores the lost will. The deadly thing about sin is that it slowly but surely destroys a person's will and the indulgence which begins as a pleasure becomes a necessity. Jesus re-creates the will.

That in fact is always what love does. The effect of a great love is always to cleanse. When people really and truly fall in love, their love compels them to goodness. They love the loved one so much that the love for their sins is broken. That is what Christ does for us. When we love him, that love re-creates and restores our will towards goodness. As Charles Wesley's great hymn 'O for a thousand tongues to sing' has it:

He breaks the power of cancelled sin,
He sets the prisoner free.

Paul closes this passage with a great discussion and explanation of that paradox which always lies at the heart of his view of the gospel. That paradox has two aspects.

(1) Paul insists that it is by grace that we are saved. We have not earned salvation, nor could we have earned it. It is the gift of God, and our part is simply to accept it. Paul's point of view is undeniably true – and for two reasons.

(a) God is perfection; and, therefore, only perfection is good enough for him. Human beings by their very nature cannot bring perfection to God; and so, if we are ever to win our way to God, it must always be God who gives and we take from him.

(b) God is love; sin is therefore a crime, not against law, but against love. Now, it is possible to make atonement for a broken law, but it is impossible to make atonement for a broken heart; and sin is not so much breaking God's law as it is breaking God's heart. It is not against God's laws that we have sinned, it is against his heart. And therefore only an act of free forgiveness of the grace of God can put us back into the right relationship with him.

(2) That is to say that actions have nothing to do with earning salvation. It is neither right nor possible to leave the teaching of Paul here – and yet that is where it is so often left. Paul goes on to say that we are re-created by God for good actions. Here is the Pauline paradox. All the good works in the world cannot put us right with God; but there is something radically wrong with the Christianity that does not result in good deeds.

There is nothing mysterious about this. It is simply an inevitable law of love. If some fine person loves us, we know that we do not and cannot deserve that love. At the same time, we know with utter conviction that we must spend our lives *trying* to be worthy of it.

That is our relationship to God. Good works can never earn salvation; but there is something radically wrong if salvation does not produce good actions. It is not that our good deeds put God in our debt; rather that God's love lays on us the obligation to try throughout our lives to be worthy of it. We know what God wants us to do; God has prepared long beforehand the kind of life he wants us to live, and has told us about it in his book and through his Son. We cannot earn God's love; but we can and must show how grateful we are for it, by seeking with our whole hearts to live the kind of life that will bring joy to God's heart.

John 3:14–21

In verses 17–21 we are faced with one of the apparent paradoxes of the Fourth Gospel – the paradox of love and judgement. We have just been thinking of the love of God (verse 16), and now suddenly we are confronted with judgement and condemnation and conviction. John has just said that it was because God so loved the world that he sent his Son into the world. Later he will go on to show us Jesus saying: 'I came into this world for judgement' (9:39). How can both things be true? It is quite possible to offer someone an experience in nothing but love and for that experience to turn out a judgement.

It is quite possible to offer someone an experience which is meant to do nothing but bring joy and bliss and yet for that experience to turn out a judgement. Suppose we love great music and get nearer to God immersed in the surge and thunder of a great symphony than anywhere else. Suppose we have friends who do not know anything about such music and we wish to introduce them to this great experience, to share it with them, and give them this contact with the invisible beauty which we ourselves enjoy. We have no aim other than to give our friends the happiness of a great new experience. We take them to a symphony concert; and in a very short time they are fidgeting and gazing around the hall, extremely bored. Those friends have passed judgement on themselves that they have no music in their souls. The experience designed to bring them new happiness has become only a judgement.

This always happens when people are confronted with greatness. We may take our friends to see some great masterpiece of art; we may take them to listen to the most eloquent of preachers; we may give them a great book to read; we may take them to gaze upon some beauty. Their reactions are a judgement; if they find no beauty and no thrill, we know that there is a blind spot in their souls. A visitor was being shown round an art gallery by one of the attendants. In that gallery there were certain masterpieces beyond all price, possessions of eternal beauty and unquestioned genius. At the end of the tour, the visitor said: 'Well, I don't think much of your old pictures.' The attendant answered quietly: 'Sir, I would remind you that these pictures are no longer on trial, but those who look at them are.' All that the man's reaction had done was to show his own pitiable blindness.

This is so with regard to Jesus. If when people are confronted with Jesus their souls respond to that wonder and beauty, they are on the way to salvation. But if when they are confronted with Jesus they see nothing lovely, they stand condemned. Their reaction has condemned them. God sent Jesus in love. He sent him for the salvation of those people; but that which was sent in love has become a condemnation. It is not God who has condemned them; God only loved them; the people have condemned themselves. Those who react in hostility to Jesus have loved the darkness rather than the light. The terrible thing about really good people is that they always have a certain unconscious element of condemnation in them. It is when we compare ourselves with them that we see ourselves as we are.

Alcibiades, the spoilt Athenian man of genius, was a companion of Socrates, and every now and again he used to break out: 'Socrates, I hate you, for every time I meet you, you let me see what I am.' Those who are engaged on evil tasks do not want a flood of light on themselves or on what they are doing; but those engaged on an honourable task do not fear the light.

Once an architect came to Plato and offered for a certain sum of money to build him a house into none of whose rooms it would be possible to see. Plato said: 'I will give you double the money to build a house into whose every room everyone can see.' It is only evildoers who do not wish to see themselves and who do not wish anyone else to see them. Such people will inevitably hate Jesus Christ, for Christ will show them what they are, and that is the last thing that they want to see. It is the concealing darkness that they love and not the revealing light.

By our reaction to Jesus Christ, we stand revealed and our souls laid bare. If we regard Christ with love, even with wistful yearning, there is hope for us; but if in Christ we see nothing attractive, we have condemned ourselves. The one who was sent in love has become our judge.

The Fifth Sunday of Lent
At Home with the World and with God
and The Amazing Paradox

Hebrews 5:5–10

The Letter to the Hebrews offers a special contribution to Christian thought – the doctrine of the high priesthood of Jesus Christ. Here the writer shows here Jesus Christ fulfils the great conditions of the priesthood.

(1) He takes the last one first. Jesus did not choose his task; God chose him for it. At his baptism, there came to Jesus the voice which said: 'You are my son; today I have begotten you' (Psalm 2:7).

(2) Jesus has gone through the most bitter human experiences and understands what it is to be human with all its strength and weakness. The writer to the Hebrews has four great thoughts about him.

(a) He remembers Jesus in Gethsemane. That is what he is thinking of when he speaks of Jesus' prayers and entreaties, his tears and his cry. The word he uses for *cry* (*kraugē*) is very significant. It is an involuntary sound, a cry that is uttered in the stress of some tremendous tension or searing pain. So, the writer to the Hebrews says that there is no agony of the human spirit through which Jesus has not come. The Rabbis had a saying: 'There are three kinds of prayers, each loftier than the preceding – prayer, crying and tears. Prayer is made in silence; crying with raised voice; but tears overcome all things.' Jesus knew even the desperate prayer of tears.

(b) Jesus learned from all his experiences because he met them all with reverence. The Greek phrase for 'He learned from what he suffered' is a linguistic jingle – *emathen aph' hōn epathen*. And this is an idea which keeps recurring in the Greek thinkers. They are always connecting *mathein*, to learn, and *pathein*, to suffer. Aeschylus, the earliest of the great Greek dramatists, had as a kind of continual text: 'Learning comes from suffering' (*pathei mathos*). He calls suffering a kind of *savage grace* from the gods. Herodotus declared that his sufferings were *acharista mathēmata*, ungracious ways of learning. A traditional Irish proverb says of the poets: 'We learn in suffering what we teach in song.' God speaks to us in many experiences of life, and not least in those which try our hearts and souls. But we can hear his voice only when we accept in reverence what comes to us. If we accept it with resentment, the rebellious cries of our own hearts make us deaf to the voice of God.

(c) By means of the experiences through which he passed, both the Authorized and the Revised Standard Versions say that Jesus *was made perfect* (*teleioun*). *Teleioun* is the verb of the adjective *teleios*. *Teleios* can quite correctly be translated as *perfect* as long as we remember what the Greeks understood by that perfection. In Greek thought, a thing was *teleios* if it perfectly carried out the purpose for which it was designed. When people used the word, they were not thinking in terms of abstract and metaphysical perfection; they were thinking in terms of *function*. What the writer to the Hebrews is saying is that all the experiences of suffering through which Jesus passed perfectly fitted him to become the Saviour of the world.

(d) The salvation which Jesus brought is an *eternal salvation*. It is something which keeps people safe both in the present time and in eternity. With Christ, we are safe forever. There are no circumstances that can snatch us from Christ's hand.

John 12:20–33

At the heart of this section is a passage (verses 23–27) which would have come as a huge shock to those who it for the first time. It begins with a saying which everyone would expect; and it finishes with a series of sayings which were the last things anyone would expect.

What was this amazing paradox which Jesus was teaching? He was saying three things, which are all variations of one central truth and all at the heart of the Christian faith and life.

(1) He was saying that only by death comes life. The grain of wheat was ineffective and unfruitful as long as it was preserved, as it were, in safety and security. It was when it was thrown into the cold ground, and buried there as if in a tomb, that it bore fruit. It was by the death of the martyrs that the Church grew. In the famous phrase: 'The blood of the martyrs was the seed of the Church.'

It is always because men and women have been prepared to die that the great things have lived. But it becomes more personal than that. It is sometimes only when we bury our personal aims and ambitions that we begin to be of real use to God. Cosmo Lang became Archbishop of Canterbury. At one time he had had great worldly ambitions. A godly friend's influence led him to abandon these and enter the Church of England. When he was studying for the ministry at Cuddesdon, one day as he was praying in the chapel he heard unmistakably a voice saying to him: 'You are wanted!' It was when he had buried his personal ambitions that he became useful to God.

By death comes life. By the loyalty which was true to death there have been preserved and born the most precious things which humanity possesses. By the death of personal desire and personal ambition we become servants of God.

(2) He was saying that only by spending life do we retain it. Those who love their lives are moved by two aims – by selfishness and by the desire for security. Not once or twice but many times, Jesus insisted that those who hoarded their lives must in the end lose them, and those who spent their lives must in the end gain

them. When Joan of Arc knew that her enemies were strong and her time was short, she prayed to God: 'I shall only last a year, use me as you can.' Again and again, Jesus laid down this law (Mark 8:35; Matthew 16:25; Luke 9:24; Matthew 10:39; Luke 17:33).

We have only to think of what this world would have lost if there had not been men and women prepared to forget their personal safety, security, selfish gain and selfish advancement. The world owes everything to people who recklessly spent their strength and gave themselves to God and to others. No doubt we will exist longer if we take things easily, if we avoid all strain, if we sit at the fire and cosset life, if we look after our health. No doubt we will *exist* longer – but we will never *live*.

(3) He was saying that only by service comes greatness. The people whom the world remembers with love are the people who serve others. Once a schoolboy was asked what parts of speech *my* and *mine* are. He answered – more truly than he knew – that they were *aggressive* pronouns. It is all too true that in the modern world the idea of service is in danger of getting lost. So many people are in business only for what they can get out of it. They may well become rich, but one thing is certain – they will never be loved, and love is the true wealth of life.

Jesus came to the Jews with a new view of life. They looked on glory as conquest, the acquisition of power, the right to rule. He looked on it as a cross. He taught men and women that only by death comes life; that only by spending life do we retain it; that only by service comes greatness. And the extraordinary thing is that when we come to think of it, Christ's paradox is nothing other than the truth of common sense.

Palm Sunday

Humiliation and Exaltation *and*
The Tragedy and the Triumph

Philippians 2:5–11

In many ways, this passage is one which extends to the very limits of theological thinking in the New Testament; but its aim was to persuade the Philippians to live a life in which disunity, discord and personal ambition had no place.

So, Paul says of Jesus that he humbled himself and became obedient to the point of death, even death on a cross. The great characteristics of Jesus' life were humility, obedience and self-renunciation. He wanted not to dominate men and women but only to serve them; he wanted not his own way but only God's way; he wanted not to exalt himself but only to renounce all his glory for the sake of the world. Again and again, the New Testament is sure that only those who humble themselves will be exalted (Matthew 23:12; Luke 14:11, 18:14). If humility, obedience and self-renunciation were the supreme characteristics of the life of Jesus, they must also be the hallmarks of Christians. Selfishness, self-seeking and self-display destroy our likeness to Christ and our fellowship with each other.

But the self-renunciation of Jesus Christ brought him the greater glory. It made certain that one day, sooner or later, every living creature in all the universe – in heaven, in earth and even in hell – would worship him. It is to be carefully noted where that worship comes from. *It comes from love.* Jesus won the hearts of men and women, not by forcing them through his power, but by showing them a love they could not resist. At the sight of this person who set aside his glory for all people and loved them to the extent of dying for them on a cross, human hearts are melted and human resistance is broken down. When people worship Jesus Christ, they fall at his feet in wondering love. They do not say: 'I cannot resist a might like that' but, as Isaac Watts expressed it in the hymn 'When I survey the wondrous cross', 'Love so amazing, so divine, demands my life, my soul, my all.' Worship is founded not on fear but on love.

Further, Paul says that, as a consequence of his sacrificial love, God gave Jesus the name which is above every name. One of the common biblical ideas is the giving of a new name to mark a new stage in a person's life. Abram became Abraham when he received the promise of God (Genesis 17:5). Jacob became Israel when God entered into the new relationship with him (Genesis 32:28). What then is the new name given to Jesus Christ? We cannot be quite certain what exactly was in Paul's mind, but most likely the new name is *Lord*.

The great title by which Jesus came to be known in the early Church was *kurios*, *Lord*, which has an illuminating history. (1) It began by meaning *master* or *owner*. (2) It became the official title of the Roman emperors. (3) It became the title of the Greek and Roman gods. (4) It was the word by which the Hebrew *Yahweh* was translated in the Greek version of the Hebrew Scriptures. So, when Jesus was called *kurios*, *Lord*, it meant that he was the Master and the Owner of all life; he was the King of Kings; he was the Lord in a way in which the gods of the old religions and the idols could never be; he was nothing less than divine.

We read that the aim of God is a day when every tongue will confess that *Jesus Christ is Lord*. These four words were the first creed that the Christian Church ever had. To be a Christian was to confess that Jesus Christ is Lord (cf. Romans 10:9). This was a simple creed, yet all-embracing. Perhaps we would do well to go back to it. Later, people tried to define more closely what it meant, and argued and quarrelled about it, calling each other heretics and fools. But it is still true that anyone who can say 'For me, Jesus Christ is Lord' is a Christian. If we can say that, we mean that for us Jesus Christ is unique and that we are prepared to give him an obedience we are prepared to give no one else. We may not be able to put into words who and what we believe Jesus to be; but, as long as there is in our hearts this wondering love and in our lives this unquestioning obedience, we are indeed Christians, because Christianity consists less in the mind's understanding than it does in the heart's love.

So we come to the end of this passage; and, when we come to its end, we come back to its beginning. The day will come when people will call Jesus *Lord*, but they will do so *to the glory of God the Father*. The whole aim of Jesus is not his own glory but God's. Paul is clear about the lonely and ultimate supremacy of God. In the first letter to the Corinthians, he writes that in the end the Son himself shall be subject to the one who put all things in subjection under him (1 Corinthians 15:28). Jesus draws men and women to himself that he may draw them to God. In the Philippian church, there were some whose aim was to gratify a selfish ambition; the aim of Jesus was to serve others, no matter what depths of self-renunciation that service might involve. In the Philippian church, there were those whose aim was to focus people's eyes upon themselves; the aim of Jesus was to focus people's eyes upon God.

So the followers of Christ must think always not of themselves but of others, not of their own glory but of the glory of God.

Mark 15:1–39

The final part of this passage reveals a scene so terrible that the sky was unnaturally darkened and it seemed that even nature could not bear to look upon what was happening. Let us look at the various people in this scene.

(1) There was Jesus. Jesus said two things.

(a) He uttered the terrible cry, 'My God! My God! Why have you abandoned me?' There is a mystery behind that cry which we cannot penetrate. Maybe it was like this. Jesus had taken this life of ours upon him. He had done our work and faced our temptations and borne our trials. He had suffered all that life could bring. He had known the failure of friends, the hatred of foes, the malice of enemies. He had known the most searing pain that life could offer. Up to this moment, Jesus had gone through every experience of life *except one – he had never known the consequence of sin*. Now if there is one thing sin does, it separates us from God. It puts between us and God a barrier like an unscalable wall. That was the one human experience through which Jesus had never passed, because he was without sin.

It may be that at this moment that experience came upon him – not because he had sinned, but because in order to be identified completely with our humanity he had to go through it. In this terrible, grim, bleak moment, Jesus really and truly identified himself with human sin. Here we have the divine paradox – Jesus knew what it was to be a sinner. And this experience must have been doubly agonizing for Jesus, because he had never known what it was to be separated from God by this barrier.

That is why he can understand our situation so well. That is why we need never fear to go to him when sin cuts us off from God. Because he has gone through it, he can help others who are going through it. There is no depth of human experience which Christ has not plumbed.

(b) There was the great shout. Both Matthew (27:50) and Luke (23:46) tell of it. John does not mention the shout but he tells us that Jesus died having said, 'It is finished' (John 19:30). In the original that would be one word; and *that one word was the great shout*. 'Finished!' Jesus died with the cry of triumph on his lips, his task accomplished, his work completed, his victory won. After the terrible dark there came the light again, and he went home to God a victor triumphant.

(2) There was the bystander who wished to see if Elijah would come. He had a kind of morbid curiosity in the face of the cross. The whole terrible scene did not move him to awe or reverence or even pity. He wanted to experiment while Jesus died.

(3) There was the centurion. A hard-bitten Roman soldier, he was the equivalent of a regimental sergeant-major. He had fought in many a campaign and he had seen many men die. But he had never seen men die like this and he was sure that Jesus was the Son of God. If Jesus had lived on and taught and healed he might have attracted many, but it is the cross which speaks straight to the hearts of men and women.

There is one other thing to note. 'The curtain of the Temple was torn in two, from top to bottom.' This was the curtain which shut off the Holy of Holies, into which no one might go. Symbolically that tells us two things. (a) The way to God was now wide open. Into the Holy of Holies only the high priest could go, and he only once a year on the Day of Atonement. But now, the curtain was torn and the way to God was wide open to everyone. (b) Within the Holy of Holies dwelt the very essence of God. Now with the death of Jesus the curtain which hid God was torn and he could be seen face to face. No longer was God hidden. There was no longer any need to guess and grope. Anyone who looked at Jesus could say, 'That is what God is like. God loves me like that.'

Easter Day
The Risen Lord *and* Tell Peter

1 Corinthians 15:1–11

Paul is repeating the main elements of the good news which he first brought to the Corinthians. It was not news which he had invented but news which had first been delivered to him, and it was news of a risen Lord. In verses 1–2, Paul says an extremely interesting series of things about the good news.

(1) It was something which the Corinthians had *received*. The gospel was never something that people invented for themselves; in a sense, people never discover it for themselves. It is something which they receive. Therein indeed is the very function of the Church. The Church is the repository and the transmitter of the good news. As one of the Church fathers had it, 'No man can have God for his Father, unless he has the Church for his mother.' The good news is something that is received within a fellowship.

(2) It was something in which the Corinthians *stood*. The very first function of the good news was to give people stability. In a slippery world, it kept them on their feet. In a tempting world, it gave them power to resist. In a hurting world, it enabled them to endure heartbreak or physical suffering and not to give in. James Moffatt finely translates Job 4:4: 'Your words have kept men on their feet.' That is precisely what the gospel does.

(3) It was something in which they were *being saved*. It is interesting to note that, in the Greek, the word used is a present tense and not past. It would be strictly correct to translate it not as 'in which you have been saved' but as 'in which you are being saved'. Salvation goes from glory to glory. It is not something which is ever completed in this world. There are many things in this life which

we can exhaust, but the meaning of salvation is something which can never be exhausted.

(4) It was something which people had *to hold tenaciously*. Life makes many attempts to take away our faith. Things happen to us and to others which baffle our understanding; life has problems to which there seem to be no solutions and questions to which there seem to be no answers; life has its dark places where there seems to be nothing to do but hold on. Faith is always a *victory*, the victory of the soul which tenaciously maintains a tight grasp on God.

(5) It was something which *must not be held haphazardly and at random*. The faith which collapses is the faith which has not thought things out and thought them through. For so many of us, faith is superficial. We tend to accept things because we are told them and to possess them merely at second hand. If we undergo the agony of thought, there may be much that we find we must discard, but what remains is really ours in such a way that nothing can ever take it from us.

In Paul's list of appearances of the risen Lord, two are specially interesting.

(1) There is the appearance to *Peter*. In the earliest account of the resurrection story, the word of the messenger in the empty tomb is: 'Go, tell his disciples *and Peter*' (Mark 16:7). In Luke 24:34, the disciples say: 'The Lord has risen indeed, and he has appeared to *Simon*.' It is an amazing thing that one of the first appearances of the risen Lord was to the disciple who had denied him. There is all the wonder of the love and grace of Jesus Christ here. Others might have hated Peter forever, but the one desire of Jesus was to set this erratic disciple of his upon his feet. Peter had wronged Jesus and then had wept his heart out; and the one desire of this amazing Jesus was to comfort him in the pain of his disloyalty. Love can go no further than to think more of the heartbreak of the person who wronged it than of the hurt that it has itself received.

(2) There is the appearance to *James*. Without doubt, this James is the brother of our Lord. It is quite clear from the gospel narrative

that Jesus' own family did not understand him and were even actively hostile to him. Mark 3:21 tells us that they actually sought to restrain him because they believed him to be mad. John 7:5 tells us that his brothers did not believe in him. One of the earliest of the gospels which did not succeed in getting into the New Testament is the Gospel according to the Hebrews. Only fragments of it remain. One fragment, preserved by the biblical scholar Jerome, reads: 'Now the Lord, when he had given the linen cloth unto the servant of the priest, went unto James and appeared unto him (for James had sworn that he would not eat bread from that hour wherein he had drunk the Lord's cup until he should see him risen again from among them that sleep).' So, the story runs, 'Jesus went to James and said: "Bring ye a table and bread." And he took bread and blessed it and broke it and gave it unto James the Just and said unto him: "My brother, eat thy bread, for the Son of Man is risen from among them that sleep." ' We can only conjecture what lies behind this. It may well be that the last days turned James' contempt into wondering admiration so that, when the end came, he was so torn with remorse for the way in which he had treated his brother that he swore that he would starve unless he came back to forgive him. Here, once again, we have the amazing grace and love of Christ. He came to bring peace to the troubled soul of the man who had called him mad and who had been his opponent.

It is one of the most heart-moving things in all the story of Jesus that two of his first appearances, after he rose from the tomb, were to men who had hurt him and were sorry for it. Jesus meets the penitent heart far more than halfway.

Mark 16:1–8

There had not been time to render the last services to the body of Jesus. The Sabbath had intervened and the women who wished to anoint the body had not been able to do so. As early as possible after the Sabbath had passed, they set out to perform this sad task.

They were worried about one thing. Tombs had no doors. When the word door is mentioned it really means *opening*. In front of the opening was a groove, and in the groove ran a circular stone as big as a cartwheel; and the women knew that it was quite beyond their strength to move a stone like that. But when they reached the tomb, the stone was rolled away, and inside was a messenger who gave them the unbelievable news that Jesus had risen from the dead.

One thing is certain – if Jesus had not risen from the dead, we would never have heard of him. The attitude of the women was that they had come to pay the last tribute to a dead body. The attitude of the disciples was that everything had finished in tragedy. By far the best proof of the resurrection is the existence of the Christian Church. Nothing else could have changed sad and despairing men and women into people radiant with joy and aflame with courage. The resurrection is the central fact of the whole Christian faith. Because we believe in the resurrection certain things follow.

(1) Jesus is not a figure in a book but a living presence. It is not enough to study the story of Jesus like the life of any other great historical figure. We may begin that way but we must end by meeting him.

(2) Jesus is not a memory but a presence. The dearest memory fades. The Greeks had a word to describe time meaning *time which wipes all things out*. Long since, time would have wiped out the memory of Jesus unless he had been a living presence forever with us. As J. G. Whittier's hymn 'Immortal Love' has it:

> And warm, sweet, tender, even yet
> A present help is he;
> And faith has still its Olivet,
> And love its Galilee.

Jesus is not someone to discuss so much as someone to meet.

(3) The Christian life is not a matter of *knowing about* Jesus, but of *knowing* Jesus. There is all the difference in the world between *knowing about* a person and *knowing* a person. Most people *know about* the Queen or the President of the United States but not so many *know* them. The greatest scholar in the world who knows everything about Jesus is less than the humblest Christian who knows him.

(4) There is an endless quality about the Christian faith. It should never stand still. Because our Lord is a living Lord there are new wonders and new truths waiting to be discovered all the time.

But the most precious thing in this passage is in two words which are in no other gospel. 'Go,' said the messenger. 'Tell his disciples *and Peter*.' How that message must have cheered Peter's heart when he received it! He must have been tortured with the memory of his disloyalty, and suddenly there came a special message for him. It was characteristic of Jesus that he thought not of the wrong Peter had done him but of the remorse he was undergoing. Jesus was far more eager to comfort the penitent sinner than to punish the sin. Someone has said, 'The most precious thing about Jesus is the way in which he trusts us on the field of our defeat.'

The Second Sunday of Easter
The Pastor's Message and the Tests of Truth *and* The Commission of Christ

1 John 1:1–2:2

John's message is about Jesus Christ; and of Jesus he has three great things to say. First, he says that Jesus was *from the beginning*. That is to say, in him eternity entered time; in him the eternal God personally entered our world. Second, that entry into the world was a real entry; it was real humanity that God took upon himself. Third, through that action there came to men and women the word of life, the word which can change death into life and mere existence into real living.

John begins by laying down the nature of the God and Father of Jesus Christ whom Christians worship. God, he says, is light, and there is no darkness in him. What does this statement tell us about God?

(1) It tells us that he is splendour and glory. There is nothing so glorious as a blaze of light piercing the darkness. To say that God is light tells us of his sheer splendour.

(2) It tells us that God is self-revealing. Above all things, light is seen; and it lights up the darkness round about it. To say that God is light is to say that there is nothing secretive or furtive about him. He wishes to be seen and to be known.

(3) It tells us of God's purity and holiness. In God, there is none of the darkness which cloaks hidden evil. That he is light speaks to us of his white purity and stainless holiness.

(4) It tells us of the guidance of God. It is one of the great functions of light to show the way. The road that is lit is the road that

can be seen clearly. To say that God is light is to say that he offers his guidance for the path we must tread.

(5) It tells us of the revealing quality in the presence of God. Light is the great revealer. Flaws and stains which are hidden in the shade are obvious in the light. Light reveals the imperfections in any piece of work or material. So, the imperfections of life are seen in the presence of God. As the poet and hymn-writer J. G. Whittier wrote,

> Our thoughts lie open to thy sight;
> And naked to thy glance;
> Our secret sins are in the light
> Of thy pure countenance.

We can never know either the depth to which life has fallen or the height to which it may rise until we see it in the revealing light of God.

In God, says John, there is no darkness at all. Darkness stands for the Christless life. It represents the life that people lived before they met Christ or the life that they live if they stray away from him. John writes to his people that, now that Christ has come, the darkness is past and the true light shines (1 John 2:8). The darkness stands for the ignorance of life apart from Christ and for the chaos of life without God. The darkness is connected with lovelessness and hate. If people hate one another, it is a sign that they walk in darkness (1 John 2:9–11). Love is sunshine, and hatred is the dark.

As John sees it, there are two great tests of truth.

(1) Truth is the creator of fellowship. If men and women are really walking in the light, they have fellowship with one another. No belief can be fully Christian if it separates people from their neighbours. No church can be exclusive and still be the Church of Christ. Anything that destroys fellowship cannot be true.

(2) Those who really know the truth are each day more and more cleansed from sin by the blood of Jesus. The Revised Standard Version is correct enough here, but it can very easily be misunderstood. It runs: 'The blood of Jesus his Son cleanses us from all sin.' That can be read as a statement of a general principle. But it is a statement of what ought to be happening in the life of every individual. The meaning is that, all the time, day by day, constantly and consistently, the blood of Jesus Christ ought to be carrying out a cleansing process in the life of the individual Christian.

The Greek for *to cleanse* is *katharizein*, which was originally a ritual word, describing the ceremonies and washings and so on that qualified an individual to approach the gods. But, as religion developed, the word came to have a moral sense; and it describes the goodness which enables people to enter into the presence of God. So, what John is saying is: 'If you really know what the sacrifice of Christ has done and are really experiencing its power, day by day you will be adding holiness to your life and becoming more fit to enter the presence of God.'

Here indeed is a great conception. It looks on the sacrifice of Christ as something which not only atones for past sin but also equips people in holiness day by day.

True religion is the means by which every day we come closer to one another and closer to God. It produces fellowship with God and fellowship with other people – and we can never have the one without the other.

John 20:19–31

It is most likely that the disciples continued to meet in the upper room where the Last Supper had been held. But they met in something very like terror. They knew the intense bitterness of the Jews who had brought about the death of Jesus, and they were afraid that their turn would come next. So they were meeting in terror, listening fearfully for every step on the stair and for every knock at the door, lest the representatives of the Sanhedrin should come to arrest them too. As they sat there, Jesus was suddenly in their midst. He gave them the normal everyday middle-eastern greeting: 'Peace be to you.' It means far more than: 'May you be saved from trouble.' It means: 'May God give you every good thing.' Then Jesus gave the disciples the commission which the Church must never forget.

(1) He said that as God had sent him forth, so he sent them forth. Here is what the New Testament scholar B. F. Westcott called 'The Charter of the Church'. It means three things.

(a) It means that Jesus Christ needs the Church, which is exactly what Paul meant when he called the Church 'the body of Christ' (Ephesians 1:23; 1 Corinthians 12:12). Jesus had come with a message for all people, and now he was going back to his Father. His message could never be taken to all men and women, unless the Church took it. The Church was to be a mouth to speak for Jesus, feet to run upon his errands, hands to do his work. Therefore, the first thing this means is that *Jesus is dependent on his Church.*

(b) It means that the Church needs Jesus. People who are to be sent out need someone to send them; they need a message to take; they need a power and an authority to back the message; they need someone to whom they may turn when they are in doubt and in difficulty. Without Jesus, the Church has no message; without him it has no power; without him it has no one to turn to when up against it; without him it has nothing to enlighten its mind, to strengthen its arm and to encourage its heart. This means that *the Church is dependent on Jesus.*

(c) There remains still another thing. The sending out of the Church by Jesus is parallel to the sending out of Jesus by God. But no one can read the story of the Fourth Gospel without seeing that the relationship between Jesus and God was continually dependent on Jesus' perfect obedience and perfect love. Jesus could be God's messenger only because he rendered to God that perfect obedience and love. It follows that the Church is fit to be the messenger and the instrument of Christ only when it perfectly loves him and perfectly obeys him. The Church must never be out to propagate *its own* message; it must be out to propagate the message of Christ. It must never be out to follow policies of human devising; it must be out to follow the will of Christ. The Church fails whenever it tries to solve some problem in its own wisdom and strength, and leaves out of account the will and guidance of Jesus Christ.

(2) Jesus breathed on his disciples and gave them the Holy Spirit. There is no doubt that, when John spoke in this way, he was thinking back to the old story of the creation. There the writer says: 'Then the Lord God formed man from the dust of the ground, and breathed into his nostrils the breath of life; and the man became a living being' (Genesis 2:7). This was the same picture as Ezekiel saw in the valley of dead, dry bones, when he heard God say to the wind: 'Come from the four winds, O breath, and breathe upon these slain, that they may live' (Ezekiel 37:9). The coming of the Holy Spirit is like the wakening of life from the dead. When he comes upon the Church, it is re-created for its task.

(3) Jesus said to the disciples: 'If you remit the sins of anyone, they are remitted; if you retain them, they are retained.' This is a saying whose true meaning we must be careful to understand. One thing is certain – no one can forgive anyone else's sins. But another thing is equally certain – it is the great privilege of the Church to convey the message of God's forgiveness to men and women. Suppose someone brings us a message from another, our assessment of the value of that message will depend on how well the bringer of the message knows the sender. If someone proposes to interpret another's thought to us, we know that the value of that

person's interpretation depends on the closeness they have to the other.

The apostles had the best of all rights to bring Jesus' message to all people, because they knew him best. If they knew that people were really penitent, they could with absolute certainty proclaim to them the forgiveness of Christ. But equally, if they knew that there was no penitence in their hearts or that they were trading on the love and the mercy of God, they could tell them that until their hearts were altered there was no forgiveness for them. This sentence does not mean that the power to forgive sins was ever entrusted to any individual or group; it means that the power to proclaim that forgiveness was so entrusted, along with the power to warn that forgiveness is not open to the impenitent. This sentence lays down the duty of the Church to convey forgiveness to the penitent in heart and to warn the impenitent that they are forfeiting the mercy of God.

The Third Sunday of Easter
Remember the Privileges of the Christian Life *and* In the Upper Room

1 John 3:1–7

John begins by demanding that his people should remember their privileges. It is their privilege that they are called *the children of God*. There is something even in a name. The fourth-century Church father, John Chrysostom, in a sermon on how to bring up children, advises parents to give their boy some great Scriptural name, to teach him repeatedly the story of the original bearer of the name, and so to give him a standard to live up to when he grows up. So, Christians have the privilege of being called the children of God. Just as to belong to a great school, a great regiment, a great church or a great household is an inspiration in life, so, even more, to bear the name of the family of God is something to keep our feet on the right way and to set us climbing. And John points out that we are not merely *called* the children of God; we *are* the children of God.

It is by the gift of God that we become children of God. By nature we are God's creatures, but it is by grace that we *become* the children of God. We are children of God only when he makes his gracious approach to us and we respond. While all men and women are children of God in the sense that they owe their lives to him, they become his children in the intimate and loving sense of the term only by an act of God's initiating grace and the response of their own hearts. Immediately, the question arises: if people have that great honour when they become Christians, why are they so despised by the world? The answer is that they are experiencing only what Jesus Christ has already experienced. When he came into the world, he was not recognized as the Son of God; the world preferred its own ideas and rejected his. The same is bound to happen to anyone who chooses to embark on the way of Jesus Christ.

John goes on to set before his people what is in many ways an even more tremendous truth – the great fact that *this life is only a beginning*. Here, John refers to the only true agnosticism. So great is the future and its glory that he will not even guess at it or try to put it into inevitably inadequate words. But there are certain things he does say about it.

(1) When Christ appears in his glory, we shall be like him. Surely, John had in mind the saying of the old creation story that human beings were made in the image and in the likeness of God (Genesis 1:26). That was God's intention, and that was human destiny. We have only to look into any mirror to see how far we have fallen short of that destiny. But John believes that, in Christ, people will finally attain it and at last bear the image and the likeness of God. It is John's belief that only through the work of Christ in their souls can men and women reach the true humanity that God meant them to reach.

(2) When Christ appears, we shall see him and be like him. The goal of all the great Christian men and women has been the vision of God. The end of all devotion is to see God. But that vision of God is not for the sake of intellectual satisfaction; it is in order that we may become like him. There is a paradox here. We cannot become like God unless we see him; and we cannot see him unless we are pure in heart, for only the pure in heart shall see God (Matthew 5:8). In order to see God, we need the purity which only he can give. We are not to think of this vision of God as something which only the great mystics can enjoy. There is somewhere a story about a poor and simple man who would often go into a cathedral to pray; and he would always pray kneeling before the crucifix. Someone noticed that, though he knelt in the attitude of prayer, his

lips never moved and he never seemed to say anything, and asked the man what he was doing kneeling like that. The man answered: 'I look at him; and he looks at me.' That is the vision of God in Christ that everyone can have; and whoever looks long enough at Jesus Christ must become like him.

We must note one other thing. John is here thinking in terms of the second coming of Christ. It may be that we can think in the same terms; or it may be that we cannot think so literally of a coming of Christ in glory. Be that as it may, there will come for every one of us the day when we shall see Christ and behold his glory. Here, there is always the veil of sense and time; but the day will come when that veil, too, will be torn in two. As Ray Palmer's hymn has it,

When death these mortal eyes shall seal,
And still this throbbing heart,
The rending veil shall thee reveal
All glorious as thou art.

Therein is the Christian hope and the vast possibility that the Christian life holds for us.

Luke 24:36b–48

Here we read of how Jesus came to his own when they were gathered in the upper room. In this passage certain great notes of the Christian faith are resonantly struck.

(1) It stresses *the reality of the resurrection*. The risen Lord was no phantom or hallucination. He was real. The Jesus who died was in truth the Christ who rose again. Christianity is not founded on the dreams of disordered minds or the visions of fevered eyes, but on one who in actual historical fact faced and fought and conquered death and rose again.

(2) It stresses *the necessity of the cross*. It was to the cross that all the Scriptures looked forward. The cross was not forced on God; it was not an emergency measure when all else had failed and when the scheme of things had gone wrong. It was part of the plan of God, for it is the one place on earth where, in a moment of time, we see his eternal love.

(3) It stresses *the urgency of the task*. Out to all people had to go the call to repentance and the offer of forgiveness. The Church was not left to live forever in the upper room; it was sent out into all the world. After the upper room came the worldwide mission of the Church. The days of sorrow were past and the tidings of joy must be taken to everyone.

(4) It stresses *the secret of power*. They had to wait in Jerusalem until power from on high came upon them. There are occasions when the Christian may seem to be wasting time, waiting in a wise passivity. Action without preparation must often fail. There is a time to wait on God and a time to work for God. Fay Inchfawn writes of the days when life is a losing contest with a thousand little things.

> I wrestle – how I wrestle! – through the hours.
> Nay, not with principalities and powers –
> Dark spiritual foes of God's and man's –
> But with antagonistic pots and pans;
> With footmarks on the hall,
> With smears upon the wall,
> With doubtful ears and small unwashen hands,
> And with a babe's innumerable demands.

And then, even in the busyness, she lays aside her work to be for a moment with God.

> With leisured feet and idle hands, I sat.
> I, foolish, fussy, blind as any bat,

Sat down to listen, and to learn. And lo,
My thousand tasks were done the better so.

The quiet times in which we wait on God are never wasted; for it is in these times when we lay aside life's tasks that we are strengthened for the very tasks we lay aside.

The Fourth Sunday of Easter
The Inseparable Commands *and*
The Rue and the False Shepherd

1 John 3:16–24

John has been speaking of the obligation of love. He now says, 'If you want to see what this love is, look at Jesus Christ. In his death for us on the cross, it is fully displayed.' In other words, the Christian life is the imitation of Christ. 'Let the same mind be in you that was in Christ Jesus' (Philippians 2:5). 'Christ also suffered for you, leaving you an example, so that you should follow in his steps' (1 Peter 2:21). No one can look at Christ and then claim not to know what the Christian life is.

But someone may say: 'How can I follow in the steps of Christ? He laid down his life upon the cross. You say I ought to lay down my life for others. But opportunities as dramatic as that do not come into my life. What then?' John's answer is: 'True. But when you see someone who is in need and you have enough, to give that person from what you have is to follow Christ. To shut your heart and to refuse to give is to show that the love of God which was in Jesus Christ has no place in you.'

John insists that we can find plenty of opportunities to reveal the love of Christ in everyday life. The New Testament scholar C. H. Dodd writes impressively on this passage: 'There were occasions in the life of the early church, as there are certainly tragic occasions at the present day, for a quite literal obedience to this precept, [that is, to lay down our life for the brothers]. But not all life is tragic; and yet the same principle of conduct must apply all through. Thus it may call for the simple expenditure of money we might have spent upon ourselves, to relieve the need of someone poorer. It is, after all, the same principle of action, though at a lower level of intensity: it is the willingness to surrender that which has value for our own life, to enrich the life of another. If such a minimum response to the law of charity, called for by such an everyday situation, is absent, then it is idle to pretend we are within the family of God, the realm in which love is operative as the principle and the token of eternal life.'

Fine words will never take the place of fine deeds; and no amount of talk of Christian love will take the place of a kindly action to someone in need, made at some personal expense or with some self-sacrifice, for in that action the principle of the cross is at work again.

At the end of this passage John speaks of the two things which are well pleasing in God's sight, the two commandments on obedience on which our relationship to God depends.

(1) We must believe in the name of his Son Jesus Christ. Here, we have that use of the word *name* which is peculiar to the biblical writers. It does not mean simply the name by which a person is called; it means the whole nature and character of that person as far as it is known to us. The psalmist writes: 'Our help is in the name of the Lord' (Psalm 124:8). Clearly, that does not mean that our help lies in the fact that God is called Yahweh; it means that our help is in the love and mercy and power which have been revealed to us as the nature and character of God. So, to believe in the *name* of Jesus Christ means to believe in the nature and character of Jesus Christ. It means to believe that he is the Son of God, that he does stand in relation to God in a way in which no other person in the universe ever stood or ever can stand, that he can perfectly reveal God to us and that he is the Saviour of our souls. To believe in the name of Jesus Christ is to accept him for what he really is.

(2) We must love one another, even as he gave us his commandment. This commandment is in John 13:34. We must love

each other with that same selfless, sacrificial, forgiving love with which Jesus Christ loved us. When we put these two commandments together, we find the great truth that the Christian life depends on the combination of right belief and right conduct. We cannot have the one without the other. There can be no such thing as a Christian theology without a Christian ethic; and equally there can be no such thing as a Christian ethic without a Christian theology. Our belief is not real belief unless it is translated into action; and our action has neither authority nor force unless it is based on belief.

We cannot begin the Christian life until we accept Jesus Christ for what he is; and we have not accepted him in any real sense of the term until our attitude to others is the same as his own attitude of love.

John 10:11–18

This passage draws the contrast between the good and the bad, the faithful and the unfaithful shepherd.

Jesus describes himself as the *good* shepherd. Now in Greek, there are two words for good. There is *agathos* which simply describes the moral quality of a thing; there is *kalos* which means that in the goodness there is a certain charm which makes it lovely. When Jesus is described as the *good* shepherd, the word is *kalos*. In him, there is more than efficiency and more than fidelity; there is loveliness. In the picture of Jesus as the good shepherd, there is loveliness as well as strength and power.

In the parable, the flock is the Church of Christ; and it suffers from a double danger. It is always liable to attack from outside, from the wolves and the robbers and the marauders. It is always liable to trouble from the inside, from the false shepherd. The Church runs a double danger. It is always under attack from outside and often suffers from the tragedy of bad leadership, from the disaster of shepherds who see their calling as a career and not as a means of service. The second danger is by far the worse; because if the shepherd is faithful and good, there is a strong defence from the attack from outside; but if the shepherd is faithless and a hireling, the enemies from outside can penetrate into and destroy the flock. The Church's first essential is a leadership based on the example of Jesus Christ.

Few passages in the New Testament tell us so much about Jesus in so short a compass than the final verses of this section.

(1) They tell us that Jesus saw his whole life as an act of obedience to God. God had given him a task to do, and he was prepared to carry it out to the end, even if it meant death. He was in a unique relationship to God which we can describe only by saying that he was the Son of God. But that relationship did not give him the right to do what he liked; it depended on his doing always, cost what it may, what God liked. Sonship for him, and our relationship to God, could never be based on anything except obedience.

(2) They tell us that Jesus always saw the cross and the glory together. He never doubted that he must die; and equally he never doubted that he would rise again. The reason was his confidence in God; he was sure that God would never abandon him. All life is based on the fact that anything worth getting is hard to get. There is always a price to be paid. Scholarship can be bought only at the price of study; skill in any craft or technique can be bought only at the price of practice; distinction in any sport can be bought only at the price of training and discipline. The world is full of people who have missed their destiny because they would not pay the price. No one can take the easy way and enter into glory or greatness; no one can take the hard way and fail to find these things.

(3) They tell us in a way that we cannot possibly mistake that Jesus' death was entirely voluntary. Jesus stresses this again and again. In the Garden of Gethsemane, he ordered his would-be

defender to put up his sword. If he had wished, he could have called in the hosts of heaven to his defence (Matthew 26:53). He made it quite clear that Pilate was not condemning him, but that he was accepting death (John 19:10–11). He was not the victim of circumstance. He was not like some animal, dragged unwillingly and without understanding to the sacrifice. Jesus laid down his life because he chose to do so.

Jesus was not helplessly caught up in a mesh of circumstances from which he could not break free. Apart from any divine power he might have called in, it is quite clear that to the end he could have turned back and saved his life. He did not lose his life; he gave it. The cross was not thrust upon him: he willingly accepted it – for us.

The Fifth Sunday of Easter
Love Human and Divine *and* The Vine and the Branches

1 John 4:7–21

Here we find John's teaching on love.

(1) Love has its origin in God (verse 7). It is from the God who is love that all love takes its source. We are never nearer to God than when we love. Clement of Alexandria said, in a startling phrase, that the real Christian 'practises being God'. Those who dwell in love dwell in God (verse 16). We are made in the image and the likeness of God (Genesis 1:26). God is love; and, therefore, to be like God and be what we were meant to be, we must also love.

(2) Love has a double relationship to God. It is only by knowing God that we learn to love, and it is only by loving that we learn to know God (verses 7–8). Love comes from God, and love leads to God.

(3) It is by love that God is known (verse 12). We cannot see God, because he is spirit; what we can see is his effect. We cannot see the wind, but we can see what it can do. The effect of God is love. It is when God comes into an individual that that person is clothed with the love of God and the love of other people, and the best demonstration of God comes not from argument but from a life of love.

(4) God's love is demonstrated in Jesus Christ (verse 9). When we look at Jesus, we see two things about the love of God. (a) It is a love which holds nothing back. In his love for men and women, God was prepared to give his only Son and make a sacrifice beyond which no sacrifice can possibly go. (b) It is a totally undeserved love. It would be no wonder if we loved God, when we remember

all the gifts he has given to us, even apart from Jesus Christ; the wonder is that he loves poor and disobedient creatures like us. As F. W. Faber's hymn has it,

> How thou canst think so well of us,
> And be the God thou art,
> Is darkness to my intellect,
> But sunshine to my heart.

(5) Human love is a response to divine love (verse 19). We love because God loved us. It is the sight of his love which wakens in us the desire to love him as he first loved us and to love our neighbours as he loves them.

(6) When love comes, fear goes (verses 17–18). Fear is the characteristic emotion of someone who expects to be punished. As long as we regard God as the Judge, the King and the Law-giver, there can be nothing in our hearts but fear, for from such a God we can expect nothing but punishment. But once we know God's true nature, fear is swallowed up in love. The fear that remains is the fear of causing him grief in his love for us.

(7) Love of God and love of other people are indissolubly connected (verses 7, 11, 20–1). John says, with almost crude bluntness, that anyone who claims to love God and hates a brother or sister is nothing but a liar. The only way to prove that we love God is to love the men and women whom God loves. The only way to prove that God is within our hearts is constantly to show the love for others within our lives.

This passage also has great things to say about Jesus Christ.

(1) It tells us that Jesus is *the bringer of life*. God sent him that through him we might have life (verse 9). There is a world of difference between existence and life. We all have existence, but we do not all have life. The very eagerness with which people seek

pleasure shows that there is something missing in their lives. Jesus gives people a purpose in life; he gives them strength by which to live; and he gives them peace in which to live. Living with Christ turns mere existence into fullness of life.

(2) It tells us that Jesus is *the restorer of the lost relationship with God*. God sent him to be the atoning sacrifice for sin (verse 10). When people sinned, the relationship with God was broken; and sacrifice was an expression of penitence, designed to restore that lost relationship. Jesus, by his life and death, made it possible for us to enter into a new relationship of peace and friendship with God. He bridged the awful gulf between us and God.

(3) It tells us that Jesus is *the Saviour of the world* (verse 14). When he came into the world, people were only too well aware of their own weakness and helplessness. People need to be saved from themselves; they need to be saved from the habits which have become their chains, from their temptations, from their fears and their anxieties and from their follies and mistakes. In every case, Jesus offers salvation; he enables us to face the present and to meet eternity.

(4) It tells us that Jesus is *the Son of God* (verse 15). Whatever that may mean, it certainly means that Jesus Christ is in a relationship to God in which no other person ever stood or ever will stand. He alone can show us what God is like; he alone can bring God's grace, love, forgiveness and strength.

This passage also teaches us about the Spirit. In verse 13, John says it is because we have a share of the Spirit that we know that we dwell in God. It is the work of the Spirit that in the beginning makes us seek God at all; it is the work of the Spirit that makes us aware of God's presence; and it is the work of the Spirit that gives us the certainty that we are truly at peace with God. It is the Spirit in our hearts which makes us dare to address God as Father (Romans 8:15–16).

John 15:1–8

Jesus, as so often, is working in this passage with pictures and ideas which were part of the religious heritage of the Jewish nation. Over and over again in the Old Testament, Israel is pictured as the vine or the vineyard of God. 'The vineyard of the Lord of hosts is the house of Israel' (Isaiah 5:7). 'Yet I planted you as a choice vine' is God's message to Israel through Jeremiah (Jeremiah 2:21). Ezekiel 15 likens Israel to the vine, as does Ezekiel 19:10. 'Israel is a luxuriant vine,' said Hosea (Hosea 10:1). 'You brought a vine out of Egypt,' sang the psalmist, thinking of God's deliverance of his people from bondage (Psalm 80:8). The vine had actually become the symbol of the nation of Israel. It was the emblem on the coins of the Maccabees. The vine was part and parcel of Jewish imagery, and the very symbol of Israel.

Jesus calls himself the *true* vine. The point of that word *alēthinos* – true, real, genuine – is this. It is a curious fact that the symbol of the vine is never used in the Old Testament apart from the idea of *degeneration*. The point of Isaiah's picture is that the vineyard has run wild. Jeremiah complains that the nation has turned 'degenerate and become a wild vine'. It is as if Jesus said: 'You think that because you belong to the nation of Israel you are a branch of the true vine of God. But the nation is a degenerate vine, as all your prophets saw. It is I who am the true vine. The fact that you are Jews will not save you. The only thing that can save you is to have an intimate living fellowship with *me*, for I am the vine of God and you must be branches joined to me.' Jesus was laying it down that not Jewish blood but faith in him was the way to God's salvation. No external qualification can set us right with God; only the friendship of Jesus Christ can do that.

When Jesus drew his picture of the vine, he knew what he was talking about. The vine was grown all over Palestine, as it still is. It is a plant which needs a great deal of attention if the best fruit is to be got out of it. It is grown commonly on terraces. The ground has to be perfectly clean. It is sometimes trained on trellises; it is sometimes allowed to creep over the ground, held up by low forked sticks; it sometimes even grows round the doors of the cottages; but wherever it grows, careful preparation of the soil is essential. It grows luxuriantly, and severe pruning is necessary. So luxuriant is it that the slips are set in the ground at least twelve feet apart, for it will creep over the ground at speed. A young vine is not allowed to fruit for the first three years and is drastically cut back each year to develop and conserve its life and energy. When mature, it is pruned in December and January. It has two kinds of branches, one that bears fruit and one that does not; and the branches that do not bear fruit are drastically pruned back, so that they will drain away none of the plant's strength.

The vine cannot produce the crop of which it is capable without severe pruning – and Jesus knew that. Further, the wood of the vine has the curious characteristic that it is good for nothing. It is too soft for any purpose. At certain times of the year, as was laid down by the law, the people must bring offerings of wood to the Temple for the altar fires. But the wood of the vine must not be brought. The only thing that could be done with the wood pruned out of a vine was to make a bonfire of it and destroy it. This adds to the picture Jesus draws.

He says that his followers are like that. Some of them are lovely fruit-bearing branches of himself; others are useless because they bear no fruit. Who was Jesus thinking of when he spoke of the fruit-less branches? There are two answers. First, he was thinking of the Jews. They were branches of God's vine. Was not that the picture found in the Old Testament, the picture that prophet after prophet had drawn (cf. Isaiah 5; Jeremiah 2:21; Ezekiel 15:1–5)? But they refused to listen to him; they refused to accept him, therefore they were withered and useless branches. Second, he was thinking of something more general. He was thinking of Christians whose

Christianity consisted of profession without practice, words without deeds; he was thinking of Christians who were useless branches, all leaves and no fruit. And he was thinking of Christians who heard the message and accepted it and then fell away, renouncing their beliefs and becoming traitors to the Master they had once pledged themselves to serve.

So then there are three ways in which we can be useless branches. We can refuse to listen to Jesus Christ at all. We can listen to him, and then render him a lip-service unsupported by any deeds. We can accept him as Master, and then, in the face of the difficulties of the way or the desire to do as we like, abandon him. One thing we must remember. It is a first principle of the New Testament that *uselessness invites disaster*. The fruitless branch is on the way to destruction.

The Sixth Sunday of Easter
The Necessary Obedience *and* The Life of Jesus' Chosen People

1 John 5:1–6

John here comes back to an idea which is never far from the surface of his mind. *Obedience is the only proof of love.* We cannot prove our love to anyone other than by seeking to please and bring joy to that person. Then, John quite suddenly says a most surprising thing. God's commandments, he says, are not heavy. We must note two general things here.

He certainly does not mean that obedience to God's commandments is easy to achieve. Christian love is no easy matter. It is never an easy thing to love people whom we do not like or people who hurt our feelings or injure us. It is never an easy thing to solve the problem of living together; and, when it becomes the problem of living together according to the Christian standard of life, it is a task of immense difficulty.

Further, there is in this saying an implied contrast. Jesus said of the scribes and Pharisees: 'They tie up heavy burdens, hard to bear, and lay them on the shoulders of others' (Matthew 23:4). The scribal and Pharisaic mass of rules and regulations could be an intolerable burden on the shoulders of any individual. There is no doubt that John is remembering that Jesus said: 'My yoke is easy, and my burden is light' (Matthew 11:30).

How is this to be explained? How can it be said that the tremendous demands of Jesus are not a heavy burden? There are three answers to that question.

(1) It is the way of God never to lay a commandment on anyone without also giving strength to carry it out. With the vision comes the power; with the need for it comes the strength. God does not give us his commandments and then go away and leave us to ourselves. He is there by our side to enable us to carry out what he has commanded. What is impossible for us becomes possible with God.

(2) Our response to God must be the response of love; and, for love, no duty is too hard and no task too great. Things that we would never do for a stranger we will willingly attempt for a loved one. There is an old story which is a kind of parable of this. Someone once met a young boy going to school long before the days when transport was available. The boy was carrying on his back a smaller boy who was clearly lame and unable to walk. The stranger said to the boy: 'Do you carry him to school every day?' 'Yes,' said the boy. 'That's a heavy burden for you to carry,' said the stranger. 'He's not a burden,' said the boy. 'He's my brother.' Love turned the burden into no burden at all. It must be so with us and Christ. His commandments are not a burden but a privilege and an opportunity to show our love.

The commandments of Christ are indeed difficult; but burdensome they are not, for Christ never laid a commandment on anyone without giving strength to carry it; and every commandment laid upon us provides another chance to show our love.

(3) The commandments of Jesus Christ are not hard to bear because with the commandment there comes the power and because we accept them in love. But there is another great truth. There is something in Christians which makes them able to conquer the world. The thing that enables us to conquer the world is *faith*.

John defines this conquering faith as the belief that Jesus is the Son of God. It is belief in the incarnation. Why should that be able to give us power to overcome? If we believe in the incarnation, it means that we believe that, in Jesus, God entered the world and took our human life upon himself. If he did that, it means that he *cared* enough for us to take upon himself the limitations of humanity, which is the act of a love that is beyond human understanding. If God did that, it means that he *shares* in all the many different activities of human life and knows the many and varied trials and temptations and sorrows of this world. Everything that happens to us is fully understood by God and that he is in this business of living along with us. Faith in the incarnation is the conviction that God shares and God cares. Once we possess that faith, certain things follow.

(1) We have a defence to resist the infections of the world. From within and from outside come the temptations which are part of the human situation in a world and a society not interested in and sometimes hostile to God. But, once we are aware of the constant presence of God in Jesus Christ with us, we have a strong protection against the infections of the world.

(2) We have a strength to stand up to the attacks of the world. The human situation is full of things which seek to take our faith away. In life there are sorrows and perplexities; there are disappointments and frustrations and, for most of us, failures and discouragements. But, if we believe in the incarnation, we believe in a God who himself went through all this, even to the cross, and who can, therefore, help others who are going through it.

(3) We have the indestructible hope of final victory. The world did its worst to Jesus. It did everything humanly possible to eliminate him – *and it failed*. After the cross came the resurrection; after the shame came the glory. That is the Jesus who is with us, one who saw life at its grimmest, to whom life did its worst – who died, who conquered death, and who offers us a share in that victory which was his. If we believe that Jesus is the Son of God, we always have Christ the Victor with us to make us victorious.

John 15:9–17

The central words of this passage are those in which Jesus says that his disciples have not chosen him, but he has chosen them. It was not we who chose God, but God who, in his grace, approached us with a call and an offer made out of his love.

Out of this passage, we can compile a list of things for which we are chosen and to which we are called.

(1) We are chosen for *joy*. However hard the Christian way is, it is, both in the travelling and in the goal, the way of joy. There is always a joy in doing the right thing. Christians are men and women of joy. It is true that Christians are sinners; but they are *redeemed* sinners, and therein lies their joy. How can any of us fail to be happy when we walk the ways of life with Jesus?

(2) We are chosen for *love*. We are sent out into the world to love one another. Sometimes we live as if we were sent into the world to compete with one another, or to dispute with, or even to quarrel with one another. But Christians are to live in such a way that they show what is meant by loving our neighbours. It is here that Jesus makes another of his great claims. He says: 'No one can show greater love than to lay down his life for his friends – and I did that.' Jesus gave us a commandment which he had himself first fulfilled.

(3) Jesus called us to be *his friends*. He tells his disciples that he does not call them slaves any more; he calls them friends. *Doulos*, the slave, the servant of God, was no title of shame; it was a title of the highest honour. Moses was the *doulos* of God (Deuteronomy 34:5); so was Joshua (Joshua 24:29); so was David (Psalm 89:20). It is a title which Paul counted it an honour to use (Titus 1:1); and so did James (James 1:1). And Jesus says: 'I have something greater for you yet: you are no longer *slaves*; you are *friends*.' Christ offers an intimacy with God which not even the greatest men and women knew before he came into the world.

(4) Jesus did not only choose us for a series of tremendous privileges. He called us to be his *partners*. Slaves could never be partners. A slave was defined in Greek law as *a living tool*. Slaves simply had to do what they were told without reason and without explanation. But Jesus said: 'You are not my slaves; you are my partners. I have told you everything; I have told you what I am trying to do, and why I am trying to do it. I have told you everything which God told me.' Jesus has given us the honour of making us partners in his task. He has shared his mind with us and opened his heart to us. The tremendous choice laid before us is that we can accept or refuse partnership with Christ in the work of leading the world to God.

(5) Jesus chose us to be *ambassadors*. 'I have chosen you', he said, '*to send you out*.' He did not choose us to live a life retired from the world, but to represent him in the world. Jesus chose us, first to come in to him, and then to go out to the world. And that must be the daily pattern and rhythm of our lives.

(6) Jesus chose us to be *advertisements*. He chose us to go out *to bear fruit*, and to bear fruit which will stand the test of time. The way to spread Christianity is to be Christian. Jesus sends us out, not to argue people into Christianity, still less to threaten them into it, but to attract them into it; so to live that its fruits may be so wonderful that others will desire them for themselves.

(7) Jesus chose us to be *privileged members of the family of God*. He chose us so that whatever we ask in his name the Father will give to us. Here again, we are face to face with one of those great sayings about prayer which we must understand aright. The New Testament lays down certain definite laws about prayer.

(a) Prayer must be *the prayer of faith* (James 5:15). When prayer is hopeless, it cannot be effective. There is little use in praying to be changed, if we do not believe it possible that we can be changed. To pray with power, we must have an invincible belief in the all-sufficient love of God.

(b) Prayer must be *in the name of Christ*. We cannot pray for things of which we know that Jesus would disapprove.

(c) Prayer must say: '*Your will be done*.' The essence of prayer is not that we say to God: 'Your will be changed,' but that we say to him: 'Your will be done.' So often, real prayer must be not that God would send us the things we wish, but that he would make us able to accept the things he wills.

(d) Prayer must never be *selfish*. When we pray, we must ask not only: 'Is this for my good?' but: 'Is this for the good of everyone?' The greatest temptation of all in prayer is to pray as if nobody but ourselves mattered.

Jesus chose us to be privileged members of the family of God. We can and must take everything to God in prayer; but when we have done so we must accept the answer which God in his perfect wisdom and perfect love sends to us. And the more we love God, the easier it will be to do that.

The Seventh Sunday of Easter
The Undeniable Witness and the Essence of Faith *and* Jesus' Prayer for His Disciples

1 John 5:9–13

Behind this passage, there are two basic ideas. There is the Old Testament idea of what constitutes an adequate witness. The law was quite clear: 'A single witness shall not suffice to convict a person of any crime or wrongdoing in connection with any offence that may be committed. Only on the evidence of two or three witnesses shall a charge be sustained' (Deuteronomy 19:15; cf. 17:6).

A triple human witness is enough to establish any fact. How much more must a triple divine witness – the witness of the Spirit, the water and the blood – be regarded as convincing? Second, the idea of witness is an integral part of John's thought. In his gospel, we find different witnesses all converging on Jesus Christ. John the Baptist is a witness to Jesus (John 1:15, 1:32–4, 5:33). Jesus' deeds are a witness to him (John 5:36). The Scriptures are a witness to him (John 5:39). The Father who sent him is a witness to him (John 5:30-2, 5:37, 8:18). The Spirit is a witness to him. 'When the Advocate comes . . . the Spirit of truth . . . he will testify on my behalf' (John 15:26).

John goes on to use a phrase which is a favourite of his in his gospel. He speaks of the person who 'believes in the Son of God'. There is a wide difference between *believing* someone and *believing in* that person. If we *believe* someone, we do no more than accept whatever statement that person may be making at the moment as true. If we *believe in* someone, we accept the whole person and all that that individual stands for in complete trust. We would be prepared not only to trust the spoken word, but also to trust ourselves to that person. To believe in Jesus Christ is not simply to accept what he says as true; it is to commit ourselves into his hands, for time and for eternity.

When we do that, the Holy Spirit within us testifies that we are acting aright. It is the Holy Spirit who gives us the conviction of the ultimate value of Jesus Christ and assures us that we are right to make this act of commitment to him. Those who refuse to do that are refusing the promptings of the Holy Spirit within their hearts.

If people refuse to accept the evidence of those who have experienced what Christ can do, the evidence of the actions of Christ, the evidence of the Scriptures, the evidence of God's Holy Spirit, the evidence of God himself, in effect, they are calling God a liar – and that is the very limit of blasphemy.

At the very end of the passage there is a statement that the essence of the Christian life is *eternal life*. The word for *eternal* is *aiōnios*. It means far more than simply *lasting forever*. A life which lasted forever might well be a curse and not a blessing, an intolerable burden and not a shining gift. There is only one person to whom *aiōnios* may properly be applied, and that is God. In the real sense of the term, it is God alone who possesses and inhabits eternity. *Eternal life* is, therefore, nothing other than *the life of God himself*. What we are promised is that, here and now, there can be given to each one of us a share in the very life of God. In God, there is peace; and, therefore, *eternal life* means *serenity*. It means a life liberated from the fears which haunt the human situation. In God, there is *power*; and, therefore, *eternal life* means *the defeat of frustration*. It means a life filled with the power of God and, therefore, victorious over circumstance. In God, there is *holiness*; and, therefore, *eternal life* means the *defeat of sin*. It means a life clothed with the purity of God and armed against contamination from a wicked world. In God, there is love; and, therefore, *eternal life* means *the end of bitterness and hatred*. It means a life which has the love of God in its heart and the undefeatable love of men and women in all its feelings and in all its actions. In God, there is *life*; and, therefore, *eternal life* means *the defeat of death*. It means a life which is indestructible because it has in it the indestructibility of God himself.

It is John's conviction that such a life comes through Jesus Christ and in no other way. Why should that be? If eternal life is the life of God, it means that we can possess that life only when we know God and are enabled to approach him and rest in him. We can do these two things only in Jesus Christ. The Son alone fully knows the Father; and, therefore, only he can fully reveal to us what God is like. As John had it in his gospel, 'No one has ever seen God. It is God the only Son, who is close to the Father's heart, who has made him known' (John 1:18). And Jesus Christ alone can bring us to God. It is in him that the new and living way into the presence of God becomes open to us (Hebrews 10:19–23). We may take a simple analogy. If we wish to meet someone whom we do not know and who moves in a completely different circle from our own, we can achieve that meeting only by finding someone who knows the other person and is willing to introduce us. That is what Jesus does for us in regard to God. Eternal life is the life of God, and we can find that life only through Jesus Christ.

John 17:6–19

The great interest of this passage is that it tells us of the things for which Jesus prayed for his disciples.

(1) The first essential is to note that Jesus did not pray that his disciples should be taken out of this world. He never prayed that

they might find escape; he prayed that they might find victory. The kind of Christianity which buries itself in a monastery or a convent would not have seemed Christianity to Jesus at all. The kind of Christianity which finds its essence in prayer and meditation and in a life withdrawn from the world would have seemed to him a sadly truncated version of the faith he died to bring. He insisted that it was in the rough and tumble of life that a people must live out their Christianity.

Of course there is need of prayer and meditation and quiet times, when we shut the door upon the world to be alone with God, but all these things are not the end that we seek in life, but means to that end; and the end is to demonstrate the Christian life in the ordinary work of the world. Christianity was never meant to withdraw people from life, but to equip them better for it. It does not offer us release from problems, but a way to solve them. It does not offer us an easy peace, but a triumphant warfare. It does not offer us a life in which troubles are escaped and evaded, but a life in which troubles are faced and conquered. However much it may be true that Christians are not of the world, it remains true that it is within the world that their Christianity must be lived out. We must never desire to abandon the world, but always desire to win it.

(2) Jesus prayed for the unity of his disciples. Where there are divisions, where there is exclusiveness, where there is competition between the churches, the cause of Christianity is harmed and the prayer of Jesus frustrated. The gospel cannot truly be preached in any congregation which is not one united band of brothers and sisters. The world cannot be evangelized by competing churches. Jesus prayed that his disciples might be as fully one as he and the Father are one; and there is no prayer of his which has been so hindered from being answered by individual Christians and by the churches than this.

(3) Jesus prayed that God would protect his disciples from the attacks of the evil one. The Bible is not a speculative book; it does not discuss the origin of evil; but it is quite certain that in this world

there is a power of evil which is in opposition to the power of God. It is uplifting to feel that God is the sentinel who stands over our lives to guard us from the assaults of evil. The fact that we fall so often is due to the fact that we try to meet life in our own strength and forget to seek the help and to remember the presence of our protecting God.

(4) Jesus prayed that his disciples might be consecrated by the truth. The word for *to consecrate* is *hagiazein*, which comes from the adjective *hagios*. In the Authorized Version, *hagios* is usually translated as *holy*, but its basic meaning is *different* or *separate*. So, *hagiazein* has two ideas in it.

(a) It means *to set apart for a special task*. When God called Jeremiah, he said to him: 'Before I formed you in the womb I knew you, and before you were born I consecrated you; I appointed you a prophet to the nations' (Jeremiah 1:5). Even before his birth, God had set Jeremiah apart for a special task. When God was instituting the priesthood in Israel, he told Moses to *ordain* the sons of Aaron and to *consecrate* them that they might serve in the office of the priests (Exodus 28:41). Aaron's sons were to be set apart for a special office and a special duty.

(b) But *hagiazein* means not only to set apart for some special office and task, it also means *to equip people with the qualities of mind and heart and character which are necessary for that task*. If they are to serve God, they must have something of God's goodness and God's wisdom in them. Those who would serve the holy God must themselves be holy too. And so God does not only choose people for his special service, and set them apart for it; he also equips them with the qualities needed to carry it out.

We must always remember that God has chosen us and dedicated us for his special service. That special service is that we should love and obey him and should bring others to do the same. And God has not left us to carry out that great task in our own strength, but out of his grace he fits us for our task, if we place our lives in his hands.

Pentecost
The Glorious Hope *and* The Work of the Holy Spirit

Romans 8:22–27

Here Paul speaks of human longing. In the experience of the Holy Spirit, men and women had a foretaste, a first instalment, of the glory that shall be; now they long with all their hearts for the full realization of what adoption into the family of God means. That final adoption will be the redemption of their bodies. In the state of glory, Paul did not think of people as disembodied spirits. In this world, every individual is a body and a spirit; and, in the world of glory, the total person will be saved. But the body will no longer be the victim of decay and the instrument of sin; it will be a spiritual body fit for the life of a spiritual person.

Then comes a great saying: 'We are saved by hope.' The blazing truth that lit life for Paul was that the human situation is not hopeless. Paul was no pessimist. The writer H. G. Wells once said: 'Man, who began in a cave behind a windbreak, will end in the disease-soaked ruins of a slum.' Not so Paul. He saw human sin and the state of the world; but he also saw God's redeeming power; and the end of it all for him was hope. Because of that, to Paul, life was not a state of permanent despair, waiting for an inevitable end in a world encompassed by sin, death and decay; life was an eager anticipation of a liberation, a renewal and a re-creation brought about by the glory and the power of God.

Verses 26–27 form one of the most important passages on prayer in the whole New Testament. Paul is saying that, because of our weakness, we do not know what to pray for, but the prayers we ought to offer are offered for us by the Holy Spirit. The New Testament scholar C. H. Dodd defines prayer in this way: 'Prayer is the divine in us appealing to the Divine above us.'

There are two very obvious reasons why we cannot pray as we ought. First, we cannot pray aright because we cannot foresee the future. We cannot see a year or even an hour ahead; and we may well pray, therefore, to be saved from things which are for our good, and we may well pray for things which would be to our ultimate harm. Second, we cannot pray aright because in any given situation we do not know what is best for us. We are often in the position of children who want something which would be bound only to hurt them; and God is often in the position of parents who have to refuse their children's requests or compel them to do something they do not want to do, because the parents know what is good for them far better than the children themselves.

Even the Greeks knew that. Pythagoras forbade his disciples to pray for themselves, because, he said, they could never in their ignorance know what was appropriate and best for them. Xenophon tells us that Socrates taught his disciples simply to pray for good things, and not to attempt to specify them, but to leave God to decide what the good things were. C. H. Dodd puts it in this way. We cannot know our own real need; we cannot with our finite minds grasp God's plan; in the last analysis, all that we can bring to God is an inarticulate sigh which the Spirit will translate to God for us.

As Paul saw it, prayer, like everything else, is of God. He knew that by no possible human effort can we justify ourselves; and he also knew that by no possible effort of the human intelligence can we know what to pray for. In the last analysis, the perfect prayer is simply: 'Father, into your hands I commend my spirit. Not my will, but yours be done.'

John 15:26–27; 16:4b–15

The disciples were bewildered and grief-stricken men. All they knew was that they were going to lose Jesus. But he told them that in the end this was all for the best, because, when he went away, the Holy Spirit, the Helper, would come. When he was in the body, he could not be everywhere with them; it was always a case of greetings and farewells. When he was in the body, he could not reach the minds and hearts and consciences of men and women everywhere; he was confined by the limitations of place and time. But there are no limitations in the Spirit. Everywhere we go, the Spirit is with us. The coming of the Spirit would be the fulfilment of the promise: 'I am with you always, to the end of the age' (Matthew 28:20). The Spirit would bring to men and women an uninterrupted fellowship forever, and would bring to Christian preachers a power and an effectiveness no matter where they preached.

We have here an almost perfect summary of the work of the Spirit. The word that John uses of the work of the Spirit is the word *elegchein*, translated as *convince* by the Revised Standard Version. The trouble is that no one word can translate it adequately. It is used for the cross-examination of a witness, or someone on trial, or an opponent in an argument. It has always this idea of cross-examining people until they see and admit their errors, or acknowledge the force of some argument which they had not yet seen. It is, for instance, sometimes used by the Greeks for the action of conscience on a person's mind and heart. Clearly such cross-examination can do two things – it can *convict* a person of the crime that has been committed or the wrong that has been done; or it can *convince* a person of the weakness of a particular case and the strength of the case which has been opposed. In this passage, we need *both* meanings, both *convict* and *convince*. Now let us go on to see what Jesus says the Holy Spirit will do.

(1) The Holy Spirit will *convict people of sin*. When the Jews crucified Jesus, they did not believe that they were sinning; they believed that they were serving God. But when the story of that crucifixion was later preached, they were pricked in their heart (Acts 2:37). They suddenly had the terrible conviction that the crucifixion was the greatest crime in history and that their sin had caused it. What is it that gives people a sense of sin? What is it that makes people humble before the cross? In an Indian village, a missionary was telling the story of Christ by means of slides projected on the whitewashed wall of a village house. When the picture of the cross was shown, one man stepped forward, as if he could not help it: 'Come down!' he cried. 'I should be hanging there – not you.' Why should the sight of a man crucified as a criminal in Palestine 2,000 years ago tear open the hearts of people throughout the centuries and still today? *It is the work of the Holy Spirit.*

(2) The Holy Spirit will *convince people of righteousness*. It becomes clear what this means when we see that it is *Jesus Christ's righteousness* of which they will be convinced. Jesus was crucified as a criminal. He was tried; he was found guilty; he was regarded by the Jews as an evil heretic, and by the Romans as a dangerous character; he was given the punishment that the worst criminals had to suffer, branded as a felon and an enemy of God. What changed that? What made people see in this crucified figure the Son of God, as the centurion saw at the cross (Matthew 27:54) and Paul on the Damascus road (Acts 9:1–9)? It is amazing that men and women should put their trust for all eternity in a crucified Jewish criminal. *It is the work of the Holy Spirit.* It is the Spirit who convinces people of the sheer righteousness of Christ, backed by the fact that Jesus rose again and went to his Father.

(3) The Holy Spirit *convinces people of judgement*. On the cross, evil stands condemned and defeated. What makes us feel certain that judgement lies ahead? *It is the work of the Holy Spirit.* It is the Spirit who gives us the inner and unshakable conviction that we shall all stand before the judgement seat of God.

(4) There remains one thing which at the moment John does not go on to mention. When we are convicted of our own sin, when we are convinced of Christ's righteousness, when we are convinced of judgement to come, what gives us the certainty that in the cross of Christ is our salvation and that with Christ we are forgiven, and saved from judgement? *This, too, is the work of the Holy Spirit.* It is the Spirit who convinces us and makes us sure that in this crucified figure we can find our Saviour and our Lord. The Holy Spirit convicts us of our sin and convinces us of our Saviour.

Trinity Sunday

Entry into the Family of God *and* Born Again

Romans 8:12–17

Here Paul is introducing us to another of the great metaphors in which he describes the new relationship of Christians to God. He speaks of Christians being adopted into the family of God. It is only when we understand how serious and complicated a step Roman adoption was that we really understand the depth of meaning in this passage.

Roman adoption was always rendered more serious and more difficult by the Roman *patria potestas*. This was the father's power over his family; it was the power of absolute disposal and control, and in the early days it was actually the power of life and death. In relation to his father, a Roman son never came of age. No matter how old he was, he was still under the *patria potestas*, in the absolute possession and under the absolute control of his father. Obviously, this made adoption into another family a very difficult and serious step. In adoption, a person had to pass from one *patria potestas* to another.

But it is the consequences of adoption which are most significant for the picture that is in Paul's mind. There were four main ones. (1) The adopted person lost all rights in his old family and gained all the rights of a legitimate son in his new family. In the most binding legal way, he got a new father. (2) It followed that he became heir to his new father's estate. Even if other sons were born afterwards, it did not affect his rights. He was co-heir with them, and no one could deny him that right. (3) In law, the old life of the adopted person was completely wiped out; for instance, all debts were cancelled. He was regarded as a new person entering into a new life in which the past had no part. (4) In the eyes of the law, he was absolutely the son of his new father. Roman history provides an outstanding case of how completely this was held to be true. The Emperor Claudius adopted Nero in order that he might succeed him to the throne; they were not in any sense blood relatives. Claudius already had a daughter, Octavia. To cement the alliance, Nero wished to marry her. Nero and Octavia were not blood relatives; yet, in the eyes of the law, they were brother and sister; and before they could marry, the Roman senate had to pass special legislation.

That is what Paul is thinking of. He uses yet another picture from Roman adoption. He says that God's spirit witnesses with our spirit that we really are his children. The adoption ceremony was carried out in the presence of seven witnesses. Now, suppose the adopting father died and there was some dispute about the right of the adopted son to inherit, one or more of the seven witnesses stepped forward and swore that the adoption was genuine. Thus the right of the adopted person was guaranteed, and he entered into his inheritance. So, Paul is saying, it is the Holy Spirit who is the witness to our adoption into the family of God.

So, we see that every step of Roman adoption was meaningful in the mind of Paul when he transferred the picture to our adoption into the family of God. Once, we were in the absolute control of our own sinful human nature; but God, in his mercy, has brought us into his absolute possession. The old life has no more rights over us; God has an absolute right. The past is cancelled and its debts are wiped out; we begin a new life with God and become heirs of all his riches. If that is so, we become joint heirs with Jesus Christ, God's own Son. Whatever Christ inherits, we also inherit. If Christ had to suffer, we also inherit that suffering; but, if Christ was raised to life and glory, we also inherit that life and glory.

It was Paul's picture that when people became Christians they entered into the very family of God. They did nothing to deserve it; God, the great Father, in his amazing love and mercy, has taken lost, helpless, poverty-stricken, debt-laden sinners and adopted them into his own family, so that the debts are cancelled and the glory inherited.

John 3:1–17

In the New Testament, and especially in the Fourth Gospel, there are four closely interrelated ideas. There is the idea of rebirth; there is the idea of the kingdom of heaven, into which people cannot enter unless they are reborn; there is the idea of being children of God; and there is the idea of eternal life.

Let us start with the *kingdom of heaven*. What does it mean? We get our best definition of it from the Lord's Prayer. There are two petitions side by side:

Your kingdom come:
Your will be done in earth as it is in heaven.

It is characteristic of Jewish style to say things twice, the second way explaining and amplifying the first. Any verse of the Psalms will show us this Jewish habit of what is technically known as parallelism:

The Lord of hosts is with us;
the God of Jacob is our refuge. (Psalm 46:7)

For I know my transgressions,
and my sin is ever before me. (Psalm 51:3)

Let us apply that principle to these two petitions in the Lord's Prayer. The second petition amplifies and explains the first; we then arrive at the definition: *the kingdom of heaven is a society where God's will is as perfectly done on earth as it is in heaven*. To be in the kingdom of heaven is therefore to lead a life in which we have willingly submitted everything to the will of God; it is to have arrived at a stage when we perfectly and completely accept the will of God.

Now let us take the idea of being a child of God. In one sense, this is a tremendous *privilege*. To those who believe, there is given the power to become God's children (John 1:12). But the very essence of being a child of God is necessarily *obedience*. 'They who have my commandments *and keep them* are those who love me' (John 14:21). The essence of this relationship is love; and the essence of love is obedience. This relationship is a privilege, but one which is entered into only when full obedience is given. So to be children of God and to be in the kingdom are one and the same thing. The children of God and the citizens of the kingdom are both people who have completely and willingly accepted the will of God.

Now let us take *eternal life*. It is far better to speak of *eternal* life than to speak of *everlasting* life. The main idea behind eternal life is not simply that of duration. It is quite clear that a life which went on forever could just as easily be hell as heaven. The idea behind eternal life is the idea of a certain quality of life. What kind? There is only one person who can properly be described by this adjective *eternal*, and that one person is God. Eternal life is the kind of life that God lives; it is God's life. To enter into eternal life is to enter into possession of that kind of life which is the life of God. It is to be lifted up above merely human, transient things into that joy and peace which belong only to God. Clearly we can enter into this close fellowship with God only when we render to him that love, that reverence, that devotion and that obedience which truly bring us into fellowship with him.

Here, then, we have three great related conceptions – entry into the kingdom of heaven, becoming children of God and eternal life – and all are dependent on and are the products of perfect obedience to the will of God. Here the idea of being *reborn* comes in. It is what links all these three conceptions together. It is quite clear that, as we are and in our own strength, we are quite unable to render to God this perfect obedience; it is only when God's grace enters into us and takes possession of us and changes us that we can give to him the reverence and the devotion we ought to give. It is through Jesus Christ that we are reborn; it is when he enters into possession of our hearts and lives that the change comes. When that happens, we are born of *water and the Spirit*.

Water is the symbol of cleansing. When Jesus takes possession of our lives, when we love him with all our heart, the sins of the past are forgiven and forgotten. *The Spirit* is the symbol of *power*. When Jesus takes possession of our lives, it is not only that the past is forgotten and forgiven; if that were all, we might well proceed to make the same mess of life all over again; but into life there enters a new power which enables us to be what by ourselves we could never be and to do what by ourselves we could never do. Water and the Spirit stand for the cleansing and the strengthening power of Christ, which wipes out the past and gives victory in the future.

Finally, John says that which is born of the flesh is flesh, and that which is born of the Spirit is spirit. Human beings by themselves are flesh, and their power is limited to what the flesh can do. By themselves, they cannot be other than defeated and frustrated; that we know only too well; it is the universal fact of human experience. But the very essence of the Spirit is power and life which are beyond human power and human life; and when the Spirit takes possession of us, the defeated life of human nature becomes the victorious life of God.

To be born again is to be changed in such a way that it can be described only as rebirth and re-creation. The change comes when we love Jesus and allow him into our hearts. Then we are forgiven for the past and armed by the Spirit for the future; then we can truly accept the will of God. And then we become citizens of the kingdom; then we become children of God; then we enter into eternal life, which is the very life of God.

The Sunday between 29 May and 4 June
Tribulation and Triumph *and*
The Clash of Ideas

2 Corinthians 4:5–12

Paul begins this passage with the thought that it might well be that the privileges which Christians enjoy might move them to pride. But life is designed to keep us from pride. However great our Christian glory, we are still mortal, still the victims of circumstance, still subject to the chances and the changes of human life, still mortal bodies with all their weakness and pain. We are like people who have precious treasure contained in earthen vessels, which are themselves weak and worthless. We talk a great deal about human power and about the vast forces which we now control. But the real characteristic of human beings is not their power but their weakness. As the French mathematician and theologian Blaise Pascal said in the seventeenth century, 'A drop of water or a breath of air can kill.'

A Triumph was for a Roman general a proud and glorious thing. But there were two things designed to keep the general from pride. First, as he rode in the chariot with the crown held over his head, the people not only shouted their applause but also, again and again, they shouted: 'Look behind you and remember you will die.' Second, at the very end of the procession there came the conquering general's own soldiers, and they did two things as they marched. They sang songs in the general's praise, but they also shouted disrespectful jibes and insults to keep him from too much pride.

Life has surrounded us with weakness, although Christ has surrounded us with glory, so that we may remember that the weakness is ours and the glory is God's, and recognize our own utter dependence on him. Paul goes on to describe this Christian life, in which our weakness is intermingled with God's glory, in a series of paradoxes.

(1) We are pressurized at every point but not hemmed in. There are all kinds of pressures on us, but we are never in so tight a corner that there is no way out. It is characteristic of Christians that, even if they are physically confined in some difficult environment or some restricting situation, there is always an escape route for the spirit to the spaciousness of God.

In 'East London', the poet Matthew Arnold writes of his meeting with a minister of Christ in the London slums.

> 'Twas August, and the fierce sun overhead
> Smote on the squalid streets of Bethnal Green,
> And the pale weaver, through his window seen
> In Spitalfields, look'd thrice dispirited.
> I met a preacher there I knew, and said:
> 'Ill and o'erwork'd, how fare you in this scene?'
> 'Bravely!' said he, 'for I of late have been
> Much cheer'd with thoughts of Christ, the living bread.'

His body might be hemmed in in a slum, but his soul reached out into the spaciousness of communion with Christ.

(2) We are persecuted by other people but never abandoned by God. One of the most notable things about the martyrs is that it was in their most difficult times that they had their sweetest times with Christ. As Joan of Arc said, when she was abandoned by those who should have stood by her, 'It is better to be alone with

God. His friendship will not fail me, nor his counsel, nor his love. In his strength, I will dare and dare and dare until I die.' As the psalmist wrote, 'If my father and mother forsake me, the Lord will take me up' (Psalm 27:10). Nothing can alter the loyalty of God.

(3) We are at our wits' end but never at our hope's end. There are times when Christians do not know what should be done, but even then they never doubt that something can be done. There are times when they cannot see clearly where life is going, but they never doubt that it is going somewhere. If they must, in Robert Browning's words, 'stoop into a dark, tremendous sea of cloud', they still know that they will emerge. There are times when, as Christians, we have to learn the hardest lesson of all, the very lesson which Jesus himself had to learn in Gethsemane – how to accept what we cannot understand and still echo another line from Browning's 'Paracelsus': 'God, Thou art love; I build my faith on that.'

The poet Francis Thompson wrote in 'The Kingdom of God' of the presence of Christ on the darkest days:

> But (when so sad thou canst not sadder)
> Cry – and upon thy so sore loss
> Shall shine the traffic of Jacob's ladder
> Pitched betwixt Heaven and Charing Cross.
> Yea, in the night, my Soul, my daughter,
> Cry – clinging Heaven by the hems;
> And lo, Christ walking on the water
> Not of Gennesareth but Thames!

We may be at our wits' end, but we can never be at our hope's end while we have the presence of Christ.

(4) We are knocked down but not knocked out. The supreme characteristic of Christians is not that they do not fall, but that every time they fall they rise again. It is not that they are never

beaten, but they are never ultimately defeated. They may lose a battle, but they know that in the end they can never lose the campaign. Robert Browning, in his 'Epilogue', describes the gallant character:

One who never turned his back but marched breast forward,
Never doubted clouds would break,
Never dreamed, though right were worsted, wrong would triumph,
Held we fall to rise, are baffled to fight better,
Sleep to wake.

Mark 2:23–3:6

The story told at the beginning of Chapter 3 is a crucial incident in the life of Jesus. It was already clear that he and the orthodox leaders of the Jews were quite at variance. For him to go back into the synagogue at all was a brave thing to do. It was the act of a man who refused to seek safety and who was determined to look a dangerous situation in the face. In the synagogue there was a deputation from the Sanhedrin. No one could miss them, for, in the synagogue, the front seats were the seats of honour and they were sitting there. It was the duty of the Sanhedrin to deal with anyone who was likely to mislead the people and seduce them from the right way; and that is precisely what this deputation conceived of themselves as doing. The last thing they were there to do was to worship and to learn; they were there to scrutinize Jesus' every action.

In the synagogue there was a man with a paralysed hand. The Greek word means that he had not been born that way but that some illness had taken the strength from him. The Gospel according to the Hebrews, a gospel which is lost except for a few fragments, tells us that the man was a stone mason and that he entreated Jesus to help him, for his livelihood was in his hands and he was ashamed to beg. If Jesus had been a cautious, prudent person he would have conveniently arranged not to see the man, for he knew that to heal him was asking for trouble.

It was the Sabbath day; all work was forbidden, and to heal was to work. The Jewish law was definite and detailed about this. Medical attention could be given only if a life was in danger. To take some examples – a woman in childbirth might be helped on the Sabbath; an infection of the throat might be treated; if a wall fell on anyone, enough might be cleared away to see whether the person was dead or alive; anyone found alive might be helped, but a dead body must be left until the next day. A fracture could not be attended to. A cut finger might be bandaged with a plain bandage but not with ointment. That is to say, at the most an injury could be kept from getting worse; it must not be made better.

Jesus knew that. This man's life was not in the least danger. Physically he would be no worse off if he were left until the next day. For Jesus this was a test case, and he met it fairly and squarely. He told the man to rise and to come out of his place and stand where everyone could see him. There were probably two reasons for that. Very likely Jesus wished to make one last effort to waken sympathy for the stricken man by showing everyone his wretchedness. Quite certainly Jesus wished to take the step he was going to take in such a way that no one could possibly fail to see it.

He asked the experts in the law two questions. *Is it lawful to do good or to do evil on the Sabbath day?* He put them in a dilemma. They were bound to admit that it was lawful to do good; and it was a good thing he proposed to do. They were bound to deny that it was lawful to do evil; and, yet, surely it was an evil thing to leave a man in wretchedness when it was possible to help him. Then he asked, *Is it lawful to save a life or to kill it?* Here he was driving the point home. *He* was taking steps to save this wretched man's life;

they were thinking out methods of killing himself. On any reckoning it was surely a better thing to be thinking about helping a man than it was to be thinking of killing a man. No wonder they had nothing to say!

This passage is fundamental because it shows the clash of two ideas of religion.

(1) To the Pharisee, religion was *ritual*: it meant obeying certain rules and regulations. Jesus broke these regulations and they were genuinely convinced that he was a bad man. It is like those who believe that religion consists in going to church, reading the Bible, saying grace at meals, having family worship, and carrying out all the external acts which are looked on as religious, and who yet never put themselves out to do anything for anyone, who have no sense of sympathy, no desire to sacrifice, who are serene in their rigid orthodoxy, and deaf to the call of need and blind to the tears of the world.

(2) To Jesus, religion was *service*. It was love of God *and* love of others. Ritual was irrelevant compared with love in action. A verse from J. G. Whittier's hymn, 'O Lord and Master of us All', sums it up:

> Our Friend, our Brother, and our Lord,
> What may Thy service be?
> Nor name, nor form, nor ritual word,
> But simply following Thee.

To Jesus, the most important thing in the world was not the correct performance of a ritual but the spontaneous answer to the cry of human need.

The Sunday between 5 and 11 June

The Secret of Endurance *and* The Conditions of Kinship

2 Corinthians 4:13–5:1

Paul sets out the reasons why he was able to do and to endure as he did.

(1) He was well aware that to share the life of Christ also meant to share the risks – that those who wished to live with Christ must be ready to die with him. Paul knew and accepted the inexorable law of the Christian life: 'no cross, no crown'.

(2) He faced everything in the memory of the power of God who raised Jesus Christ from the dead. He was able to speak with such courage and such disregard for personal safety because he believed that, even if death took him, the God who raised up Jesus Christ could and would also raise him up. He was certain that he could draw on a power which was sufficient for life and greater than death.

(3) He bore everything in the conviction that, through his sufferings and trials, others were being led into the light and love of God. In the USA, the great Boulder Dam (now known as the Hoover Dam) scheme brought fertility to vast areas which had once been desert. In the making of it, there were inevitably those who lost their lives. When the scheme was completed, a tablet was set into the wall of the dam bearing the names of the workmen who had died, and below stands the inscription: 'These died that the desert might rejoice and blossom as the rose.' Paul could go through what

he did because he knew that it was not for nothing; he knew that it was to bring others to Christ. When we have the conviction that what is happening to us is happening literally for Christ's sake, we can face anything.

And he continues by revealing the secret of endurance.

(1) All through life, inevitably, our physical strength fades away; but all through life it ought to happen that our souls keep growing. The sufferings which leave us with weakened bodies may be the very things which strengthen our inner selves. It was the prayer of the poet Karle Wilson in her poem 'Old Lace': 'Let me grow lovely growing old.' From the physical point of view, life may be a slow but inevitable slipping down the slope that leads to death. But, from the spiritual point of view, life is climbing up the hill that leads to the presence of God. No one need fear the years, for they bring us nearer, not to death, but to God.

(2) Paul was convinced that anything he had to suffer in this world would be as nothing compared with the glory he would enjoy in the next. He was certain that God would never be in anyone's debt. Alistair MacLean, minister father of the famous author of *HMS Ulysses* and other adventure stories, tells of an old highland woman who had to leave the clean air and the blue waters and the purple hills and live in the slum of a great city. She still lived close to God, and one day she said: 'God will make it up to me, and I will see the flowers again.'

In 'Christmas Eve and Easter Day', Robert Browning writes of the martyr whose story was set out 'on the rude tablet overhead'.

I was born sickly, poor and mean,
A slave; no misery could screen
The holders of the pearl of price
From Caesar's envy; therefore twice
I fought with beasts and three times saw
My children suffer by his law;

At last my own release was earned;
I was some time in being burned,
But at the close a Hand came through
The fire above my head, and drew
My soul to Christ, whom now I see.
Sergius, a brother, writes for me
This testimony on the wall –
For me, I have forgot it all.

Earth's suffering was forgotten in the glory of heaven. It is a notable fact that, in all the gospel story, Jesus never foretold his death without foretelling his resurrection. Those who suffer for Christ will share his glory. God's own honour is pledged to that.

(3) For that very reason, our eyes must always be fixed not on the things that are seen, but on the things that are unseen. The things that are seen, the things of this world, have their day and cease to be; the things that are unseen, the things of heaven, last forever.

There are two ways of looking at life. We can look at it as a slow but inexorable journey away from God. Wordsworth, in his *Ode on the Intimations of Immortality*, had the idea that, when a child came into this world, that child had some memory of heaven which the years slowly took away.

Trailing clouds of glory do we come,

but,

Shades of the prison house begin to close
About the growing boy.

And, in the end, the man is earthbound and heaven is forgotten. In his poem 'I Remember, I Remember', Thomas Hood wrote with wistful pathos:

I remember, I remember
The fir-trees dark and high;
I used to think their slender tops
Were close against the sky.
It was a childish ignorance
But now 'tis little joy
To know, I'm farther off from heaven
Than when I was a boy.

If we think only of the things that are visible, we are bound to see
life that way. But there is another way. The writer to the Hebrews
said of Moses: 'He persevered as though he saw him who is invisible' (Hebrews 11:27). Robert Louis Stevenson tells of an old farmer.
Someone was sympathizing with him about his daily work amid
the muck of the cowshed and asking him how he could go on
doing it day in and day out, and the old man answered: 'He that
has something ayont [beyond] need never weary.'

Mark 3:20–35

Sometimes someone drops a remark which cannot be interpreted
otherwise than as the product of bitter experience. Once when
Jesus was enumerating the things which might have to be faced for
following him, he said, 'One's foes will be members of one's own
household' (Matthew 10:36). His own family had come to the conclusion that he had taken leave of his senses and that it was time
he was taken home.

By his actions Jesus had made it clear that the three laws by which
most people tend to organize their lives meant nothing to him.

(1) He had thrown away *security*. The one thing that most people
in this world want more than anything else is just that. They want

above all things a job and a position which are secure, and where there are as few material and financial risks as possible.

(2) He had thrown away *safety*. Most people tend at all times to play safe. They are more concerned with the safety of any course of action than with its moral quality, its rightness or its wrongness. A course of action which involves risk is something from which they instinctively shrink.

(3) He had shown himself utterly indifferent to *the verdict of society*. He had shown that he did not much care what people said about him. In point of fact, as the writer H. G. Wells said, for most people 'the voice of their neighbours is louder than the voice of God'. 'What will people say?' is one of the first questions that most of us are in the habit of asking.

What appalled Jesus' family and friends was the risks that he was taking, risks which, as they thought, no one with any sense would take.

So Jesus lays down the conditions of true kinship. It is not solely a matter of flesh and blood. It is possible to be much nearer to someone who is no blood relation at all than to those who are bound to us by the closest ties of kin and blood. Wherein lies this true kinship?

(1) True kinship lies in a *common experience*, especially when it is an experience where two people have really come through things together. It has been said that two people really become friends when they are able to say to each other, 'Do you remember?' and then to go on and talk about the things they have come through together. Someone once met an old woman. An acquaintance of hers had died. 'You will be sorry', he said, 'that Mrs So-and-so is dead.' 'Yes,' she said, but without showing any great grief. 'I saw you just last week,' he said, 'laughing and talking with each other. You must have been great friends.' 'Yes,' she said, 'I was friendly with her. I used to laugh with her; but to be real friends folks have got to weep together.' That is profoundly true. The basis of true

kinship lies in a common experience, and Christians have the common experience of being forgiven sinners.

(2) True kinship lies in *a common interest*. The ecumenical activist A. M. Chirgwin tells us a very interesting thing in *The Bible in World Evangelism*. One of the greatest difficulties that booksellers and distributors of the Scriptures have is not so much to sell their books as to keep people reading them. He goes on, 'A colporteur [bookseller] in pre-Communist China had for years been in the habit of going from shop to shop and house to house. But he was often disappointed because many of his new Bible readers lost their zeal, until he hit upon the plan of putting them in touch with one another and forming them into a worshipping group which in time became a duly organized Church.' Only when these isolated units became part of a group which was bound together by a common interest did real kinship come into being. Christians have that common interest because they are all people who desire to know more about Jesus Christ.

(3) True kinship lies in *a common obedience*. The disciples were a very mixed group. All kinds of beliefs and opinions were mixed up among them. A tax-collector like Matthew and a fanatical nationalist like Simon the Zealot ought to have hated each other like poison and no doubt at one time did. But they were bound together because both had accepted Jesus Christ as Master and Lord. Any platoon of soldiers will be made up of men from different backgrounds and from different walks of life and holding very different opinions: yet, if they are long enough together, they will be welded into a band of comrades because of the common obedience which they all share. Those who share a common leader can become friends. We can love each other only when we all love Jesus Christ.

(4) True kinship lies in *a common goal*. There is nothing for binding people together like a common aim. Here there is a great lesson for the Church. The churches will never draw together so long as they

argue about the ordination of their ministers, the form of church government, the administration of the sacraments and all the rest of it. The one thing on which they can all come together is the fact that all of them are seeking to win men and women for Jesus Christ. If kinship comes from a common goal then Christians above all others possess its secret, for all are seeking to know Christ better and to bring people within his kingdom. Wherever else we differ, on that we can agree.

The Sunday between 12 and 18 June

Judgement to Come *and* The Unseen Growth and the Certain End

2 Corinthians 5:6–10, 14–17

Verses 1–5 have shown that Paul regards the body as merely a tent, a temporary dwelling place, in which we stay until the day comes when it is dissolved and we enter into the real dwelling place of our souls. He is waiting for the day when God will give him a new body, a spiritual body, in which he will still be able, even in the heavenly places, to serve and to adore God.

Paul saw eternity not as release into permanent inaction, but as the entry into a body in which service could be complete. Christians can enjoy the foretaste of the life everlasting. It is given to Christians to be citizens of two worlds; and the result is not that they despise this world, but that they find it wrapped round with a shining glory which is the reflection of the greater glory to come.

Then comes the note of sternness. Even when Paul was thinking of the life to come, he never forgot that we are on the way not only to glory, but also to judgement. 'We must all appear before the judgement seat of Christ.' The word for *judgement seat* is *bema*. Paul may be thinking simply of the tribunal of the Roman magistrate before which he himself had stood, or he may be thinking of the Greek way of justice.

All Greek citizens were legally bound to be called to serve as judges, or, as we would say, to do jury service. When an Athenian sat in judgement on a case, he was given two bronze discs. Each had a cylindrical axis. One axis was hollow, and that disc stood for condemnation; one was solid, and that disc stood for acquittal. On the *bema*, there stood two urns. One, of bronze, was called 'the decisive urn', for into it the judge dropped the disc which stood for his verdict. The other, of wood, was called 'the inoperative urn', for into it the judge dropped the disc which he desired to discard. So, at the end the jury dropped into the bronze urn either the disc that stood for acquittal or the one that stood for condemnation. To an onlooker, they looked exactly alike and none could tell the verdict the judges gave. Then the discs were counted and the verdict was given.

In the same way, some day we shall await the verdict of God. When we remember that, life becomes a tremendous and a thrilling prospect, for in it we are making or marring a destiny, winning or losing a crown. Time becomes the testing ground of eternity.

Paul goes on to the motive which is the driving force of the whole Christian life. Christ died for all. To Paul, the Christian is, in his favourite phrase, *in Christ*; and therefore the old self of the Christian died in that death and a new person arose, as new as if freshly created by the hands of God. In this newness of life, Christians have acquired a new set of standards. They no longer judge things by the standards the world uses. There was a time when Paul had judged Christ by human standards and had set out to eliminate the Christian faith from the world. But not now. Now his standards are different. Now the man whose name he had sought to obliterate is to him the most wonderful person in the world, because he had given to him that friendship of God which he had longed for all his life.

Mark 4:26–34

This first parable is the only one which Mark alone relates to us. The kingdom of God really means *the reign of God*; it means the day when God's will will be done as perfectly on earth as it is in heaven. That is the goal of God for the whole universe. This parable is short but it is filled with unmistakable truths.

(1) It tells us of *human helplessness*. The farmer does not make the seed grow. In the last analysis he does not even understand how it grows. It has the secret of life and of growth within itself. No one has ever possessed the secret of life; no one has ever created anything in the full sense of the term. We can discover things; we can rearrange them; we can develop them; but create them we cannot. We do not create the kingdom of God; the kingdom is God's. It is true that we can frustrate it and hinder it, or we can make a situation in the world where it is given the opportunity to come more fully and more speedily. But behind all things is God and the power and will of God.

(2) It tells us something about the *kingdom*. It is a notable fact that Jesus so often uses illustrations from the growth of nature to describe the coming of the kingdom of God.

(a) Nature's growth is often *imperceptible*. If we see a plant every day, we cannot see its growth taking place. It is only when we see it, and then see it again after an interval of time, that we notice the difference. It is so with the kingdom. The growth of the kingdom may, like that of the plant, be imperceptible from day to day; but over the years it is plain.

(b) Nature's growth is *constant*. Night and day, while we sleep, growth goes on. There is nothing spasmodic about God. The great trouble about human effort and human goodness is that they are spasmodic. One day we take one step forward; the next day we take two steps back. But the work of God goes on quietly; unceasingly God unfolds his plan. In the words of the well-known hymn,

God is working his purpose out, as year succeeds to year:
God is working his purpose out, and the time is drawing near –
Nearer and nearer draws the time – the time that shall surely be,

When the earth shall be filled with the glory of God as the waters cover the sea.

(c) Nature's growth is *inevitable*. There is nothing so powerful as growth. A tree can split a concrete pavement with the power of its growth. A weed can push its green head through an asphalt path. Nothing can stop growth. It is so with the kingdom. In spite of human rebellion and disobedience, God's work goes on; and nothing in the end can stop the purposes of God.

(3) It tells us that there is *a consummation*. There is a day when the harvest comes. Inevitably when the harvest comes, two things happen – which are opposite sides of the same thing. The good fruit is gathered in, and the weeds and the tares are destroyed. Harvest and judgement go hand in hand. When we think of this coming day, three things are laid upon us.

(a) It is a summons to *patience*. We are creatures of the moment and inevitably we think in terms of the moment. God has all eternity in which to work. 'A thousand years in your sight are like yesterday when it is past, or like a watch in the night' (Psalm 90:4). Instead of our petulant, fretful, irritable human hastiness we should cultivate in our souls the patience which has learned to wait on God.

(b) It is a summons to *hope*. We are living today in an atmosphere of despair. People despair of the Church; they despair of the world; they look with shuddering dread on the future. Between the two World Wars, Sir Philip Gibbs wrote a book in which he looked forward, thinking of the possibility of a war of poison gas. He said something like this. 'If I smell poison gas in High Street, Kensington, I am not going to put on a gas-mask. I am going to go out and breathe deeply of it, because I will know that *the game is up*.' So many people feel that for humanity the game is up. Now no one can think like that *and* believe in God. If God is the God we believe him to be, there is no room for pessimism. There may be remorse, regret; there may be penitence, contrition; there may be heart-searching, the awareness of failure and of sin; but there can never be despair. The hymn-writer F. W. Faber wrote:

> Workman of God! O lose not heart,
> But learn what God is like,
> And, in the darkest battle-field,
> Thou shalt know where to strike.
> For right is right, since God is God,
> And right the day must win:
> To doubt would be disloyalty,
> To falter would be sin.

(c) It is a summons to *preparedness*. If there comes the consummation, we must be ready for it. It is too late to prepare for it when it is upon us. We have literally to prepare to meet our God. If we live in patience which cannot be defeated, in hope which cannot despair, and in preparation which always sees life in the light of eternity, we shall, by the grace of God, be ready for his consummation when it comes.

The Sunday between 19 and 25 June
A Blizzard of Troubles *and* The Peace of the Presence

2 Corinthians 6:1–13

In all the chances and changes of life, Paul had only one concern – to show himself a sincere and profitable minister of Jesus Christ. Even as he made that claim, his mind's eye went back across what John Chrysostom called 'the blizzard of troubles' through which he had come and through which he was still struggling. Every word in this tremendous catalogue, which has been called 'the hymn of the herald of salvation', has its background in Paul's adventurous life.

Paul speaks about three groups, each of three things, in which this victorious endurance is practised.

(1) There are the internal conflicts of the Christian life.

(a) *The things which press sore upon us.* There are things which weigh down the spirit like the sorrows which are a burden on the heart and the crushing disappointments which squeeze the life out of us. The triumphant endurance can cope with them all.

(b) *The inescapable pains of life.* Certain burdens can be avoided, but others are inescapable. There are certain things which must be borne. The greatest of these are sorrow, for only the life which has never known love will never know that – and death, which comes to us all. The triumphant endurance enables us to face all that is involved in being human.

(c) *Anxieties.* Even then, the triumphant endurance makes us able to breathe the spaciousness of heaven.

(2) There are the external tribulations of life.

(a) *Stripes.* For Paul, the Christian life meant not only spiritual suffering but also physical suffering. There are still some for whom it is physical agony to be a Christian; and it is always true that, as the second-century theologian Tertullian said, 'the blood of the martyrs is the seed of the Church'.

(b) *Prisons.* From Acts, we know that before he wrote to the Corinthians Paul was in prison in Philippi, and afterwards in Jerusalem, in Caesarea and in Rome. The pageant of Christians who were imprisoned stretches from the first to the twenty-first century. There have always been those who would abandon their liberty sooner than abandon their faith.

(c) *Tumults.* Over and over again, we have the picture of the Christian facing not the sternness of the law but the violence of the mob. The mob has often been the enemy of Christianity; but nowadays it is not the violence but the mockery or the amused contempt of the crowd against which Christians must stand fast.

(3) There is the effort of the Christian life.

(a) *Toils.* The word Paul uses describes toil to the point of sheer exhaustion, the kind of toil which takes everything of body, mind and spirit that we have to give. Christians are God's labourers.

(b) *Sleepless nights.* Some would be spent in prayer, some in a situation of danger or discomfort where sleep was impossible. At all times, Paul was ready to be the unsleeping sentinel of Christ.

(c) *Fastings.* No doubt, what Paul means here is not deliberately chosen fastings but times when he went hungry for the work's sake.

Paul completes this lyrical passage with a series of contrasts. He begins with *in honour and in dishonour.* The word he uses for *dishonour* is normally used in Greek for loss of rights as a citizen (*atimia*). Paul says: 'I may have lost all the rights and privileges which the world can confer, but I am still a citizen of the kingdom of God.' *In ill report and in good report.* There are those who criticize his every action and who hate his very name; but his fame with God is sure. *Deceivers, and yet true.* The Greek word (*planos*) literally means a wandering quack and impostor. That is what others call him; but he knows that his message is God's truth. *Unknown, yet well known.* The Jews who slandered him said he was an insignificant nobody whom no one had ever heard of; yet, to those to whom he had brought Christ, he was known with gratitude. *Dying, and lo! we live.* Danger was his companion and the prospect of death his comrade; and yet by the grace of God he was triumphantly alive with a life that death could never kill. *Chastened, but not killed.* Things happened to him that might have chastened anyone's spirit; but they could not kill the spirit of Paul. *Grieved, but always rejoicing.* Things happened that might have broken anyone's heart; but they could not destroy Paul's joy. *Poor, yet making many rich.* He might seem to be penniless; but he brought with him that which would enrich the souls of men and women. *Having nothing, yet possessing all things.* He might seem to have nothing; but, having Christ, he had everything that mattered in this world and the next.

Mark 4:35–41

The Lake of Galilee was notorious for its storms. They came literally out of the blue with shattering and terrifying suddenness. A writer describes them like this: 'It is not unusual to see terrible squalls hurl themselves, even when the sky is perfectly clear, upon these waters which are ordinarily so calm. The numerous ravines which to the north-east and east debouch [open out] upon the upper part of the lake operate as so many dangerous defiles in which the winds from the heights of Hauran, the plateaux of Trachonitis, and the summit of Mount Hermon are caught and compressed in such a way that, rushing with tremendous force through a narrow space and then being suddenly released, they agitate the little Lake of Gennesaret in the most frightful fashion.' The voyager across the lake was always liable to encounter just such sudden storms as this.

Jesus was in the boat in the position in which any distinguished guest would be conveyed. We are told that, 'In these boats . . . the place for any distinguished stranger is on the little seat placed at the stern, where a carpet and cushion are arranged. The helmsman stands a little farther forward on the deck, though near the stern, in order to have a better look-out ahead.'

It is interesting to note that the words Jesus addressed to the wind and the waves are exactly the same as he addressed to the demon-possessed man in Mark 1:25. Just as an evil demon possessed that man, so the destructive power of the storm was, so people in Palestine believed in those days, the evil power of the demons at work in the realm of nature.

We do this story far less than justice if we merely take it in a literalistic sense. If it describes no more than a physical miracle in which an actual storm was stilled, it is very wonderful and it is something at which we must marvel, but it is something which happened once and cannot happen again. In that case it is quite external to us. But if we read it in a symbolic sense, it is far more valuable. When the disciples realized the presence of Jesus with them, the storm became a calm. Once they knew he was there, fearless peace entered their hearts. To voyage with Jesus was to voyage in peace even in a storm. Now that is universally true. It is not something which happened once; it is something which still happens and which can happen for us. In the presence of Jesus, we can have peace even in the wildest storms of life.

(1) He gives us peace in the storm of *sorrow*. When sorrow comes as come it must, he tells us of the glory of the life to come. He changes the darkness of death into the sunshine of the thought of

life eternal. He tells us of the love of God. There is an old story of a gardener who in his garden had a favourite flower which he loved much. One day he came to the garden to find that flower gone. He was vexed and angry and full of complaints. In the midst of his resentment he met the master of the garden and hurled his complaints at him. 'Hush!' said the master, 'I plucked it for myself.' In the storm of sorrow Jesus tells us that those we love have gone to be with God, and gives us the certainty that we shall meet again those whom we have loved and lost awhile.

(2) He gives us peace when life's *problems* involve us in a tempest of doubt and tension and uncertainty. There come times when we do not know what to do; when we stand at some crossroads in life and do not know which way to take. If then we turn to Jesus and say to him, 'Lord, what will you have me to do?' the way will be clear. The real tragedy is not that we do not know what to do; but that often we do not humbly submit to Jesus' guidance. To ask his will and to submit to it is the way to peace at such a time.

(3) He gives us peace in the storms of *anxiety*. The chief enemy of peace is worry, worry for ourselves, worry about the unknown future, worry about those we love. But Jesus speaks to us of a Father whose hand will never cause his child a needless tear and of a love beyond which neither we nor those we love can ever drift. In the storm of anxiety, he brings us the peace of the love of God.

The Sunday between 26 June and 2 July
An Appeal for Generosity *and*
In the Hour of Need

2 Corinthians 8:7–15

One of the schemes that lay closest to Paul's heart was the collection that he was organizing for the church of Jerusalem. This was the mother church; but it was poor, and it was Paul's desire that all the Gentiles' churches should remember and help that church which was their mother in the faith. So, here he reminds the Corinthians of their duty and urges them to be generous. He appeals to them to give worthily.

(1) He cites the example of Jesus Christ. For Paul, the sacrifice of Jesus did not begin on the cross. It did not even begin with his birth. It began in heaven, when he laid his glory to one side and consented to come to earth. Paul's challenge to Christians is: 'With that tremendous example of generosity before you, how can you hold back?'

(2) He cites their own past record. They have led the way in everything. Can they then lag behind in this? If people were only true to their own highest standards, if we all lived always at our best, what a difference it would make!

(3) He stresses the necessity of translating fine feeling into fine action. The Corinthians had been the first to feel the appeal of this scheme. But a feeling which remains only a feeling, a pity which remains a pity only of the heart, a fine desire that never turns into a fine deed, is a sadly unfinished and frustrated thing. The tragedy

of life so often is not that we have no high impulses, but that we fail to turn them into actions.

(4) He reminds them that life has a strange way of evening things up. Far more often than not, we find that it is measured to us with the same measure as we measure to others. Life has a way of repaying generosity with generosity, and the sparing spirit with the sparing spirit.

No gift can be in any real sense a gift unless the giver gives with it a bit of himself or herself. That is why personal giving is always the highest kind, and that is the kind of giving of which Jesus Christ is the supreme example. The Old Testament quotation with which Paul concludes this passage is from Exodus 16:18, which tells how, when the Israelites gathered the manna in the wilderness, whether they gathered little or much, it was enough.

Mark 5:21–43

This story has all the elements of tragedy. It is always tragic when a child is ill. The story tells us that the ruler's daughter was twelve years of age. According to the Jewish custom, a girl became a woman at twelve years and one day. This girl was just on the threshold of womanhood, and when death comes at such a time it is doubly tragic.

The story tells us something about this man who was the ruler of the synagogue. He must have been a person of some considerable importance. The ruler was the administrative head of the synagogue. He was the president of the board of elders responsible for the good management of the synagogue. He was responsible for the conduct of the services, for the allocation of duties and for seeing that they were carried out with all seemliness and good order.

He was one of the most important and most respected men in the community. But something happened to him when his daughter fell ill and he thought of Jesus.

(1) His *prejudices* were forgotten. There can be no doubt that he must have regarded Jesus as an outsider, as a dangerous heretic, as one to whom the synagogue doors were rightly closed, and one whom anyone who valued his orthodoxy would do well to avoid. But he was a big enough man to abandon his prejudices in his hour of need. Prejudice really means *a judging beforehand*. It is a judging before the evidence has been examined, or a verdict given because of refusal to examine it. Few things have done more to hold things up than this. Nearly every forward step has had to fight against initial prejudice. A prejudiced mind shuts out many a blessing.

(2) His *dignity* was forgotten. He, the ruler of the synagogue, came and threw himself at the feet of Jesus, the wandering teacher. He was not the first man who had to forget his dignity to save his life and to save his soul. In the old story, that is precisely what Naaman had to do (2 Kings 5). He had come to Elisha to be cured of his leprosy. Elisha's prescription was that he should go and wash in the Jordan seven times. That was no way to treat the Syrian prime minister! Elisha had not even delivered the message personally; he had sent it by a messenger! And, had they not far better rivers in Syria than the muddy little Jordan? These were Naaman's first thoughts; but he swallowed his pride and lost his leprosy.

It frequently happens that those who stand on their dignity fall from grace.

(3) His *pride* was forgotten. It must have taken a conscious effort of humiliation for this ruler of the synagogue to come and ask for help from Jesus of Nazareth. No one wishes to be indebted to anyone else; we would like to run our lives on our own. The very first step of the Christian life is to become aware that we cannot be anything other than indebted to God.

(4) Here we enter the realm of speculation, but it seems to me that we can say of this man that his *friends* were forgotten. It may well be that, to the end, they objected to him calling in Jesus. It is rather strange that he came himself and did not send a messenger. It seems unlikely that he would consent to leave his daughter when she was on the point of death. Maybe he came because no one else would go. His household were suspiciously quick to tell him not to trouble Jesus any more. It sounds almost as if they were glad not to call upon his help. It may well be that this ruler defied public opinion and home advice in order to call in Jesus. It is often the case that we are wisest when our worldly-wise friends think we are acting like fools.

Here was a man who forgot everything except that he wanted the help of Jesus; and because of that forgetfulness he would remember forever that Jesus is a Saviour.

This is also a story of contrasts.

(1) There is the contrast between *the despair* of the mourners and *the hope* of Jesus. 'Don't bother the Teacher,' they said. 'There's nothing anyone can do now.' 'Don't be afraid,' said Jesus, 'only believe.' In the one place it is the voice of despair that speaks, in the other the voice of hope.

(2) There is the contrast between *the unrestrained distress* of the mourners and *the calm serenity* of Jesus. They were wailing and weeping and tearing their hair and rending their garments in a paroxysm of distress; he was calm and quiet and serene and in control.

Why this difference? It was due to Jesus' perfect confidence and trust in God. The worst human disaster can be met with courage and gallantry when we meet it with God. They laughed him to scorn because they thought his hope was groundless and his calm mistaken. But the great fact of the Christian life is that what looks completely impossible to us is possible with God. What on merely human grounds is far too good to be true becomes blessedly true when God is there. They laughed him to scorn, but their laughter must have turned to amazed wonder when they realized what God can do. There is nothing beyond facing, and there is nothing beyond conquest – not even death – when it is faced and conquered in the love of God which is in Christ Jesus our Lord.

The Sunday between 3 and 9 July
The Thorn and the Grace *and*
Without Honour in His Own Country

2 Corinthians 12:2–10

If we have any sensitivity, we should read this passage with a certain reverence, for in it Paul lays bare his heart and shows us at one and the same time his glory and his pain. Against his will, he is still setting out his credentials, and he tells of an experience at which we can only wonder and which we cannot even try to probe. In the strangest way, he seems to stand outside himself and look at himself. 'I know a man,' he says. The man is Paul himself; and yet he can look at the man who had this amazing experience with a kind of wondering detachment. For the mystic, the great aim of all religious experience is the vision of God and union with him. We cannot even guess what happened to Paul. We need not form theories about the number of heavens because of the fact that he speaks of the third heaven. He simply means that his spirit rose to an unsurpassable ecstasy in its nearness to God.

After the glory came the pain. The Authorized Version and the Revised Standard Version speak of *the thorn* in the flesh. The word (*skolops*) can mean *thorn*, but it is more likely to mean *stake*. Sometimes criminals were impaled upon a sharp stake. It was a stake like that that Paul felt was twisting in his body. What was it? Many answers have been given. First, we look at those which great Christian thinkers have held but which, in the light of the evidence, we must discard.

(1) The thorn has been taken to mean *spiritual temptations* – the temptation to doubt and to shirk the duties of the apostolic life,

and the sting of conscience when temptation conquered. That was the sixteenth-century reformer John Calvin's view.

(2) It has been taken to mean *the opposition and persecution* which he had to face, the constant battle with those who tried to undo his work. That was Martin Luther's view.

(3) It has been taken to mean *sexual temptations*. When the monks and the hermits shut themselves up in their monasteries and their cells, they found that the last instinct that could be tamed was that of sex. They wished to eliminate it, but it preyed on their minds. They held that Paul was like that. None of these solutions can be right, for three reasons. (a) The very word 'stake' indicates an almost savage pain. (b) The whole picture before us is one of physical suffering. (c) Whatever the thorn was, it was intermittent, for, although it sometimes laid Paul low, it never kept him wholly from his work. So, let us look at the other suggestions.

(4) It has been suggested that the thorn was Paul's *physical appearance*. 'His bodily presence is weak' (2 Corinthians 10:10). It has been suggested that he suffered from some disfigurement which made him ugly and hindered his work. But that does not account for the sheer pain that must have been there.

(5) One of the most common solutions is *epilepsy*. It is painful and recurrent, but between attacks sufferers can go about their business. It produces visions and trances such as Paul experienced. It can be repellent; in the ancient world, it was attributed to demons. In the ancient world, when people saw an epileptic, they spat to ward off the evil demon. In Galatians 4:14, Paul says that when the Galatians saw his infirmity they did not *reject* him. The Greek word literally means *you did not spit at me*. But this theory has consequences which are hard to accept. It would mean that Paul's visions were epileptic trances, and it is hard to believe that the visions which changed the world were due to epileptic attacks.

(6) The oldest of all theories is that Paul was overcome by *severe headaches*. The early Christian fathers Tertullian and Jerome both believed that.

(7) That may well lead us to the truth, for still another theory is that Paul suffered from *eye trouble*, and this would explain the headaches. After the glory on the Damascus Road passed, he was blind (Acts 9:9). It may be that his eyes never recovered again. Paul said of the Galatians that they would have plucked out their eyes and would have given them to him (Galatians 4:15). At the end of Galatians, he writes: 'See what large letters I make when I am writing in my own hand' (Galatians 6:11), as if he was describing the great sprawling characters of someone who could hardly see.

(8) By far the most likely thing is that Paul suffered from chronically recurrent attacks of a certain virulent malarial fever which haunted the coasts of the eastern Mediterranean. The people of the country, when they wished to harm their enemies, prayed to their gods that the enemies should be 'burnt up' with this fever. One who has suffered from it describes the headache that accompanies it as being like 'a red-hot bar thrust through the forehead'. Another speaks of 'the grinding, boring pain in one temple, like the dentist's drill – the phantom wedge driven in between the jaws', and says that, when the pain became acute, it 'reached the extreme point of human endurance'. That, in truth, deserves the description of a thorn in the flesh, and even of a stake in the flesh. The man who endured so many other sufferings had this agony to contend with all the time.

Paul prayed that it might be taken from him, but God answered that prayer as he answers so many prayers – he did not take the thing away but gave Paul strength to bear it. That is how God works. He does not spare us things, but makes us able to conquer them. To Paul came the promise and the reality of the all-sufficient grace. It is the glory of the gospel that in our weakness we may find this wondrous grace, for always that which is the greatest challenge to our strength is God's opportunity.

Mark 6:1–13

When Jesus came to Nazareth, he put himself to a very severe test. He was coming to his home town; and there are no severer critics than those who have known us since childhood. It was never meant to be a private visit simply to see his old home and his own people. He came attended by his disciples. That is to say he came as a Rabbi. The Rabbis moved about the country accompanied by their little circle of disciples, and it was as a teacher, with his disciples, that Jesus came. He went into the synagogue and he taught. His teaching was greeted not with wonder but with a kind of contempt. 'They took offence at him.' They were scandalized that a man who came from a background like Jesus should say and do things such as he did. Familiarity had bred a mistaken contempt.

They refused to listen to what he had to say for two reasons.

(1) They said, 'Is not this the carpenter?' The word used for *carpenter* does mean a worker in wood, but it means more than merely a joiner. It means a *craftsman*. In the past, there could be found in little towns and villages a craftsman who would build you anything from a chicken-coop to a house; the kind of man who could build a wall, mend a roof, repair a gate; the craftsman, the handyman, who with few or no instruments and with the simplest tools could turn his hand to any job. That is what Jesus was like. But the point is that the people of Nazareth despised Jesus *because he was a working man*. He was a man of the people, a layman, an ordinary man – and therefore they despised him.

To us that is his glory, because it means that God, when he came to earth, claimed no exemptions. He took upon himself the common life with all its common tasks.

The accidents of birth and fortune and pedigree have nothing to do with our true worth. As Alexander Pope had it:

Worth makes the man, and want of it the fellow;
The rest is all but leather or prunello.

We must always beware of the temptation to evaluate one another by externals and incidentals, and not by native worth.

(2) They said, 'Is not this Mary's son? Do we not know his brothers and his sisters?' The fact that they called Jesus *Mary's son* tells us that Joseph must have been dead. Therein we have the key to one of the enigmas of Jesus' life. Jesus was only thirty-three when he died; and yet he did not leave Nazareth until he was thirty (Luke 3:23). Why this long delay? Why this lingering in Nazareth while a world waited to be saved? The most likely reason was that Joseph died young and Jesus took upon himself the support of his mother and of his brothers and sisters; and only when they were old enough to fend for themselves did he go forth. He was faithful in this small matter, and therefore in the end God gave him much to do.

But the people of Nazareth despised him because they knew his family. Thomas Campbell was a very considerable poet. His father had no sense of poetry at all. When Thomas' first book emerged with his name on it, he sent a copy to his father. The old man took it up and looked at it. It was really the binding and not the contents at all that he was looking at. 'Who would have thought', he said in wonder, 'that our Tom could have made a book like that?' Sometimes when familiarity should breed a growing respect it breeds an increasing and easy-going familiarity. Sometimes we are too near people to see their greatness.

The result of all this was that Jesus could do no mighty works in Nazareth. The atmosphere was wrong, and there are some things that cannot be done unless the atmosphere is right.

(1) It is still true that people cannot be healed if they refuse to be healed. Margot Asquith tells of the death of Neville Chamberlain. It is well known that his policy turned out in such a way that it broke his heart. Margot Asquith met his doctor, Lord Horder. 'You can't be much of a doctor,' she said, 'as Neville Chamberlain was only a few years older than Winston Churchill, and I should have said he was a strong man. Were you fond of him?' Lord Horder replied, 'I was very fond of him. I like all unlovable men. I have seen too many of the other kind. Chamberlain suffered from shyness. He did not want to live; and when a man says that, *no doctor can save him*.' We may call it faith; we may call it the will to live; but without it none of us can survive.

(2) There can be no preaching in the wrong atmosphere. Our churches would be different places if congregations would only remember that they preach far more than half the sermon. In an atmosphere of expectancy, the poorest effort can catch fire. In an atmosphere of critical coldness or bland indifference, the most Spirit-packed utterance can fall lifeless to the earth.

(3) There can be no peace-making in the wrong atmosphere. If those gathered together have come together to hate, they will hate. If they have come together to refuse to understand, they will misunderstand. If they have come together to see no other point of view but their own, they will see no other. But if they have come together, loving Christ and seeking to love each other, even those who are most widely separated can come together in him.

There is laid on us the tremendous responsibility that we can either help or hinder the work of Jesus Christ. We can open the door wide to him – or we can slam it in his face.

The Sunday between 10 and 16 July

The Goal of History *and* Three Verdicts on Jesus

Ephesians 1:3–14

In verse 9 Paul says, as the Authorized Version has it, that God has made known to us 'the mystery of his will'. The New Testament uses the word *mystery* in a special sense. It is not something mysterious in the sense that it is hard to understand. It is something which has long been kept secret and has now been revealed, but is still incomprehensible to the person who has not been initiated into its meaning.

Let us take an example. Suppose someone who knew nothing whatever about Christianity was brought into a communion service. To that person, it would be a complete mystery; he or she would not understand in the least what was going on. But to anyone who knows the story and the meaning of the Last Supper, the whole service has a meaning which is quite clear. So, in the New Testament sense, a mystery is something which is hidden to non-Christians but clear to Christians.

What, for Paul, was the mystery of the will of God? It was that the gospel was open to the Gentiles too. In Jesus, God has revealed that his love and care, his grace and mercy, are meant not only for the Jews but for the whole world. Now Paul, in one sentence, introduces his great thought. Up until now, people had been living in a divided world. There was division between the animals and human beings. There was division between Jews and Gentiles, Greeks and barbarians. All over the world, there was strife and tension. Jesus came into the world to wipe out the divisions. That, for Paul, was the secret of God. It was God's purpose that all the many different strands and all the warring elements in this world should be gathered into one in Jesus Christ.

Here, we have another tremendous thought. Paul says that all history has been a working out of this process. He says that all through the ages there has been an arranging and an administering of things so that this day of unity should come. The word which Paul uses for this preparation is intensely interesting. It is *oikonomia*, which literally means *household management*. The *oikonomos* was the steward who saw to it that the family affairs ran smoothly.

It is the Christian conviction that history is the working out of the will of God. That is by no means what every historian or thinker has been able to see. In one of his epigrams, the Irish playwright and poet Oscar Wilde said: 'You give the criminal calendar of Europe to your children under the name of history.' The historian and poet Sir George Clark, in his inaugural lecture at Oxford, said: 'There is no secret and no plan in history to be discovered. I do not believe that any future consummation could make sense of all the irrationalities of preceding ages. If it could not explain them, still less could it justify them.' In the introduction to *A History of Europe*, H. A. L. Fisher writes: 'One intellectual excitement, however, has been denied to me. Men wiser and more learned than I have discovered in history a plot, a rhythm, a predetermined pattern. These harmonies are concealed from me. I can see only one emergency following another, as wave follows upon wave, only one great fact with respect to which, since it is unique, there can be no generalizations, only one safe rule for the historian: that he should recognize in the development of human destinies the play of the contingent and the unforeseen.' The French novelist and biographer André Maurois says: 'The universe is indifferent. Who created it? Why are we here on this puny mud-heap spinning in infinite space? I have not the slightest idea, and I am quite convinced that no one has the least idea.'

It so happens that we are living in an age in which many people have lost their faith in any purpose for this world. But it is the faith of Christians that in this world God's purpose is being worked out; and Paul's conviction is that it is God's purpose that one day all things and all people should be one family in Christ. As Paul sees it, that mystery was not even grasped until Jesus came, and now it is the great task of the Church to work out God's purpose of unity, revealed in Jesus Christ.

Mark 6:14–29

News of Jesus had penetrated all over the country. The tale had reached the ears of Herod. The reason why he had not up to this time heard of Jesus may well be due to the fact that his official residence in Galilee was in Tiberias. Tiberias was largely a Gentile city, and, as far as we know, Jesus never set foot in it. But the mission of the Twelve (Mark 6: 7–13) had taken Jesus' fame all over Galilee, so that his name was upon everyone's lips. In this passage, we have three verdicts upon Jesus.

(1) There is the verdict of a guilty conscience. Herod had been guilty of allowing the execution of John the Baptizer, and now he was haunted by what he had done. Whenever people commit evil acts, the whole world becomes their enemy. Inwardly, they cannot command their thoughts; and, whenever they allow themselves to think, their thoughts return to the wicked things that they have done. We cannot avoid living with ourselves; and when we are filled with self-accusations, life becomes intolerable. Outwardly, we live in the fear that we will be found out and that some day the consequences of our evil deeds will catch up with us.

Some time ago, a convict escaped from a Glasgow prison. After forty-eight hours of liberty he was recaptured, cold and hungry and exhausted. He said that it was not worth it. 'I didn't have a minute,' he said. 'Hunted, hunted all the time. You don't have a chance. You can't stop to eat. You can't stop to sleep.'

Hunted – that is the word which so well describes the lives of those who have done some evil thing. When Herod heard of Jesus, the first thing that flashed into his mind was that this was John the Baptizer whom he had killed, come back to reckon with him. Because the sinning life is the haunted life, sin is never worth the cost.

(2) There is the verdict of the nationalist. Some thought that this Jesus was Elijah come again. The Jews waited for the Messiah. There were many ideas about the Messiah, but the commonest of all was that he would be a conquering king who would first give the Jews back their liberty and who would then lead them on a triumphant campaign throughout the world. It was an essential part of that belief that, before the coming of the Messiah, Elijah, the greatest of the prophets, would come again to be his herald and his forerunner. Even to this day, when Jews celebrate the Passover Feast, they leave at the table an empty chair called Elijah's chair. They place it there with a glass of wine before it, and at one part of their celebration they go to the door and fling it wide open, that Elijah may come in and bring at last the long-awaited news that the Messiah has come.

This is the verdict of those who desire to find in Jesus the realization of *their own ambitions*. They think of Jesus not as someone to whom they must submit and whom they must obey; they think of Jesus as someone they can use. Such people think more of their own ambitions than of the will of God.

(3) There is the verdict of those who are waiting for the voice of God. There were those who saw in Jesus a prophet. In those days, the Jews were only too well aware that for 300 years the voice of proph-

ecy had been silent. They had listened to the arguments and the legal disputations of the Rabbis; they had listened to the moral lectures of the synagogue; but it was three long centuries since they had listened to a voice which proclaimed, 'Thus says the Lord.' People in those days were listening for the authentic voice of God – and in Jesus they heard it. It is true that Jesus was more than a prophet. He did not bring only the voice of God. He brought the very power and the very life and the very being of God. But those who saw in Jesus a prophet were at least more right than the conscience-stricken Herod and the expectant nationalists. If they had got that far in their thoughts of Jesus, it was not impossible that they might take the further step and see in him the Son of God.

The Sunday between 17 and 23 July

The End of Barriers *and* The Pathos of the Crowd

Ephesians 2:11–22

The ancient world had its barriers. So, too, has our modern world. In any Christless society, there can be nothing but middle walls of partition. Paul says that in Christ these barriers are down.

How did Christ destroy them?

(1) Paul says of Jesus: 'He is our peace.' What did he mean by that? Let us use a human analogy. Suppose two people have a difference and go to law about it; and the experts in the law draw up a document, which states the rights of the case, and ask the two conflicting parties to come together on the basis of that document. All the chances are that the division will remain unhealed, for peace is seldom made on the basis of a legal document. But suppose that someone whom both of these conflicting parties love comes and talks to them, there is every chance that peace will be made. When two parties are at variance, the surest way to bring them together is through someone whom they both love.

That is what Christ does. *He* is our peace. It is in a shared love of him that people come to love each other. That peace is won at the price of his blood, for the great awakener of love is the cross. The sight of that cross awakens in the hearts of men and women of all nations love for Christ, and only when they all love Christ will they love each other. It is not through treaties and organizations that peace comes. There can be peace only in Jesus Christ.

(2) Paul says of Jesus that he wiped out the law of the command-ments with all its decrees. What does that mean? The Jews believed that only by keeping the Jewish law was an individual considered good and able to achieve the friendship and fellowship of God. That law had been worked out into thousands and thousands of commandments and decrees. The only people who fully kept the Jewish law were the Pharisees, and there were only 6,000 of them. A religion based on all kinds of rules and regulations, about sacred rituals and sacrifices and days, can never be a universal religion. But, as Paul said elsewhere, 'Christ is the end of the law' (Romans 10:4). Jesus ended legalism as a principle of religion.

In its place, he put love for God and love for other people. Jesus came to tell people that they cannot earn God's approval by simply keeping the ceremonial law, but must accept the forgiveness and fellowship which God in mercy freely offers them. A religion based on love can immediately become a universal religion. Jesus abol-ished all religion founded on rules and regulations and brought to everyone a religion whose foundation is love.

Paul goes on to tell of the priceless gifts which come with the new unity in Christ.

(1) He made both Jew and Gentile into one new being. The word that Paul uses here is *kainos*, which means new in terms of *quality*. A thing which is *kainos* is new in the sense that it brings into the world a new quality in itself which did not exist before. He says that Jesus brings together Jew and Gentile and from them both produces one new kind of person. This is very interesting and very significant; it is not that Jesus makes all the Jews into Gentiles, or all the Gentiles into Jews; he produces a new kind of person out of both, although they remain Gentiles and Jews.

The unity which Jesus achieves is not achieved by blotting out all racial characteristics; it is achieved by making all people of all nations into Christians. Their unity lies in their Christianity. The oneness in Christ is in Christ and not in any external change.

(2) He reconciled both to God. The word Paul uses is the word used of bringing together friends who have been estranged. The work of Jesus is to show all men and women that God is their friend and that, therefore, they must be friends with each other. Reconciliation with God involves and necessitates reconciliation with one another.

(3) Through Jesus, both Jew and Gentile have the right of access to God. The word Paul uses for *access is prosagoge*, and it is a word of many pictures. It is the word used of bringing a sacrifice to God; it is the word used of bringing people into the presence of God so that they may be consecrated to his service; it is the word used for introducing a speaker or an ambassador into a national assembly; and above all it is the word used for introducing a person into the presence of a king. It is a priceless privilege to have the right to go to some lovely and wise and saintly person at any time, to have the right to break in upon that person and to bring with us our troubles, our problems, our loneliness and our sorrow. That is exactly the right that Jesus gives us with regard to God.

The unity in Christ produces Christians whose Christianity is above all their local and racial differences; it produces people who are friends with each other because they are friends with God; it produces individuals who are one because they meet in the presence of God to whom they all have access.

Mark 6:30–34, 53–56

When the disciples came back from their mission, they reported to Jesus all that they had done. The demanding crowds were so insistent that they had no time even to eat; so Jesus told them to come with him to a lonely place on the other side of the lake that they might have peace and rest for a little time.

Here we see what might be called the *rhythm of the Christian life*. The Christian life is a continuous going into the presence of God from the presence of men and women and coming out into the presence of men and women from the presence of God. It is like the rhythm of sleep and work. We cannot work unless we have our time of rest; and sleep will not come unless we have worked until we are tired.

There are two dangers in life. First, there is the danger of a too constant activity. We cannot work without rest; and we cannot live the Christian life unless we give ourselves time with God. It may well be that the whole trouble in our lives is that we give God no opportunity to speak to us, because we do not know how to be still and to listen; we give God no time to recharge us with spiritual energy and strength, because there is no time when we wait upon him. How can we bear life's burdens if we have no contact with him who is the Lord of all good life? How can we do God's work unless in God's strength? And how can we receive that strength unless we seek in quietness and in loneliness the presence of God?

Second, there is the danger of too much withdrawal. Devotion that does not issue in action is not real devotion. Prayer that does not issue in work is not real prayer. We must never seek God's fellowship in order to avoid human fellowship but in order to fit ourselves better for it. The rhythm of the Christian life is the alternate meeting with God in the secret place and serving one another in the market place.

But the rest which Jesus sought for himself and for his disciples was not to be. The crowds saw Jesus and the Twelve going away. At this particular place, it was four miles across the lake by boat and ten miles round the top of the lake on foot. On a windless day, or with a contrary wind, a boat might take some time to make the passage, and an energetic person could walk round the top of the lake and be there before the boat arrived. That is exactly what happened; and when Jesus and his disciples stepped out of the boat, the very crowd from which they had sought some little peace was there waiting for them.

Any ordinary man would have been intensely annoyed. The rest Jesus so much desired and which he had so well earned was denied to him. His privacy was invaded. Any ordinary man would have resented it all, but Jesus was moved with pity at the pathos of the crowd. He looked at them; they were so desperately in earnest; they wanted so much what he alone could give them; to him they were like sheep who had no shepherd. What did he mean?

(1) A sheep without the shepherd cannot find the way. Left to ourselves, we get lost in life. John Cairns, Principal of the United Presbyterian Trinity Hall, Edinburgh, spoke of people who feel like 'lost children out in the rain'. In the *Inferno*, Dante has a line where he says, 'I woke up in the middle of the wood, and it was dark, and there was no clear way before me.' Life can be so bewildering. We can stand at some crossroads and not know which way to take. It is only when Jesus leads and we follow that we can find the way.

(2) A sheep without the shepherd cannot find its pasture and its food. In this life, we are bound to seek for sustenance. We need the strength which can keep us going; we need the inspiration which can lift us out of ourselves and above ourselves. When we seek it elsewhere, our minds are still unsatisfied, our hearts still restless, our souls still unfed. We can gain strength for life only from him who is the living bread.

(3) A sheep without the shepherd has no defence against the dangers which threaten it. It can defend itself neither from robbers nor from wild animals. If life has taught us one thing, it must be that we cannot live it alone. No one has a sure defence against the temptations which assail us and from the evil of the world which attacks us. Only in the company of Jesus can we walk in the world and remain untainted by it. Without him we are defenceless; with him we are safe.

The Sunday between 24 and 30 July
The Infinite Love of Christ *and*
The Meaning of a Miracle

Ephesians 3:14–21

Paul is here praying that the people within the Church may be such that the whole Church will be the body of Christ. He prays that his people may be strengthened in their inner *being*. What did he mean? The inner *being* was a phrase by which the Greeks understood three things.

(1) There was human *reason*. It was Paul's prayer that Jesus Christ should strengthen the reason of his friends. He wanted them to be better able to discern between what was right and what was wrong. He wanted Christ to give them the wisdom which would keep life pure and safe.

(2) There was *conscience*. It was Paul's prayer that the conscience of his people should become increasingly sensitive. It is possible to disregard conscience for so long that in the end it becomes dulled. Paul prayed that Jesus should keep our consciences sensitive and on the alert.

(3) There was the *will*. So often we know what is right, and mean to do it, but our will is not strong enough to back up our knowledge and to carry out our intentions. As the American poet John Drinkwater wrote in 'A Prayer':

> Grant us the will to fashion as we feel,
> Grant us the strength to labour as we know,
> Grant us the purpose, ribbed and edged with steel,

To strike the blow.
Knowledge we ask not, knowledge Thou hast lent,
But, Lord, the will – there lies our deepest need,
Grant us the power to build, above the high intent,
The deed, the deed!

The inner being is the reason, the conscience, the will. The strengthening of the inner being comes when Christ takes up his permanent residence in an individual. The word Paul uses for Christ *dwelling* in our hearts is the Greek *katoikein*, which is the word used for permanent, as opposed to temporary, residence. Henry Lyte wrote, as one of the less familiar and now rarely sung verses of that great hymn 'Abide with me':

Not a brief glance I beg, a passing word,
But as thou dwell'st with thy disciples, Lord,
Familiar, condescending, patient, free,
Come, not to sojourn, but abide with me.

The secret of strength is the presence of Christ within our lives. Christ will gladly come into our lives – but he will never force his way in. He must await our invitation to bring us his strength.

Paul prays that Christians may be able to grasp the meaning of the breadth, depth, length and height of the love of Christ. It is as if Paul invited us to look at the universe – to the limitless sky above, to the limitless horizons on every side, to the depth of the earth and of the seas beneath us, and said: 'The love of Christ is as vast as that.'

It is unlikely that Paul had any more definite thought in his mind than the sheer vastness of the love of Christ. But many people have taken this picture and have read meanings, some of them very beautiful, into it. One ancient commentator sees the cross as the symbol of this love. The upper arm of the cross points up; the lower arm points down; and the crossing arms point out to the widest horizons. The fourth-century biblical scholar Jerome said that the love of Christ reaches up to include the holy angels, that it reaches down to include even the evil spirits in hell, that in its length it covers all who are striving on the upward way, and in its breadth it covers those who are wandering away from Christ.

If we want to work this out, we might say that in the *breadth* of its sweep, the love of Christ includes every individual of every kind in every age in every world; in the *length* to which it would go, the love of Christ accepted even the cross; in its *depth*, it descended to experience even death; in its *height*, he still loves us in heaven, where he lives always to make intercession for us (Hebrews 7:25). No one is outside the love of Christ; no place is beyond its reach.

Then Paul comes back again to the thought which dominates the letter to the Ephesians. Where is that love to be experienced? We experience it *with all God's consecrated people*. That is to say, we find it in the fellowship of the Church. The founder of Methodism, John Wesley, had a saying which was true: 'God knows nothing of solitary religion.' 'No man', he said, 'ever went to heaven alone.' The Church may have its faults; church members may be very far from what they ought to be; but in the fellowship of the Church we find the love of God.

Paul ends with a hymn of praise to God, who can do for us more than we can dream of, and who does it for us in the Church and in Christ. Let us think of Paul's glorious picture of the Church. This world is not what it was meant to be; it is torn apart by opposing forces and by hatred and bitter conflict. Nation is against nation, neighbour is against neighbour, class is against class. Within every individual, the fight rages between the evil and the good. It is God's design that all people and all nations should become one in Christ. To achieve this end, Christ needs the Church to go out and tell the world of his love and of his mercy. And the Church cannot do that until its members, joined together in fellowship, experience the limitless love of Christ.

John 6:1–21

We will never know exactly what happened on that grassy plain near Bethsaida Julias. We may look at it in three ways.

(a) We may regard it simply as a miracle in which Jesus multiplied loaves and fishes. Some may find that hard to conceive of; and some may find it hard to reconcile with the fact that that is just what Jesus refused to do at his temptations (Matthew 4:3–4). If we can believe in the sheer miraculous character of this miracle, then let us continue to do so. But if we are puzzled, there are two other explanations.

(b) It may be that this was really a sacramental meal. In the rest of the chapter, the language of Jesus is exactly that of the Last Supper, when he speaks about eating his flesh and drinking his blood. It could be that at this meal it was but a morsel, like the sacrament, that each person received; and that the thrill and wonder of the presence of Jesus and the reality of God turned the sacramental crumb into something which richly nourished their hearts and souls – as happens at every communion service to this day.

(c) There may be another and very lovely explanation. It is scarcely to be thought that the crowd left on a nine-mile expedition without making any preparations at all. If there were pilgrims with them, they would certainly possess supplies for the way. But it may be that they would not produce what they had, for they selfishly – and very humanly – wished to keep it all for themselves. It may then be that Jesus, with that rare smile of his, produced the little store that he and his disciples had; with sunny faith he thanked God for it and shared it out. Moved by his example, everyone who had anything did the same; and in the end there was enough, and more than enough, for all. It may be that this is a miracle in which the presence of Jesus turned a crowd of selfish men and women into a fellowship of sharers. It may be that this story represents the biggest miracle of all – one which changed not loaves and fishes, but men and women.

However that may be, there were certain people there without whom the miracle would not have been possible.

(1) There was Andrew. There is a contrast between Andrew and Philip. Philip was the man who said: 'The situation is hopeless; nothing can be done.' Andrew was the man who said: 'I'll see what I can do; and I'll trust Jesus to do the rest.'

It was Andrew who brought that young boy to Jesus, and by bringing him made the miracle possible. No one ever knows what will come out of it when we bring someone to Jesus. If parents train up their children in the knowledge and the love and the fear of God, no one can say what mighty things those children may some day do for God and for others. If a Sunday School teacher brings a child to Christ, no one knows what that child may some day do for Christ and his Church.

There is a tale of an old German schoolmaster who, when he entered his class of boys in the morning, used to remove his cap and bow ceremoniously to them. One asked him why he did this. His answer was: 'You never know what one of these boys may some day become.' He was right – one of them was the founder of the Reformation, Martin Luther. Andrew did not know what he was doing when he brought that boy to Jesus that day, but he was providing material for a miracle. We never know what possibilities we are releasing when we bring someone to Jesus.

(2) There was the boy. He had not much to offer, but in what he had Jesus found the materials of a miracle. There would have been one great deed fewer in history if that boy had withheld his loaves and fishes.

Jesus needs what we can bring him. It may not be much, but he needs it. It may well be that the world is denied miracle after miracle and triumph after triumph because we will not bring to Jesus what we have and what we are. If we would lay ourselves on the altar of his service, there is no saying what he could do with us and through us. We may be sorry and embarrassed that we have not more to bring – and rightly so; but that is no reason for failing to bring what we have. Little is always much in the hands of Christ.

The Sunday between 31 July and 6 August
The Basis of Unity *and* The Only True Work

Ephesians 4:1–16

Paul here sets down the basis on which Christian unity is founded.

(1) There is one body. Christ is the head and the Church is the body. No brain can work through a body which is split into fragments. Unless there is a co-ordinated oneness in the body, the plans and intentions of the head are frustrated. The oneness of the Church is essential for the work of Christ. That does not need to be a mechanical oneness of administration and of human organization; but it does need to be a oneness founded on a common love of Christ and of every part for the other.

(2) There is one Spirit. The word *pneuma* in Greek means both *spirit* and breath; it is in fact the usual word for breath. Unless the breath is in the body, the body is dead; and the life-giving breath of the body of the Church is the Spirit of Christ. There can be no Church without the Spirit; and there can be no receiving of the Spirit without prayerful waiting.

(3) There is one hope in our calling. We are all proceeding towards the same goal. This is the great secret of the unity of Christians. Our methods, our organization, even some of our beliefs may be different; but we are all striving towards the one goal of a world redeemed in Christ.

(4) There is one Lord. The nearest approach to a creed which the early Church possessed was the short sentence: 'Jesus Christ is Lord' (Philippians 2:11). As Paul saw it, it was God's dream that there should come a day when everyone would make this confession. The word used for *Lord* is *kurios*. It was used for *master* as distinct from *servant* or *slave*; and it was the regular way of referring to the Roman emperor. Christians are joined together because they are all in the possession and in the service of the one Master and King.

(5) There is one faith. Paul did not mean that there is one *creed*. Very seldom indeed in the New Testament does the word *faith* mean a *creed*. By *faith*, the New Testament nearly always means the complete commitment of Christians to Jesus Christ. Paul means that all Christians are bound together because they have made a common act of complete surrender to the love of Jesus Christ. They may describe their act of surrender in different terms; but, however they describe it, that surrender is the one thing common to all of them.

(6) There is one baptism. In the early Church, baptism was usually adult baptism, because men and women were coming direct from the worship of other gods into the Christian faith. Therefore, above all, baptism was a public confession of faith. There was only one way for a Roman soldier to join the army: he had to take the oath that he would be true forever to his emperor. Similarly, there was only one way to enter the Christian Church – the way of public confession of Jesus Christ.

(7) There is one God. See what Paul says about the God in whom we believe. He is the *Father* of all; in that phrase is enshrined the *love* of God. The greatest thing about the Christian God is not that he is king, nor that he is judge, but that he is Father. The Christian idea of God begins in love.

He is *above* all; in that phrase is enshrined the *control* of God. No matter what things may look like, God is in control. There may be floods; but 'The Lord sits enthroned over the flood' (Psalm 29:10).

He is *through* all; in that phrase is enshrined the *providence* of God. God did not create the world and set it going as we might wind up a clockwork toy and leave it to run down. God is all through his world, guiding, sustaining, loving.

He is *in* all; in that phrase is enshrined the *presence* of God in all life. It may be that Paul took the germ of this idea from the Stoics who believed that God was a fire purer than any earthly fire; they believed that what gave human beings life was that a spark of that fire which was God came and dwelt in their bodies. It was Paul's belief that in everything there is God.

It is the Christian belief that we live in a God-created, God-controlled, God-sustained, God-filled world.

In every church, there are certain members who must be protected. There are those who are like children: they are dominated by a desire for novelty at the mercy of the latest fashion in religion. It is the lesson of history that popular fashions in religion come and go but the Church continues forever. The solid food of religion is always to be found within the Church.

In every church, there are certain people who have to be guarded against. There are always those who by ingenious arguments seek to lure people away from their faith. It is one of the characteristics of our age that people talk about religion more than they have done for many years; and Christians, especially young Christians, often have to meet the clever arguments of those who are against the Church and against God. There is only one way to avoid being blown about by the latest religious fashion and to avoid being seduced by the convincing but wrong arguments of clever people, and that is by continual growth into Christ.

The only thing which can keep the individual Christian solid in the faith and secure against persuasive arguments that lead people astray, the only thing which can keep the Church healthy and efficient, is an intimate association with Jesus Christ, who is the head and the directing mind of the body.

John 6:24–35

When Jesus spoke about the works of God, the Jews immediately thought in terms of 'good' works. It was their conviction that by living a good life it was possible to earn the favour of God. They held that people could be divided into three classes – those who were good, those who were bad and those who were in between, who, by doing one more good work, could be transferred to the category of the good. So, when the Jews asked Jesus about the work of God, they expected him to lay down lists of things to do. But that is not what Jesus says at all.

Jesus' answer is extremely compressed, and we must expand it and see what lies behind it. He said that God's work was to believe in him whom he had sent. Paul would have put it this way – the one work that God desires from us is *faith*. Now what does faith mean? It means being in such a relationship with God that we are his friends, not terrified of him any more but knowing him as our Father and our friend and giving him the trust and the obedience and the submission which naturally arise from this new relationship. How does believing in Jesus tie up with that? It is only because Jesus came to tell us that God is our Father and loves us and wants nothing more than to forgive, that the old distance and enmity are taken away and the new relationship with him is made possible.

But that new relationship issues in a certain kind of life. Now we know what God is like, our lives must answer to that knowledge. That answer will be in three directions, each of which corresponds to what Jesus told us of God.

(1) God is love. Therefore in our lives there must be love and service of others corresponding to the love and the service of God, and forgiveness of others corresponding to the forgiveness of God.

(2) God is holiness. Therefore in our lives there must be purity corresponding to the holiness of God.

(3) God is wisdom. Therefore in our lives there must be complete submission and trust corresponding to the wisdom of God.

The essence of the Christian life is a new relationship to God, a relationship offered by him and made possible by the revelation which Jesus gave us of him, a relationship which issues in that service, purity and trust which are the reflection of God. This is the work which God wishes us and enables us to perform.

Jesus had just made a great claim. The true work of God was to believe in him. 'Very well,' said the Jews, 'this is in effect a claim to be the Messiah. Prove it.'

Their minds were still on the feeding of the crowd, and inevitably that turned their thoughts to the manna in the wilderness. They could hardly help connecting the two things. The manna had always been regarded as the bread of God (Psalm 78:24; Exodus 16:15); and there was a strong Rabbinic belief that when the Messiah came he would again give the manna. The giving of the manna was held to be the supreme work in the life of Moses, and the Messiah was bound to surpass it. 'As was the first redeemer so was the final redeemer; as the first redeemer caused the manna to fall from heaven, even so shall the second redeemer cause the manna to fall.' 'Ye shall not find the manna in this age, but ye shall find it in the age that is to come.' 'For whom has the manna been prepared? For the righteous in the age that is coming. Everyone who believes is worthy and eateth of it.' It was the belief that a pot of the manna had been hidden in the ark in the first Temple, and that, when the Temple was destroyed, Jeremiah had hidden it away and would produce it again when the Messiah came. In other words, the Jews were challenging Jesus to produce bread from God in order to substantiate his claims. They did not regard the bread which had fed the 5,000 as bread from God; it had begun in earthly loaves and issued in earthly loaves. The manna, they held, was a different thing and a real test.

Jesus' answer was twofold. First, he reminded them that it was not *Moses* who had given them the manna; it was *God*. Second, he told them that the manna was not really the bread of God; it was only the symbol of the bread of God. The bread of God was he who came down from heaven and gave men and women not simply satisfaction from physical hunger, but life. Jesus was claiming that the only real satisfaction was in him.

The Sunday between 7 and 13 August
The Imitation of God *and*
The Bread of Life

Ephesians 4:25–5.2

Paul has just been saying that when people become Christians, they must put off their old life as they would put off a coat for which they have no further use. Here, he speaks of the things which must be banished from the Christian life.

(1) There must be no more falsehood. There is more than one kind of lie in this world. There is the lie of speech, sometimes deliberate and sometimes almost unconscious. There is also the lie of silence, and maybe it is even more common. It may be that in some discussion we, by our silence, give approval to some course of action which we know is wrong. It may be that we withhold warning or rebuke when we know quite well we should have given it.

Paul gives the reason for telling the truth. It is because we are all members of the same body. We can live in safety only because the senses and the nerves pass true messages to the brain. If they took to passing false messages – if, for instance, they told the brain that something was cool and touchable when in fact it was hot and burning – life would very soon come to an end. A body can function healthily only when each part of it passes true messages to the brain. If we are all bound into one body, that body can function properly only when we speak the truth.

(2) There must be anger in the Christian life, but it must be the right kind of anger. Bad temper and irritability are indefensible;

but there is an anger without which the world would be a poorer place. The world would have lost much without the blazing anger of William Wilberforce against the slave trade of the British Empire or of Lord Shaftesbury against the working conditions of the nineteenth century. There were times when Jesus was terribly and majestically angry. He was angry when the scribes and Pharisees were watching to see if he would heal the man with the withered hand on the Sabbath day (Mark 3:5). It was not their criticism of himself at which he was angry; he was angry that their rigid orthodoxy wanted to impose unnecessary suffering on a fellow human being.

The anger which is selfish and uncontrolled is sinful and hurtful and must be banished from the Christian life. But the selfless anger which is disciplined into the service of Christ and of other people is one of the great dynamic forces of the world.

(3) Paul goes on to say that Christians must never let the sun set upon their anger. There was a Jewish Rabbi whose prayer it was that he might never go to sleep with any bitter thought against a fellow human being within his mind. Paul's advice is sound, because the longer we postpone putting right a quarrel, the less likely we are ever to sort things out. If we have been in the wrong, we must pray to God to give us grace to admit it; and, even if we are in the right, we must pray to God to give us the graciousness which will enable us to take the first step to put matters right.

(4) Thieves must become honest workers. This was necessary advice, for in the ancient world stealing was rampant. Interestingly, Paul does not say: 'Become an honest worker so that you may support yourself.' He says: 'Become an honest worker so that you may have something to give away to those who are poorer than yourself.' Here is a new idea and a new ideal – that of working in order to give away. In modern society, not many of us have a great deal to give away; but we do well to remember that the Christian ideal is that we work not to accumulate things but to be able, if need be, to give them away.

(5) Paul forbids all foul-mouthed speaking, and then goes on to put the same thing positively. The Christian should be characterized by words which help others. As James Moffatt's translation has it, Eliphaz the Temanite paid Job a tremendous compliment. 'Your words', he said, 'have kept men on their feet' (Job 4:4). Such are the words that every Christian ought to speak.

(6) Paul urges us not to grieve the Holy Spirit. The Holy Spirit is the guide of life. When we act against the counsel of our parents when we are young, we hurt them. Similarly, to act against the guidance of the Holy Spirit is to grieve the Spirit and to hurt the heart of God, the Father, who, through the Spirit, sent his word to us.

Paul sets before his Christian people the highest standard in all the world; he tells them they must be imitators of God. When Paul talked of imitation, he was using language which the wisest Greeks could understand. The main part of training for an orator was the study and the imitation of the masters who had gone before. It is as if Paul said: 'If you were to train to be an orator, you would be told to imitate those who are experts in making speeches. Since you are training in life, you must imitate the Lord of all good life.'

Above all, Christians must imitate the love and the forgiveness of God. Paul uses a typical Old Testament phrase, 'odour of a sweet savour', which goes back to a very old idea, as old as sacrifice itself. A sacrifice which had the odour of a sweet savour was specially pleasing and specially acceptable to the god to whom it was offered. Paul takes this time-honoured phrase and uses it of the sacrifice that Jesus brought to God. The sacrifice of Jesus was well pleasing to God.

What was that sacrifice? It was a life of perfect obedience to God and of perfect love to all men and women, an obedience so absolute and a love so infinite that they accepted the cross. What Paul says is: 'Imitate God. And you can do so only by loving one another with the same sacrificial love with which Jesus loved, and forgiving one another in love as God has done.'

John 6:35, 41–51

What did Jesus mean when he said: 'I am the bread of life'? It is not enough to regard this as simply a beautiful and poetical phrase. Let us analyse it step by step. (1) Bread sustains life. It is that without which life cannot go on. (2) But what is life? Clearly by life is meant something far more than mere physical existence. What is this new spiritual meaning of life? (3) Real life is the new relationship with God, that relationship of trust and obedience and love. (4) That relationship is made possible only by Jesus Christ. Apart from him, no one can enter into it. (5) That is to say, without Jesus there may be existence, but not life. (6) Therefore, if Jesus is the essential of life, he may be described as the bread of life. The hunger of the human situation is ended when we know Christ and through him know God. The restless soul is at rest; the hungry heart is satisfied.

This passage also shows the reasons why the Jews rejected Jesus and, in rejecting him, rejected eternal life.

(1) They judged things by human values and by external standards. Their reaction in face of the claim of Jesus was to produce the fact that he was a carpenter's son and that they had seen him grow up in Nazareth. They were unable to understand how one who was a tradesman and who came from a poor home could possibly be a special messenger from God.

We must take care that we never neglect a message from God because we despise or do not care for the messenger. We would hardly refuse a sizable cheque because it happened to be enclosed in an envelope which did not conform to the most aristocratic standards of notepaper. God has many messengers. His greatest message came through a Galilaean carpenter, and for that very reason the Jews disregarded it.

(2) The Jews argued *with each other*. They were so taken up with their private arguments that it never struck them to refer the

decision to God. They were exceedingly eager to let everyone know what they thought about the matter; but not in the least anxious to know what God thought. It might well be that sometimes in a court or committee, when those present are desirous of pushing their opinions down one another's throats, we would be better to be quiet and ask God what he thinks and what he wants us to do. After all, it does not matter so very much what we think; but what God thinks matters intensely; and we so seldom take steps to find it out.

(3) The Jews listened, *but they did not learn*. There are different kinds of listening. There is the listening of criticism; there is the listening of resentment; there is the listening of superiority; there is the listening of indifference; there is the listening of those who listen only because for the moment they cannot get the chance to speak. The only listening that is worth while is that which hears and learns; and that is the only way to listen to God.

(4) The Jews resisted *being drawn to God*. Only those accept Jesus whom God draws to him. The word which John uses for *to draw* is *helkuein*. It is the word used in the Greek translation of the Hebrew when Jeremiah hears God say, as the Authorized Version has it: 'With lovingkindness have I drawn thee' (Jeremiah 31:3). The interesting thing about the word is that it almost always implies some kind of resistance. It is the word for drawing a heavily laden net to the shore (John 21:6, 11). It is used of Paul and Silas being dragged before the magistrates in Philippi (Acts 16:19). It is the word for drawing a sword from the belt or from its scabbard (John 18:10). Always there is this idea of resistance. God can draw men and women, but their resistance can defeat God's pull.

Jesus is the bread of life; which means that he is the essential for life; therefore to refuse the invitation and command of Jesus is to miss life and to die. The Rabbis had a saying: 'The generation in the wilderness have no part in the life to come.' In the old story in Numbers, the people who cravenly refused to brave the dangers of the promised land, after the report of the scouts, were condemned to wander in the wilderness until they died. Because they would not accept the guidance of God, they were forever shut out from the promised land. The Rabbis believed that their ancestors who died in the wilderness not only missed the promised land but also missed the life to come. To refuse the offer of Jesus is to miss life in this world and in the world to come; whereas to accept his offer is to find real life in this world and glory in the world to come.

The Sunday between 14 and 20 August
The Christian Fellowship *and* His Body and His Blood

Ephesians 5:15–20

Paul exhorts his converts to live like the wise. The times in which they are living are evil; they must rescue as much time as they can from the evil uses of the world.

He goes on to draw a contrast between a typical gathering in a society that worshipped the gods of Greece and Rome and a Christian gathering. The first gathering is apt to be a drunken revel. It is significant that we still use the word *symposium* for a discussion of a subject by a number of people; the Greek word *sumposion* literally means a drinking party. A certain preacher was preaching on the text: 'Be filled with the Spirit.' He began with one startling sentence: 'You've got to fill a man with something.' Those who were not Christians found their happiness in filling themselves with wine and with worldly pleasures; Christians found their happiness in being filled with the Spirit.

From this passage, we can gather certain facts about the Christian gatherings in the early days.

(1) The early Church was a *singing church*. Its characteristic was psalms and hymns and spiritual songs; it had a happiness which made people sing.

(2) The early Church was a *thankful church*. The instinct was to give thanks for all things and in all places and at all times. John Chrysostom, the great preacher of the Church of a later day, had

the curious thought that Christians could give thanks even for hell, because hell was a warning to keep them in the right way. The early Church was a thankful church because its members were still dazzled with the wonder that God's love had stooped to save them; and it was a church that gave thanks because its members had an awareness of being in the hands of God.

(3) The early Church was a church where people *honoured and respected each other*. Paul says that the reason for this mutual honour and respect was that they reverenced Christ. They saw each other not in the light of their professions or social standing but in the light of Christ; and therefore they recognized the dignity of everyone.

John 6:51–58

There are two ways in which we may take this rather difficult passage.

(1) We may take it in a quite general sense. Jesus spoke about eating his flesh and drinking his blood. Now the flesh of Jesus was his complete humanity. John insisted that we must grasp and never let go the full humanity of Jesus, that he was bone of our bone and flesh of our flesh. What does this mean? Jesus was the mind of God become a person. This means that in Jesus we see God taking human life upon him, facing our human situation, struggling with our human problems, battling with our human temptations, working out our human relationships.

Therefore it is as if Jesus said: 'Feed your heart, feed your mind, feed your soul on the thought of my humanity. When you are discouraged and in despair, when you are beaten to your knees and disgusted with life and living – remember I took that life of yours and these struggles of yours on me.' Suddenly life and the flesh are clad with glory, for they are touched with God. It was and is the great belief of the Greek Orthodox christology that Jesus deified our flesh by taking it on himself. To eat Christ's body is to feed on the thought of his humanity until our own humanity is strengthened and cleansed and irradiated by his.

Jesus said we must drink his blood. In Jewish thought, *the blood stands for the life*. It is easy to understand why. As the blood flows from a wound, life ebbs away; and to the Jews, *the blood belonged to God*. That is why to this day a true Jew will never eat any meat which has not been completely drained of blood. 'Only, you shall not eat flesh with its life, that is, its blood' (Genesis 9:4). 'Its blood, however, you must not eat' (Deuteronomy 15:23). Now see what Jesus is saying – 'You must drink my blood – you must take my life into the very centre of your being – and that life of mine is the life which belongs to God.' When Jesus said we must drink his blood, he meant that we must take his life into the very core of our hearts.

What does that mean? Think of it this way. Here in a bookcase is a book which you never read. It may be the glory and the wonder of the tragedies of Shakespeare; but as long as it remains unread upon your bookshelves, it is external to you. One day, you take it down and read it. You are thrilled and fascinated and moved. The story sticks to you; the great lines remain in your memory; now when you want to, you can take that wonder out from inside yourself and remember it and think about it and feed your mind and your heart upon it. Once the book was outside you. Now it is inside you and you can feed upon it. It is that way with any great experience in life. It remains external until we take it within ourselves.

It is so with Jesus. As long as he remains a figure in a book, he is external to us; but when he enters into our hearts, we can feed upon the life and the strength and the dynamic vitality that he gives to us. Jesus said that we must drink his blood. He is saying: 'You must stop thinking of me as a subject for theological debate;

you must take me into you, and you must come into me; and then you will have real life.' That is what Jesus meant when he spoke about us abiding in him and himself abiding in us.

When he told us to eat his flesh and drink his blood, he was telling us to feed our hearts and souls and minds on his humanity, and to revitalize our lives with his life until we are filled with the life of God.

(2) But John meant more than that, and was thinking also of the Lord's Supper. He was saying: 'If you want life, you must come and sit at that table where you eat that broken bread and drink that poured-out wine which somehow, in the grace of God, bring you into contact with the love and the life of Jesus Christ.' But – and here is the sheer wonder of his point of view – *John has no account of the Last Supper*. He brings in his teaching about it, not in the narrative of the upper room, but in the story of a picnic meal on a hillside near Bethsaida Julias by the blue waters of the Sea of Galilee.

There is no doubt that John is saying that for the true Christian *every meal has become a sacrament*. It may well be that there were those who – if the phrase is allowed – were making too much of the sacrament within the Church, making a magic of it, implying that it was the only place where we might enter into the nearer presence of the risen Christ. It is true that the sacrament is a special appointment with God; but John held with all his heart that every meal in the humblest home, in the richest palace, beneath the canopy of the sky with only the grass for carpet, was a sacrament. He refused to limit the presence of Christ to an ecclesiastical environment and a correctly liturgical service. He said: 'At any meal you can find again that bread which speaks of the humanity of the Master, that wine which speaks of the blood which is life.'

In John's thought, the communion table and the dinner table and the picnic on the seashore or the hillside are all alike in that at all of them we may taste and touch and handle the bread and the wine which brings us Christ. Christianity would be a poor thing if Christ were confined to churches. It is John's belief that we can find him anywhere in a Christ-filled world. It is not that he belittles the sacrament; but he expands it, so that we find Christ at his table in church, and then go out to find him everywhere where men and women meet together to enjoy the gifts of God.

The Sunday between 21 and 27 August
The Armour of God *and* Attitudes to Christ

Ephesians 6:10–20

As Paul takes leave of his people, he thinks of the greatness of the struggle which lies before them. Undoubtedly, life was much more terrifying for the people of those times than it is for us today. They believed implicitly in evil spirits, which filled the air and were determined to bring harm to people.

The words which Paul uses – powers, authorities, world rulers – are all names for different classes of these evil spirits. To him, the whole universe was a battle ground. Christians not only had to contend with the attacks from other people; they had to contend with the attacks of spiritual forces that were fighting against God. We may not take Paul's actual language literally; but our experience will tell us that there is an active power of evil in the world. We have all felt the force of that evil influence which seeks to make us sin.

Paul suddenly sees a picture staring him in the face. All this time, he was chained by the wrist to a Roman soldier. Night and day, a soldier was there to ensure that he would not escape. Paul was literally an ambassador in chains. Now, he was the kind of man who could get along with anyone; and without a doubt he had often talked to the soldiers who were compelled to be so near him. As he writes, the soldier's armour suggests a picture to him. Christians too have armour; and item by item Paul takes the armour of the Roman soldier and translates it into Christian terms.

There is the belt of truth. It was the belt which went round the soldier's tunic and from which his sword hung and which gave him freedom of movement. Others may guess and feel their way; Christians move freely and quickly because they know the truth.

There is the breastplate of righteousness. When we are clothed in righteousness, we are impregnable. Words are no defence against accusations, but a good life is. Once, a man accused Plato of certain crimes. 'Well then,' said Plato, 'we must live in such a way as to prove that his accusations are a lie.' The only way to meet the accusations against Christianity is to show how good a Christian can be.

There are the sandals. Sandals were the sign of one equipped and ready to move. The sign of Christians is that they are eager to be on the way to share the gospel with others who have not heard it.

There is the shield. The word Paul uses is not that for the comparatively small round shield; it is the word used for the great oblong shield which the heavily armed warrior wore. One of the most dangerous weapons in ancient warfare was the fiery dart. It was a dart tipped with fibres of rope dipped in pitch. The pitch-soaked rope was set alight and the dart was thrown. The great oblong shield was made of two sections of wood, glued together. When the shield was presented to the dart, the dart sank into the wood and the flame was put out. Faith can deal with the darts of temptation. For Paul, faith is always complete trust in Christ. When we walk closely with Christ, we are safe from temptation.

There is salvation for a helmet. Salvation is not something which only looks back. The salvation which is in Christ gives us forgiveness for the sins of the past and strength to conquer sin in the days to come.

There is the sword; and the sword is the word of God. The word of God is both our weapon of defence against sin and our weapon of attack against the sins of the world. During the English Civil

War, Oliver Cromwell's Ironsides fought with a sword in one hand and a Bible in the other. We can never win God's battles without God's book.

Lastly, Paul comes to the greatest weapon of all – and that is prayer. We note three things that he says about prayer. (1) It must be constant. Our tendency is so often to pray only in the great crises of life; but it is from daily prayer that Christians will find daily strength. (2) It must be intense. Unfocused prayer never got anyone anywhere. Prayer demands the concentration of every faculty upon God. (3) It must be unselfish. The Jews had a saying: 'Let a man unite himself with the community in his prayers.' Often, our prayers are too much for ourselves and too little for others. We must learn to pray as much for others and with others as for ourselves.

Finally, Paul asks for the prayers of his friends for himself. And he asks not for comfort or for peace but that he may yet be allowed to proclaim God's secret, that his love is for all men and women. We do well to remember that all Christian leaders and all Christian preachers need their people to hold up their hands in prayer.

John 6:56–69

The final section of this passage is charged with tragedy, for in it is the beginning of the end. There was a time when people came to Jesus in large numbers. When he was in Jerusalem at the Passover, many saw his miracles and believed in his name (2:23). So many came to be baptized by his disciples that the numbers were embarrassing (4:1–3). In Samaria, great things happened (4:1, 39, 45). In Galilee, the crowds flocked after him just the day before (6:2). But the tone of things had changed; from now on there was a growing hatred which was going to culminate in the cross. Already John launches us on the last act of the tragedy. It is circumstances like these which reveal people's hearts and show them in their true colours. In these circumstances, there were three different attitudes to Jesus.

(1) There was *defection*. Some turned back and walked with him no more. They drifted away for various reasons. Some saw quite clearly where Jesus was heading. It was not possible to challenge the authorities as he was doing and get away with it. He was heading for disaster and they were getting out in time. They were fairweather followers. It has been said that the test of an army is how it fights when it is tired. Those who drifted away would have stuck by Jesus as long as his career was on the upward way, but at the first shadow of the cross they left him.

Some shirked the challenge of Jesus. Fundamentally their point of view was that they had come to Jesus to get something from him; when it came to suffering *for* him and giving *to* him they quit. No one can give so much as Jesus, but if we come to him solely to get and never to give we will certainly turn back. Those who would follow Jesus must remember that in following him there is always a cross.

(2) There was *deterioration*. It is in Judas above all that we see this. Jesus must have seen in him a man whom he could use for his purposes. But Judas, who might have become the hero, became the villain; he who might have become a saint became a name of shame.

There is a terrible story about an artist who was painting the Last Supper. It was a great picture and it took him many years. As a model for the face of Christ, he used a young man with a face of transcendent loveliness and purity. Bit by bit the picture was filled in, and one after another the disciples were painted. The day came when he needed a model for Judas, whose face he had left to the last. He went out and searched in the lowest haunts of the city and in the dens of vice. At last he found a man with a face so depraved and vicious as matched his requirement. When the sittings were at an end, the man said to the artist: 'You painted me before.' 'Surely not,' said the artist. 'O yes,' said the man, 'I sat for your Christ.' The years had brought terrible deterioration. The years can be cruel. They can take away our ideals and our enthusiasms and our dreams and our loyalties. They can leave us with a life that has grown smaller and not bigger. They can leave us with hearts that are shrivelled instead of expanded in the love of Christ. There can be a lost loveliness in life – God save us from that!

(3) There was *determination*. This is John's version of Peter's great confession at Caesarea Philippi (Mark 8:27; Matthew 16:13; Luke 9:18). It was just such a situation as this that called out the loyalty of Peter's heart. To him, the simple fact was that there was just no one else to go to. Jesus alone had the words of life.

Peter's loyalty was based on a personal relationship to Jesus Christ. There were many things he did not understand; he was just as bewildered and puzzled as anyone else. But there was something about Jesus for which he would willingly die. In the last analysis, Christianity is not a philosophy which we accept, nor a theory to which we give allegiance. It is a personal response to Jesus Christ. It is the allegiance and the love which we give because our hearts will not allow us to do anything else.

The Sunday between
28 August and 3 September
Hearing and Doing, The True Law and True Worship *and* The Real Defilement
James 1:17–27

James presents us with two of the vivid pictures of which he is such a master. First of all, he speaks of those who go to the church meeting and listen to the reading and expounding of the word, and who think that that listening has made them Christians. They have shut their eyes to the fact that what is read and heard in church must then be lived out. It is still possible to identify church attendance and Bible reading with Christianity, but this is to take ourselves less than half the way; the really important thing is to turn that to which we have listened into action.

Second, James says such people are like those who look at themselves in a mirror, see the smuts which disfigure their faces and the dishevelment of their hair, and go away and forget what they actually look like, and so fail to do anything about it. Listening to the true word reveals to individuals what they are and what they ought to be. They see what is wrong and what must be done to put it right; but, if they are only hearers, they remain just as they are, and all the hearing has been to no avail.

James does well to remind us that what is heard in the holy place must be lived in the market place – or there is no point in hearing at all.

In verse 25 we have the kind of passage in James which Martin Luther disliked so much. He disliked the idea of law altogether, for with Paul he would have said: 'Christ is the end of the law'

(Romans 10:4). 'James', said Luther, 'drives us to law and works.' And yet there is a sense in which James is right. There is an ethical law which Christians must seek to put into action. That law is to be found first in the Ten Commandments and then in the teaching of Jesus. James calls that law two things.

(1) He calls it the *perfect law*. There are three reasons why the law is perfect. (a) It is God's law, given and revealed by him. The way of life which Jesus laid down for his followers is in accordance with the will of God. (b) It is perfect in that it cannot be bettered. The Christian law is the law of love, and the demand of love can never be satisfied. We know well, when we love someone, that even if we gave them all the world and served them for a lifetime, we still could not satisfy or deserve their love. (c) But there is still another sense in which the Christian law is perfect. The Greek word is *teleios*, which nearly always describes perfection towards some given end. Now, if men and women obey the law of Christ, they will fulfil the purpose for which God sent them into the world; they will be the people they ought to be and will make the contribution to the world they ought to make. They will be perfect in the sense that they will, by obeying the law of God, achieve their God-given destiny.

(2) He calls it the *law of liberty*; that is, the law in the keeping of which people find their true liberty. All the great philosophers and scholars have agreed that it is only in obeying the law of God that an individual becomes truly free. 'To obey God', said Seneca, 'is liberty.' Philo said: 'All who are under the tyranny of anger or desire or any other passion are altogether slaves; all who live with the law are free.' As long as human beings have to obey their own passions and emotions and desires, they are nothing less than slaves. It is when we accept the will of God that we become really free – for then we are free to be what we ought to be. God's service is perfect freedom, and in doing his will is our peace.

We must be careful to understand what James is saying in the next two verses.

The Revised Standard Version translates the phrases at the beginning of verse 27: '*Religion* that is pure and undefiled is . . .' The word translated as *religion* is *thrēskeia*, and its meaning is not so much *religion as worship* in the sense of the outward expression of religion in ritual and liturgy and ceremony. What James is saying is: 'The finest ritual and the finest liturgy you can offer to God is service of the poor and personal purity.' To James, real worship did not lie in elaborate vestments or in magnificent music or in a carefully planned service; it lay in the practical service of others and in the purity of one's own personal life. It is perfectly possible for a church to be so taken up with the beauty of its buildings and the splendour of its liturgy that it has neither the time nor the money for practical Christian service – and that is what James is condemning.

In fact, James is condemning only what the prophets had condemned long ago. God, said the psalmist, is 'father of orphans and protector of widows' (Psalm 68:5). It was Micah's complaint that all ritual sacrifices were useless if the people did not do justice and love kindness and walk humbly before God (cf. Micah 6:6–8).

All through history, people have tried to make ritual and liturgy a substitute for sacrifice and service. They have made religion splendid *within* the church at the expense of neglecting it *outside* the church. This is by no means to say that it is wrong to seek to offer the noblest and the most splendid worship within God's house, but it is to say that all such worship is empty and idle unless it sends people out to love God by loving one another and to walk more purely in the tempting ways of the world.

Mark 7:1–8, 14, 15, 21–23

Jesus has been arguing with the legal experts about different aspects of the traditional law. He has shown the irrelevance of the elaborate hand-washings. He has shown how rigid adherence to the traditional law can actually mean disobedience to the law of God. But here he says something more startling yet. He declares that nothing that goes into a person can possibly cause defilement, for it is received only into the body, which rids itself of it in the normal, physical way.

In effect, Jesus was saying that *things* cannot be either unclean or clean in any real religious sense of the term. Only *persons* can be really defiled; and what defiles people are their own actions, which are the product of their own hearts. This was new doctrine and shatteringly new doctrine. With one sweeping pronouncement, Jesus declared that uncleanness has nothing to do with what people take into their bodies but everything to do with what comes out of their hearts. Let us look at the things Jesus lists as coming from the heart and making people unclean.

He begins with *evil designs*. Every outward act of sin is preceded by an inward act of choice; therefore Jesus begins with the evil thought from which the evil action comes. Next come *fornications*; later he is to list acts of *adultery*; but this first word is a wide word – it means every kind of traffic in sexual vice. There follow *thefts*. The kind of thief described here is a mean, deceitful, dishonourable pilferer, without even the redeeming quality of a certain audacious gallantry that a brigand must have. *Murders* and *adulteries* come next in the list and their meaning is clear.

Then come *covetous deeds*. The word used here comes from two Greek words meaning to *have more*. It has been defined as *the accursed love of having*. It has been defined as 'the spirit which snatches at that which it is not right to take', 'the baneful appetite for that which belongs to others'. It is the spirit which snatches at things, not to hoard them like a miser, but to spend them in lust and luxury. It has been defined as 'Rapacious appetite for gain, not for its own sake, but for the pleasure of refunding it immediately through all the channels of pride and luxury.' It is not the desire for money and things; it includes the desire for power, the insatiable lust of the flesh.

There follow *evil deeds*. The word for evil used here refers to a person in whose heart there is the desire to do harm. That person is, as the eighteenth-century German theologian Johann Bengel said, 'trained in every crime and completely equipped to inflict evil on any man'. In the seventeenth century, Jeremy Taylor defined this *evil* as 'aptness to do shrewd turns, to delight in mischiefs and tragedies; loving to trouble our neighbour, and to do him ill offices; crossness, perverseness and peevishness of action in our intercourse'. *Such evil* not only corrupts the person who has it; it corrupts others too.

Next comes *guile*. It comes from a word which means *bait*; it is used for trickery and deceit. It is used for instance of a mousetrap. When the Greeks were besieging Troy and could not gain entry, they sent the Trojans the present of a great wooden horse, as if it was a token of goodwill. The Trojans opened their gates and took it in. But the horse was filled with Greeks who in the night broke out and dealt death and devastation to Troy. That is *guile*. It is crafty, cunning, deceitful, clever treachery.

Next on the list is *wanton wickedness*. The Greeks defined this as 'a disposition of soul that resents all discipline', as 'a spirit that acknowledges no restraints, dares whatsoever its caprice and wanton insolence may suggest'. Evil men and women may hide their sin, but those who have wanton wickedness sin without a qualm and never hesitate to shock other people. Jezebel was the classic example when she built a pagan shrine in Jerusalem the holy city.

Envy is literally *the evil eye*, the eye that looks on the success and happiness of another in such a way that it would cast an evil spell upon it if it could. The next word when used of words against others means *slander*; when it is used of words against God, it means *blasphemy*. It means insulting other people or God.

There follows *pride*. The Greek word literally means 'showing oneself above'. It describes the attitude of people 'who have a certain contempt for everyone except themselves'. The interesting thing about this word, as the Greeks used it, is that it describes an attitude that may never become *public*. It may be that in their heart of hearts these people are always secretly comparing themselves with others. They might even ape humility and yet in their hearts be proud. Sometimes, of course, the pride is evident. The Greeks had a legend of this pride. They said that the Giants, the sons of Tartarus and Gē, in their pride sought to storm heaven and were cast down by Hercules. Such pride is setting oneself up against God; it is 'invading God's prerogatives'. That is why it has been called 'the peak of all the vices', and why 'God opposes the proud' (James 4:6).

Last comes *folly*. This does not mean the foolishness that is due to weakness of intellect and lack of brains; it means moral folly. It describes not those who are brainless fools, but those who choose to play the fool. It is a truly terrible list which Jesus cites of the things that come from the human heart. When we examine it, a shudder surely passes over us. Nonetheless it is a summons, not to a fastidious shrinking from such things, but to an honest self-examination of our own hearts.

The Sunday between 4 and 10 September
Faith and Works *and* The Forecast of a World for Christ

James 2:1–10, 14–17

There is no doubt that there must have been social problems in the early Church. The Church was the only place in the ancient world where social distinctions did not exist. There must have been a certain initial awkwardness when a master found himself sitting next to his slave or when a master arrived at a service in which his slave was actually the leader and the dispenser of the sacrament. The gap between the slave, who in law was nothing more than a living tool, and the master was so wide as to cause problems of approach on either side. Further, in its early days the Church was predominantly poor and humble, and therefore if a rich man was converted and came to the Christian fellowship, there must have been a very real temptation to make a fuss of him and treat him as a special trophy for Christ.

The Church must be the one place where all distinctions are wiped out. There can be no distinctions of rank and prestige when we meet in the presence of the King of glory. There can be no distinctions of merit when we meet in the presence of the supreme holiness of God. In his presence, all earthly distinctions are less than the dust and all earthly righteousness is as filthy rags. In the presence of God, all are one.

At the end of this section, James reminds his readers of two great facts of the Christian life.

(1) Christians live under the law of liberty, and it is by the law of liberty that they will be judged. What he means is this. Unlike the Pharisees and the orthodox Jews, Christians are not men and women whose lives are governed by the external pressure of a whole series of rules and regulations imposed on them from outside. They are governed by the inner compulsion of love. They follow the right way, the way of love to God and love to other people, not because any external law compels them to do so nor because any threat of punishment frightens them into doing so, but because the love of Christ within their hearts makes them want to do so.

(2) Christians must always remember that only those who show mercy will find mercy. This is a principle which runs through all Scripture. Ben Sirach wrote: 'Forgive your neighbour the wrong he has done, and then your sins will be pardoned when you pray. Does anyone harbour anger against another, and expect healing from the Lord? If one has no mercy to another like himself, can he then seek pardon for his own sins?' (Sirach 28:2–5). Jesus said: 'Blessed are the merciful, for they will receive mercy' (Matthew 5:7). 'Do not judge, so that you may not be judged. For with the judgement you make you will be judged' (Matthew 7:1–2). He tells of the condemnation which fell upon the unforgiving servant, and ends the parable by saying: 'So, my heavenly Father will also do to every one of you, if you do not forgive your brother or sister from your heart' (cf. Matthew 18:23– 35).

Scripture teaching is agreed that those who would find mercy must themselves be merciful. And James goes even further, for in the end he says that mercy triumphs over judgement – by which he means that in the day of judgement those who have shown mercy will find that their mercy has even blotted out their own sin.

The one thing that James cannot stand is a claim to faith without putting it into practice, words without deeds. He chooses a vivid illustration of what he means. Suppose a person has neither clothes for protection nor food for sustenance, and suppose a so-called friend expresses the sincerest sympathy for such a sad plight, and suppose that sympathy stops with words and no effort is made to ease the plight of the unfortunate individual, what use is that? What use is sympathy without some attempt to turn that sympathy into practical effect?

In his approach to this subject, James is profoundly right. There is nothing more dangerous than the repeated experiencing of a fine emotion with no attempt to put it into action. It is a fact that every time we feel a generous impulse without taking action, we become less likely ever to take action. In a sense, it is true to say that we have no right to feel sympathy unless we at least attempt to put that sympathy into action. An emotion is not something in which to luxuriate; it is something which at the cost of effort and of toil and of discipline and of sacrifice must be turned into the stuff of life.

Mark 7:24–37

When the first incident is seen against its background, it becomes one of the most moving and extraordinary in the life of Jesus.

Tyre and Sidon were cities of Phoenicia, which was a part of Syria. Phoenicia stretched north from Carmel, right along the coastal plain. Although the Phoenician cities were part of Syria, they were all independent, and they were all rivals. They had their own kings, their own gods and their own coinage. Within a radius of fifteen or twenty miles, they were supreme. Outwardly they looked to the sea; inland they looked to Damascus, and the ships of the sea and the caravans of many lands flowed into them. In the end, Sidon lost trade and greatness to Tyre and sank into a demoralized degeneracy. But the Phoenician sailors will always be famous as the men who first found their way by following the stars.

(1) So, then, the first tremendous thing which meets us is that *Jesus is in Gentile territory*. Is it any accident that this incident comes here? The previous incident in Chapter 7 shows Jesus wiping out the distinction between clean and unclean foods. Can it be that here, in symbol, we have him wiping out the difference between clean and unclean people? Just as Jews would never soil their lips with forbidden foods, so they would never soil their lives by contact with the unclean Gentile. It may well be that here Jesus is saying by implication that the Gentiles are not unclean but that they, too, have their place within the kingdom.

Jesus must have come north to this region for temporary escape. In his own country, he was under attack from every side. The scribes and Pharisees had branded him as a sinner because he broke through their rules and regulations. Herod regarded him as a menace. The people of Nazareth treated him with scandalized dislike. The hour would come when he would face his enemies with blazing defiance, but that was not yet. Before it came, he would seek the peace and quiet of seclusion, and in that withdrawal from the enmity of the Jews the foundation of the kingdom of the Gentiles was laid. It is the forecast of the whole history of Christianity. The Jews' rejection had become the opportunity of the Gentiles.

(2) But there is more to it than that. Ideally, these Phoenician cities were part of the realm of Israel. When, under Joshua, the land was being partitioned out, the tribe of Asher was allocated the land "as far as Great Sidon . . . to the fortified city of Tyre' (Joshua 19:28–9). They had never been able to subdue their territory and they had never entered into it. Again is it not symbolic? Where the might of arms was helpless, the conquering love of Jesus Christ was victorious. The earthly Israel had failed to gather in the people of Phoenicia; now the true Israel had come upon them. It was not a strange land into which Jesus came; it was a land which long ago God had given him for his own. He was not so much coming among strangers as entering into his inheritance.

(3) The story itself must be read with insight. The woman came asking Jesus' help for her daughter. His answer was that it was not right to take the children's bread and give it to dogs. At first it is an almost shocking saying. The dog was not the well-loved companion that it is today; more commonly it was a symbol of dishonour. To a Greek, the word *dog* meant a shameless and audacious woman. To a Jew, it was equally a term of contempt. 'Do not give to dogs what is holy' (Matthew 7:6; cf. Philippians 3:2; Revelation 22:15). The word *dog* was in fact sometimes a Jewish term of contempt for the Gentiles. No matter how you look at it, the term *dog* is an insult. How, then, are we to explain Jesus' use of it here?

(a) He did not use the usual word; he used a diminutive word which described not the wild dogs of the streets, but the little pet lap-dogs of the house. In Greek, diminutives are characteristically affectionate. Jesus took the sting out of the word.

(b) Without a doubt, his tone of voice made all the difference. The same word can be a deadly insult and an affectionate address, according to the tone of voice. We can call someone 'an old rascal' in a voice of contempt or a voice of affection. Jesus' tone took all the poison out of the word.

(c) In any event, Jesus did *not* shut the door. *First*, he said, the children must be fed, but only first; there is meat left for the household pets. True, Israel had the *first* offer of the gospel, but only the first; there were others still to come. The woman was a Greek, and the Greeks had a gift of repartee; and she saw at once that Jesus was speaking with a smile. She knew that the door was swinging on its hinges. In those days, people did not have knives or forks or table-napkins. They ate with their hands; they wiped the soiled hands on chunks of bread and then flung the bread away and the house-dogs ate it. So the woman said, 'I know the children are fed first, but can't I even get the scraps the children throw away?' And Jesus loved it. Here was a sunny faith that would not take no for an answer, here was a woman with the tragedy of an ill daughter at home, and there was still light enough in her heart to reply with a smile. Her faith was tested and her faith was real, and her prayer was answered. Symbolically, she stands for the Gentile world which so eagerly seized on the bread of heaven which the Jews rejected and threw away.

The Sunday between 11 and 17 September
Blessing and Cursing *and* The Tempter Speaks in the Voice of a Friend

James 3:1–12

It might be argued against James' terror of the tongue that it is a very small part of the body to make such a fuss about and to which to attach so much importance. To combat that argument, James uses two pictures.

(1) We put a bit into the mouth of a horse, knowing that if we can control its mouth we can control its whole body. So James says that if we can control the tongue we can control the whole body, but if the tongue is uncontrolled the whole life is set on the wrong path.

(2) A rudder is very small in comparison with the size of a ship; and yet, by exerting pressure on that little rudder, the steersman can alter the course of the ship and direct it to safety. Long before James wrote, Aristotle had used this same picture when he was talking about the science of mechanics: 'A rudder is small and it is attached to the very end of the ship, but it has such power that by this little rudder, and by the power of one man – and that a power gently exerted – the great bulk of ships can be moved.' The tongue also is small, yet it can direct the whole course of a person's life.

The Jewish writer Philo called the mind the charioteer and steersman of an individual's life; it is when the mind controls every word and is itself controlled by Christ that life is safe. James is not for a moment saying that silence is better than speech. He is not pleading for a life where speech is forbidden, as it would be for Trappist monks. He is pleading for the control of the tongue. Aristippus, the Greek philosopher, had a wise saying: 'The conqueror of pleasure is not the man who never uses it. He is the man who uses pleasure as a rider guides a horse or a steersman directs a ship, and so directs them wherever he wishes.' Abstention from anything is never a complete substitute for control in its use. James is pleading not for the silence that comes from a fear of saying something wrong or hurtful but for a wise use of speech.

We know only too well from experience that there is a split in human nature. In human beings there is something of the ape and something of the angel, something of the hero and something of the villain, something of the saint and much of the sinner. It is James' conviction that nowhere is this contradiction more evident than in the tongue.

With it, he says, we bless God. This was especially relevant to a Jew. Whenever the name of God was mentioned, a Jew had to respond: 'Blessed be he!' Three times a day, devout Jews had to repeat the *Shemoneh Esreh*, the famous eighteen prayers called *Eulogies*, every one of which begins: 'Blessed be thou, O God.' God was indeed *the Blessed One*, the one who was continually blessed. And yet the very mouths and tongues which had frequently and piously blessed God were the very same mouths and tongues which cursed their neighbours. To James, there was something unnatural about this; it was as unnatural as for a stream to gush out both fresh and salt water or a bush to bear different kinds of fruit. Unnatural and wrong such things might be, but they were tragically common.

Peter could say: 'Even though I must die with you, I will not deny you' (Matthew 26:35) – and that very same tongue of his denied Jesus with oaths and curses (Matthew 26:69–75). The John who said: 'Little children, love one another' was the same who had once wanted to call down fire from heaven in order to destroy a Samaritan village (Luke 9:51–6). Even the tongues of the apostles could say very different things.

John Bunyan tells us of Talkative: 'He was a saint abroad and a devil at home.' Many people speak with perfect courtesy to strangers and may even preach love and gentleness, and yet snap with impatient irritability at their own families. It has not been unknown for someone to speak with piety on Sunday and to curse a team of workers on Monday. It has not been unknown for someone to utter the most pious sentiments one day and to repeat the most questionable stories the next. It has not been unknown for someone to speak with sweet graciousness at a religious meeting and then to go outside to destroy another person's reputation with a malicious tongue.

These things, said James, should not be. Some drugs are both poisons and cures; they are benefits to a patient when wisely controlled by a doctor, but harmful when used unwisely.

The tongue can bless or curse; it can wound or soothe; it can speak the fairest or the foulest things. It is one of life's hardest and plainest duties to see that the tongue does not contradict itself but speaks only such words as we would want God to hear.

Mark 8:27–38

When Jesus connected Messiahship with suffering and death, he was making statements that were to the disciples both incredible and incomprehensible. All their lives they had thought of the Messiah in terms of irresistible conquest, and they were now being presented with an idea which staggered them. That is why Peter protested so violently. To him the whole thing was impossible.

Why did Jesus rebuke Peter so sternly? Because he was putting into words the very temptations which were assailing Jesus. Jesus did not want to die. He knew that he had powers which he could use for conquest. At this moment, he was refighting the battle of temptations in the wilderness. This was the devil tempting him again to fall down and worship him, to take his way instead of God's way.

245

It is a strange thing, and sometimes a terrible thing, that the tempter sometimes speaks to us in the voice of a well-meaning friend. We may have decided on a course which is the right course but which will inevitably bring trouble, loss, unpopularity, sacrifice. And some well-meaning friend tries with the best intentions in the world to stop us. I knew a man who decided to take a course which would almost inevitably land him in trouble. A friend came to him and tried to dissuade him. 'Remember', said the friend, 'that you have a wife and a family. You can't do this.' It is quite possible for our friends to love us so much that they want us to avoid trouble and to play safe.

The tempter can make no more terrible attack than in the voice of those who love us and who think they seek only our good. That is what happened to Jesus that day; that is why he answered so sternly. Not even the pleading voice of love must silence for us the imperious voice of God.

Two things stand out here even at first sight.

(1) There is the almost startling honesty of Jesus. No one could ever say that they were induced to follow Jesus by false pretences. Jesus never tried to bribe anyone by the offer of an easy way. He did not offer peace; he offered glory. To tell the disciples they must be ready to take up a cross was to tell them they must be ready to be regarded as criminals and to die.

The honesty of great leaders has always been one of their characteristics. In the days of the Second World War, when Sir Winston Churchill took over the leadership of the country, all that he offered was 'blood, toil, tears and sweat'.

Jesus never sought to lure anyone to him by the offer of an easy way; he sought to challenge men and women, to waken the boldness and moral courage in their souls, by the offer of a way than which none could be higher and harder. He came not to make life easy but to challenge people to greatness.

246

(2) There is the fact that Jesus never called on anyone to do or face anything which he was not prepared to do and face himself. That indeed is the characteristic of the leader whom people will follow. There was a famous Roman general, Quintus Fabius Cunctator. He was discussing with his staff how to take a difficult position. Someone suggested a certain course of action. 'It will only cost the lives of a few men,' this counselor said. Fabius looked at him. 'Are you', he said, 'willing to be one of the few?'

Jesus was not the kind of leader who sat remote and played with people's lives like expendable pawns. What he demanded that they should face, he, too, was ready to face. Jesus had a right to call on us to take up a cross, for he himself first bore one.

(3) Jesus said of those who would be his disciples, 'Let them deny themselves.' We will understand the meaning of this demand best if we take it very simply and literally. 'Let them say no to self.' If we would follow Jesus Christ we must say no to ourselves and yes to Christ. We must say no to our own natural love of ease and comfort. We must say no to every course of action based on self-seeking and self-will.

We must say no to the instincts and the desires which prompt us to touch and taste and handle the forbidden things. We must unhesitatingly say yes to the voice and the command of Jesus Christ. We must be able to say with Paul, 'It is no longer I who live, but it is Christ who lives in me' (Galatians 2:20). We live no longer to follow our own will, but to follow the will of Christ, and in that service we find perfect freedom.

The Sunday between 18 and 24 September

Human Pleasure or God's Will? *and* The True Ambition

James 3:13–4:3, 7–8a

At the beginning of Chapter 4 James is setting before his people a basic question – whether their aim in life is to submit to the will of God or to gratify their own desires for the pleasures of this world. He warns that, if pleasure is the policy of life, nothing but strife and hatred and division can possibly follow. He says that the result of the overriding search for pleasure is *polemoi* (wars) and *machai* (battles). He means that the feverish search for pleasure results in long-drawn-out resentments, which are like wars, and sudden explosions of enmity, which are like battles. The ancient moralists would have thoroughly agreed with him.

When we look at human society, we so often see a seething mass of hatred and strife. The Jewish scholar Philo writes: 'Consider the continual war which prevails among men even in times of peace, and which exists not only between nations and countries and cities, but also between private houses, or, I might rather say, is present with every individual man; observe the unspeakable raging storm in men's souls that is excited by the violent rush of the affairs of life; and you may well wonder whether anyone can enjoy tranquillity in such a storm, and maintain calm amid the surge of this billowing sea.'

The root cause of this endless and bitter conflict is nothing other than desire. Lucian, the Greek satirist, writes: 'All the evils which come upon man – revolutions and wars, stratagems and slaughters – spring from desire. All these things have as their fountain-head the desire for more.' Plato writes: 'The sole cause of wars and revolutions and battles is nothing other than the body and its desires.' Cicero, the Roman orator, writes: 'It is insatiable desires which overturn not only individual men, but whole families, and which even bring down the state. From desires there spring hatred, schisms, discords, seditions and wars.' Desire is at the root of all the evils which ruin life and cause divisions.

The New Testament is clear that this overriding desire for the pleasures of this world is always a threatening danger to the spiritual life. It is the cares and riches and pleasures of this life which combine to choke the good seed (Luke 8:14). People can become slaves to passions and pleasures – and, when that happens, malice and envy and hatred enter into life (cf. Titus 3:3).

The ultimate choice in life lies between pleasing oneself and pleasing God, and a world in which people seek first and foremost to please themselves is a battle ground of savagery and division.

This life dominated by pleasure has certain inevitable consequences.

(1) It sets people at each other's throats. Desires, as James sees it, are fundamentally warring powers. He does not mean that they war within a person – although that is also true – but that they set individuals warring against each other. The basic desires are for the same things – for money, for power, for prestige, for worldly possessions, for the gratification of physical lusts. When everyone is striving to possess the same things, life inevitably becomes a competitive arena. People trample each other down in the rush to grasp what they want. They will do anything to eliminate a rival. Obedience to the will of God draws people together, for it is that will that they should love and serve one another; obedience to the craving for pleasure drives them apart, for it drives them to rivalry for the same things.

(2) The craving for pleasure drives people to shameful deeds. It drives them to envy and to enmity – and even to murder. Before reaching the point of action, there must be a certain driving emotion in the heart. People may restrain themselves from the things that the desire for pleasure incites them to do, but as long as that desire is in their hearts they are not safe. It may at any time burst free and lead to ruinous action.

The steps of the process are simple and terrible. We allow ourselves to desire something. That thing begins to dominate our thoughts; we find ourselves involuntarily thinking about it in our waking hours and dreaming of it when we sleep. It begins to be what is aptly called a *ruling passion*. We begin to form imaginary schemes to obtain it; and these plans may well involve ways of eliminating those who stand in our way. For some time, all this may go on in the mind. Then one day the imaginings may blaze into action; and we may find ourselves taking the terrible steps necessary to obtain our desire. Every crime in this world has come from desire which was first only a feeling in the heart but which, being nourished long enough, in the end resulted in action.

(3) The craving for pleasure in the end shuts the door of prayer. If our prayers are simply for the things which will gratify our desires, they are essentially selfish – and, therefore, it is not possible for God to answer them. The true end of prayer is to say to God: 'Your will be done.' The prayer of the person who is dominated by pleasure is: 'My desires be satisfied.' It is one of the grim facts of life that a selfish person can hardly ever pray aright; no one can ever pray aright until self has been removed from the centre of life and God has been put there instead.

In this life, we have to choose whether to make our main object our own desires or the will of God. And, if we choose our own desires, we have thereby separated ourselves from other people and from God.

Mark 9:30–37

Nothing so well shows how far the disciples were from realizing the real meaning of Jesus' Messiahship as this does. Repeatedly he had told them what awaited him in Jerusalem, and yet they were still thinking of his kingdom in earthly terms and of themselves as his chief ministers of state. There is something heartbreaking in the thought of Jesus going towards a cross and his disciples arguing about who would be greatest.

Yet in their heart of hearts they knew they were wrong. When he asked them what they had been arguing about, they had nothing to say. It was the silence of shame. They had no defence. It is strange how a thing takes its proper place and acquires its true character when it is set in the eyes of Jesus. So long as they thought that Jesus was not listening and that Jesus had not seen, the argument about who should be greatest seemed fair enough, but when that argument had to be stated in the presence of Jesus it was seen in all its unworthiness.

If we took everything and set it in the sight of Jesus, it would make all the difference in the world. If of everything we did, we asked, 'Could I go on doing this if Jesus was watching me?'; if of everything we said, we asked, 'Could I go on talking like this if Jesus was listening to me?', there would be many things which we would be saved from doing and saying. And the fact of Christian belief is that there is no 'if' about it. All deeds are done, all words are spoken in his presence. God keep us from the words and deeds which we would be ashamed that he should hear and see.

Jesus dealt with this very seriously. It says that he sat down and called the Twelve to him. When a Rabbi was teaching as a Rabbi, as a master teaches his scholars and disciples, when he was really making a pronouncement, he sat to teach. Jesus deliberately took up the position of a Rabbi teaching his pupils before he spoke. And then he told them that if they sought for greatness in his kingdom they must find it, not by being first but by being last, not by being masters but by being servants of all. It was not that Jesus abolished ambition. Rather, he recreated and sublimated ambition. For the ambition to rule, he substituted the ambition to serve. For the ambition to have things done for us, he substituted the ambition to do things for others.

So far from being an impossibly idealistic view, this is a view of the soundest common sense. The really great people, those who are remembered as having made a real contribution to life, are the ones who said to themselves, not, 'How can I use the state and society to further my own prestige and my own personal ambitions?' but, 'How can I use my personal gifts and talents to serve the state?'

True selflessness is rare, and when it is found it is remembered. The Greeks had a story of a Spartan called Paedaretos. Three hundred men were to be chosen to govern Sparta, and Paedaretos was a candidate. When the list of the successful was announced his name was not on it. 'I am sorry', said one of his friends, 'that you were not elected. The people ought to have known what a wise officer of state you would have made.' 'I am glad', said Paedaretos, 'that in Sparta there are 300 men better than I am.' Here was a man who became a legend because he was prepared to give to others the first place and to bear no ill-will.

Every economic problem would be solved if people lived for what they could do for others and not for what they could get for themselves. Every political problem would be solved if human ambition was only to serve the state and not to enhance individual prestige. The divisions and disputes which tear the Church asunder would for the most part never occur if the only desire of its office-bearers and its members was to serve it without caring what position they occupied. When Jesus spoke of the supreme greatness and value of the one whose ambition was to be a servant, he laid down one of the greatest practical truths in the world.

The Sunday between
25 September and 1 October
The Truth Which Must Be Done *and*
A Lesson in Tolerance

James 5:13–20

At the end of this passage, there is set down the great differentiating characteristic of Christian truth. It is something from which people can *wander*. It is not only intellectual, philosophical and abstract; it is always moral truth.

This comes out very clearly when we go to the New Testament and look at the expressions which are used in connection with truth. Truth is something which people must *love* (2 Thessalonians 2:10); it is something which people must *obey* (Galatians 5:7); it is something which must be *openly stated* (2 Corinthians 4:2); it is something which must be *spoken in love* (Ephesians 4:15); it is something which must be *testified to* (John 18:37); it is something which must be *manifested in a life of love* (1 John 3:19); it is something which *liberates* (John 8:32); and it is something which is *the gift of the Holy Spirit*, sent by Jesus Christ (John 16:13–14).

Clearest of all is the phrase in John 3:21, *those who do what is true*. That is to say, *Christian truth is something which must be done*. It is not only the object of the search of the mind; it is always moral truth leading to action. It is not only something to be studied but something to be done; not only something to which we must submit only our minds but something to which we must submit our entire lives.

James finishes his letter with one of the greatest and most uplifting thoughts in the New Testament, and yet one which occurs more than once in the Bible. Suppose someone goes wrong and strays away, and suppose a fellow Christian rescues that person from error and brings the sinner back to the right path. That Christian has not only saved the other person's soul but has covered a multitude of his or her own sins. In other words, to save another's soul is the surest way to save one's own.

Origen, the third-century biblical scholar, has a wonderful passage in one of his Homilies in which he indicates these six ways in which people may gain forgiveness of their sins – by baptism, by martyrdom, by almsgiving (Luke 11:41), by the forgiveness of others (Matthew 6:14), by love (Luke 7:47) and by converting a sinner from evil ways. God will forgive much to anyone who has been the means of leading another brother or sister back to him.

This is a thought which shines forth every now and then from the pages of Scripture. Jeremiah says: 'If you utter what is precious, and not what is worthless, you shall serve as my mouth' (Jeremiah 15:19). Daniel writes: 'Those who are wise shall shine like the brightness of the sky, and those who lead many to righteousness, like the stars for ever and ever' (Daniel 12:3). The advice to the young Timothy is: 'Pay close attention to yourself and to your teaching . . . for in doing this you will save both yourself and your hearers' (1 Timothy 4:16).

There is a saying of the Jewish fathers: 'Whosoever makes a man righteous, sin prevails not over him.' Clement of Alexandria says that true Christians reckon that which benefits their neighbours to be their own salvation. It is told that a zealous evangelical lady once asked William Wilberforce, the liberator of the slaves in the British Empire, if his soul was saved. 'Madame,' he answered, 'I have been so busy trying to save the souls of others that I have had no time to think of my own.' It has been said that those who bring sunshine into the lives of others cannot keep it from themselves, and certainly those who bring the lives of others to God cannot keep God out of their own. The highest honour God can give is bestowed upon those who lead others to God; for everyone who does that does nothing less than share in the work of Jesus Christ, the Saviour of all.

Mark 9:38–50

In the time of Jesus everyone believed in demons. Everyone believed that both mental and physical illness was caused by the malign influence of these evil spirits. Now there was one very common way to exorcise them. If one could get to know the name of a still more powerful spirit and command the evil demon in that name to come out of a person, the demon was supposed to be powerless to resist. It could not stand against the might of the more powerful name. This is the kind of picture we have at the beginning of this section. John had seen a man using the all-powerful name of Jesus to defeat the demons and he had tried to stop him, because he was not one of the intimate band of the disciples. But Jesus declared that no one could do a mighty work in his name and be altogether his enemy. Then Jesus laid down the great principle that 'Whosoever is not against us is for us.'

Here is a lesson in tolerance, and it is a lesson that nearly everyone needs to learn.

(1) We all have a right to our own thoughts. We all have a right to think things out and to think them through until we come to our own conclusions and our own beliefs. And that is a right we should respect. We are often too apt to condemn what we do not understand. The Quaker William Penn once said, 'Neither despise nor oppose what thou dost not understand.' Kingsley Williams, in *The New Testament in Plain English*, translates a phrase in Jude 10 like this – 'Those who speak abusively of everything they do not understand.' There are two things we must remember.

(a) There is far more than one way to God. 'God', as Tennyson has it, 'fulfils himself in many ways.' The Spanish novelist

Cervantes once said, 'Many are the roads by which God carries his own to heaven.' The world is round, and two people can get to precisely the same destination by starting out in precisely opposite directions. All roads, if we pursue them long enough and far enough, lead to God. It is a fearful thing for any individual or any church to claim a monopoly on salvation.

(b) It is necessary to remember that truth is always bigger than any individual's grasp of it. No one can possibly grasp all truth. The basis of tolerance is not a lazy acceptance of anything. It is not the feeling that there cannot be assurance anywhere. The basis of tolerance is simply the realization of the magnitude of truth itself. The politician and journalist John Morley wrote, 'Toleration means reverence for all the possibilities of truth, it means acknowledgment that she dwells in divers mansions, and wears vesture of many colours, and speaks in strange tongues. It means frank respect for freedom of indwelling conscience against mechanical forms, official conventions, social force. It means the charity that is greater than faith or hope.' Intolerance is a sign both of arrogance and ignorance, for it is a sign that people believe that there is no truth beyond the truth they see.

(2) Not only must we concede the right of each one of us to do our own thinking, we must also concede the right to do our own speaking. Of all democratic rights, the dearest is that of liberty of speech. There are, of course, limits. If people are spreading doctrines calculated to destroy morality and to remove the foundations from all civilized and Christian society, they must be combated. But the way to combat them is certainly not to eliminate them by force but to prove them wrong. Once Voltaire laid down the conception of freedom of speech in a vivid sentence. 'I hate what you say,' he said, 'but I would die for your right to say it.'

(3) We must remember that any doctrine or belief must finally be judged by the kind of people it produces. Thomas Chalmers once put the matter in a nutshell. 'Who cares', he demanded, 'about

any Church but as an instrument of Christian good?' The question must always ultimately be, not, 'How is a Church governed?' but, 'What kind of people does a Church produce?' No one can entirely condemn beliefs which make people good. If we remember that, we may be less intolerant.

(4) We may hate a person's beliefs, but we must never hate the person. We may wish to eliminate the teaching, but we must never wish to eliminate the teacher.

> He drew a circle that shut me out –
> Rebel, heretic, thing to flout.
> But love and I had the wit to win –
> We drew a circle that took him in.

The Sunday between 2 and 8 October

The Recovery of Our Lost Destiny *and* Of Such is the Kingdom of Heaven

Hebrews 1:1–4; 2:5–12

The basic idea of the Letter to the Hebrews is that Jesus Christ alone brings to men and women the full revelation of God and that he alone enables them to enter into the very presence of God. The writer begins here by contrasting Jesus with the prophets who had gone before. He talks about him coming *in the end of these days*. The Jews divided all time into two ages – the present age and the age to come. In between, they set the day of the Lord. The present age was wholly bad; the age to come was to be the golden age of God. The day of the Lord was to be like the birth-pangs of the new age. So, the writer to the Hebrews says: 'The old time is passing away; the age of incompleteness is gone; the time of guessing and feeling our way is at an end; the new age, the age of God, has dawned in Christ.' He sees the world and human thought enter, as it were, into a new beginning with Christ. In Jesus, God has entered humanity, eternity has invaded time, and things can never be the same again.

The second section from chapter 2 begins with a quotation from Psalm 8:4–6. If we are ever to understand this passage correctly, we must understand one thing: *the whole reference of Psalm 8 is to human beings*. It sings of the glory that God gave to *men and women*. There is no reference to the Messiah.

There is a phrase in the psalm which makes it difficult for us to grasp that. The phrase is literally translated as *the son of man*. We are so used to hearing that phrase applied to Jesus that we tend always to take it to refer to him. But, in Hebrew, *a son of man* always means simply a *man*. We find, for instance, that, in the Revised Standard Version, in the book of the prophet Ezekiel, more than eighty times God addresses Ezekiel as *son of man*. 'Son of man, set your face toward Jerusalem' (Ezekiel 21:2). 'Son of man, prophesy, and say . . .' (Ezekiel 30:2).

In the psalm quoted here, the two parallel phrases which can be translated as 'What is man that you remember him?' and 'Or the son of man that you visit him?' are different ways of saying exactly the same thing. The psalm is a great lyric cry of the glory of human life as God meant it to be. It is, in fact, an expansion of the great promise of God at creation in Genesis 1:28, when he said to Adam: 'Have dominion over the fish of the sea and over the birds of the air and over every living thing that moves upon the earth.'

The glory of human beings, incidentally, is even greater than the Authorized Version would lead us to understand. It tells us that God has made them 'a little lower than the angels' (Psalm 8:5). That is a correct translation of the *Greek* but not of the *original Hebrew*. In the original Hebrew, it is said that they are made a little lower than the *Elohim*; and *Elohim* is the regular word for *God*. What the psalmist really wrote was that human beings had been made 'little less than God', which, in fact, is the translation of the Revised Standard Version. So, this psalm sings of the glory of human beings, who were made little less than divine and whom God meant to have dominion over everything in the world.

But, the writer to the Hebrews goes on, the situation with which we are confronted is very different. Men and women were meant to have dominion over everything – *but they have not*. They are creatures who are frustrated by their circumstances, defeated by their temptations and surrounded by their own weaknesses. The ones who should be free are bound; the ones who should be rulers are slaves. As the writer G. K. Chesterton said, whatever else is or is not true, this one thing is certain: we are not what we were meant to be.

The writer to the Hebrews goes further. Into this situation came Jesus Christ. He suffered and he died; and, because he suffered and died, he entered into glory. And that suffering and death and glory are all for us, because he died to make us what we ought to be. He died to rid us of our frustration and our bondage and our weakness and to give us the dominion we ought to have. He died to re-create us until we become what we were originally created to be.

In this passage, there are three basic ideas. (1) God created men and women only a little less than himself, to have control over all things. (2) Through their sin, they entered into defeat instead of control. (3) Into this state of defeat came Jesus Christ in order that by his life and death and glory he might make men and women what they were meant to be.

We may put it another way. The writer to the Hebrews shows us three things. (1) He shows us *the ideal of what we should be* – kin to God and rulers of the universe. (2) He shows us *the actual human condition* – the frustration instead of the control, the failure instead of the glory. (3) He shows us *how the actual can be changed into the ideal through Christ*. The writer to the Hebrews sees in Christ the one who by his sufferings and his glory can make us what we were meant to be and what, without him, we could never be.

Mark 10:2–16

It was natural that Jewish mothers should wish their children to be blessed by a great and distinguished Rabbi. Especially they brought their children to such a person on their first birthday. It was in this way that they brought the children to Jesus on this day.

We will fully understand the almost poignant beauty of this passage only if we remember when it happened. Jesus was on the way to the cross – and he knew it. Its cruel shadow can never have been far from his mind. It was at such a time that he had time for the children. Even with such a tension in his mind as that, he had time to take them in his arms and he had the heart to smile into their faces and maybe to play with them for a while.

The disciples were not boorish and ungracious men. They simply wanted to protect Jesus. They did not quite know what was going on, but they knew quite clearly that tragedy lay ahead and they could see the tension under which Jesus laboured. They did not want him to be bothered. They could not conceive that he could want the children about him at such a time as that. But Jesus said, 'Let the children come to me.' Incidentally, this tells us a great deal about Jesus. It tells us that he was the kind of person who cared for children and for whom children cared. He could not have been a stern and gloomy and joyless person. There must have been a kindly sunshine on him. He must have smiled easily and laughed joyously. Somewhere the writer George Macdonald says that he does not believe in people's Christianity if the children are never to be found playing around their doors. This little, precious incident throws a flood of light on the human kind of person Jesus was.

'Of such', said Jesus 'is the kingdom of God.' What is it about children that Jesus liked and valued so much?

(1) There is the child's *humility*. There is the child who is an exhibitionist, but such a child is rare and almost always the product of misguided adult treatment. Ordinarily children are embarrassed by prominence and publicity. They have not yet learned to think in terms of place and pride and prestige. They have not yet learned to discover the importance of themselves.

(2) There is the child's *obedience*. True, children are often disobedient, but, paradox though it may seem, their natural instinct is to obey. They have not yet learned the pride and the false independence which separate us from one another and from God.

(3) There is the child's *trust*. That is seen in two things.

(a) It is seen in the child's acceptance of authority. There is a time when children believe that their father and mother know everything and that they are always right. To our shame, they soon grow out of that. But instinctively children realize their own ignorance and their own helplessness and trust the ones who, as they think, know.

(b) It is seen in the child's confidence in other people. Children do not expect people to be bad. They will make friends with a perfect stranger. A great man once said that the greatest compliment ever paid him was when a little boy came up to him, a complete stranger, and asked him to tie his shoelace. Children have not yet learned to suspect the world. They still believe the best about others. Sometimes that very trust leads them into danger, for there are those who are totally unworthy of it and who abuse it, but that trust is a lovely thing.

(4) The child has *a short memory*. Children have not yet learned to bear grudges and nourish bitterness. Even when they are unjustly treated – and who among us is not sometimes unjust to their children? – they forget, and forget so completely that they do not even need to forgive. Indeed, of such is the kingdom of God.

The Sunday between 9 and 15 October
The Perfect High Priest *and*
The Perils of Riches

Hebrews 4:12–16

Here we find the great concept of Jesus as the perfect high priest. His task is to bring the voice of God to men and women, and to usher them into the presence of God. The high priest at one and the same time must perfectly know what it is to be human and also know God. That is what this epistle claims for Jesus.

(1) This passage begins by stressing the sheer greatness and absolute deity of Jesus. He is great in his nature, not by worldly honours or by any external trappings but in his own essential being. He has passed through the heavens. That may mean one of two things. In the New Testament, the word *heaven* can mean the heaven of the sky, and it can also mean the heaven of the presence of God. This may mean that Jesus has passed through every heaven that may be and is in the very presence of God. It can mean what Christina Rossetti meant in the carol 'In the bleak midwinter' when she said: 'Heaven cannot hold Him.' Jesus is so great that even heaven is too small a place for him. No one ever stressed the sheer greatness of Jesus in the same way as the writer to the Hebrews.

(2) Then he turns to the other side. No one was ever surer of Jesus' complete identity with human beings. He went through everything that an individual has to go through and is like us in all things – except that he emerged from it all completely sinless. There is one thing we must note here. The fact that Jesus was without sin means that

263

he knew depths and tensions and assaults of temptation which we never can know. Far from his battle being easier, it was immeasurably harder. Why? For this reason – we fall to temptation long before the tempter has put out the whole of his power. We never know temptation at its fiercest because we fall long before that stage is reached. But Jesus was tempted far beyond anything we might experience; for in his case the tempter put everything he possessed into the attack.

Faced with temptation, we collapse; but Jesus went to our limit of temptation and far beyond it and still did not collapse. It is true to say that he was tempted in all things, just as we are; but it is also true to say that no one was tempted as he was.

(2) This experience of Jesus had three effects.

(a) It gave him *the gift of sympathy*. Here is something which we must understand but which we find very difficult. The Christian idea of God as a loving Father is interwoven into the very fabric of our mind and heart; but *it was a new idea*. To the Jews, the basic idea of God was that he was *holy* in the sense of being *different*. In no sense did he share our human experience – and he was in fact incapable of sharing it, simply because he was God.

It was even more so with the Greeks. The Stoics, the highest Greek thinkers, said that the primary attribute of God was the essential inability to feel anything at all. They argued that if people could feel sorrow or joy, it meant that others were able to influence them. If so, the other people must, at least for that moment, be greater than they. No one, therefore, must be able in any sense to affect God, for that would be to make such a person greater than God; and so God had to be completely beyond all feeling. The other Greek school was the Epicureans. They held that the gods lived in perfect happiness and blessedness. They lived in the spaces between the worlds; and they were not even aware of the world.

The Jews had their *different* God, the Stoics had their *feeling-less* gods, and the Epicureans had their completely *detached* gods. Into that world of thought came Christianity with its incredible conception of a God who had deliberately undergone every human experience. Christianity depicted God as not simply involved but as identified with the suffering of this world. It is almost impossible for us to realize the revolution that Christianity brought about in the relationship of men and women to God. For century after century, they had been confronted with the idea of the untouchable God; and now they discovered a God who had gone through all that they must go through.

(b) That had two results. It gave God *the quality of mercy*. It is easy to see why. It was because God *understands*. Some people have lived sheltered lives; they have been protected from the temptations that come to those for whom life is not easy. Some people are placid and find it easy to control their emotions; others have a passionate nature that makes life more dangerous. The person who has lived the sheltered life and who has the more easy-going nature finds it hard to understand why the other person slips up. Such people are faintly disgusted and cannot help condemning what they cannot understand. *But God knows*. 'To know all is to forgive all' – of no one is that truer than of God.

There is no part of human experience of which God cannot say: 'I have been there.' When we have a sad and sorry tale to tell, when life has drenched us with tears, we do not go to a God who is incapable of understanding what has happened; we go to a God who has been there. That is why – if we may put it in this way – God finds it easy to forgive.

(c) It makes God *able to help*. He knows our problems because he has come through them. The best person to give you advice and help on a journey is someone who has already travelled that way. God can help because he knows it all. Jesus is the perfect high priest because he is perfectly God, and perfectly one with us. Because he has known our life, he can give us sympathy, mercy and power. He brought God to men and women, and he can bring them to God.

Mark 10:17–31

The ruler who had refused the challenge of Jesus had walked sorrowfully away, and, no doubt, the eyes of Jesus and the company of the apostles followed him until his figure receded into the distance. Then Jesus turned and looked round his own disciples. 'How very difficult it is', he said, 'for someone who has money to enter into the kingdom of God.' The word used for money is *chremata*, which is defined by Aristotle as, 'All those things of which the value is measured by coinage.'

We may perhaps wonder why this saying so astonished the disciples. Twice their amazement is stressed. The reason for their amazement was that Jesus was turning accepted Jewish standards completely upside down. Popular Jewish morality was simple. It believed that prosperity was the sign of a good man. If a man was rich, God must have honoured and blessed him. Wealth was proof of excellence of character and of favour with God. The psalmist sums it up, 'I have been young, and now am old, yet I have not seen the righteous forsaken or their children begging bread' (Psalm 37:25).

No wonder the disciples were surprised! They would have argued that the more prosperous people were, the more certain they were of entry into the kingdom. So Jesus repeated his saying in a slightly different way to make clearer what he meant. 'How difficult it is', he said, 'for those who have put their trust in riches to enter the kingdom.' No one ever saw the dangers of prosperity and of material things more clearly than Jesus did. What are these dangers?

(1) Material possessions tend to fix our hearts to this world. We have so large a stake in it, we have so great an interest in it, that it is difficult for us to think beyond it, and it is specially difficult for us to contemplate leaving it. Dr Johnson was once shown round a famous castle and its lovely grounds. After he had seen it all, he turned to his friends and said, 'These are the things that make

it difficult to die.' The danger of possessions is that they fix our thoughts and interests to this world.

(2) If our main interest is in material possessions, it tends to make us think of everything in terms of price. A hill shepherd's wife wrote a most interesting letter to a newspaper. Her children had been brought up in the loneliness of the hills. They were simple and unsophisticated. Then her husband got a position in a town, and the children were introduced to the town. They changed very considerably – and they changed for the worse. The last paragraph of her letter read – 'Which is preferable for a child's upbringing – a lack of worldliness, but with better manners and sincere and simple thoughts, or worldliness and its present-day habit of knowing the price of everything and the true value of nothing?'

If our main interest is in material things, we will think in terms of price and not in terms of value. We will think in terms of what money can get. And we may well forget that there are values in this world far beyond money, that there are things which have no price, and that there are precious things that money cannot buy. It is fatal to begin to think that everything worth having has a monetary value.

(3) Jesus would have said that the possession of material goods is two things.

(a) It is an acid test of character. For every 100 who can stand adversity only one can stand prosperity. Prosperity can so very easily make people arrogant, proud, self-satisfied, worldly. It takes a really big and good person to bear it worthily.

(b) It is a responsibility. We will always be judged by two standards – how we got our possessions and how we use them. The more we have, the greater the responsibility that rests upon us. Will we use what we have selfishly or generously? Will we use it as if we had undisputed possession of it, or remembering that we hold it in stewardship from God? The reaction of the disciples was that if what Jesus was saying was true, to be saved at all was well-nigh impossible.

Then Jesus stated the whole doctrine of salvation in a nutshell. 'If', he said, 'salvation depended on a person's own efforts it would be impossible for anyone. But salvation is the gift of God and all things are possible to him.' Those who trust in themselves and in their possessions can never be saved. Those who trust in the saving power and the redeeming love of God can enter freely into salvation. This is the thought that Jesus stated. This is the thought that Paul wrote in letter after letter. And this is the thought which is still for us the very foundation of the Christian faith.

The Sunday between 16 and 22 October
The Essential Characteristics of a Priest *and* The Price of Salvation

Hebrews 5:1–10

This passage sets out three essential qualifications of the priest in any age and in any generation.

(1) Priests are appointed on behalf of others to deal with the things concerning God. Professor A. J. Gossip of Trinity College, Glasgow, used to tell his students that when he was ordained to the ministry he felt as if the people were saying to him: 'We are forever involved in the dust and the heat of the day; we have to spend our time getting and spending; we have to serve at the counter, to toil at the desk, to make the wheels of industry go round. We want you to be set apart so that you can go in to the secret place of God and come back every Sunday with a word from him to us.' The priest is the link between God and the world.

In Israel, the priest had one special function – to offer sacrifice for the sins of the people. Sin disturbs the relationship which should exist between men and women and God and puts up a barrier between them. The sacrifice is meant to restore that relationship and remove that barrier. But we must note that the Jews were always quite clear that the sins for which sacrifice could atone were *sins of ignorance*. The deliberate sin did not find its atonement in sacrifice. The writer to the Hebrews himself says: 'For if we wilfully persist in sin after having received the knowledge of the truth, *there no longer remains a sacrifice for sins*' (Hebrews 10:26). This is a conviction that emerges again and again in the sacrificial laws of the Old Testament. Again and again, they begin: 'When anyone sins unintentionally in any of the Lord's commandments about things not to be done . . .' (Leviticus 4:2, cf. verse 13). Numbers 15:22–31 is a key passage. There, the necessary sacrifices are laid down 'if you unintentionally fail to observe all these commandments'. But at the end it is laid down: 'But whoever acts high-handedly . . . affronts the Lord . . . shall be utterly cut off and bear the guilt.' Deuteronomy 17:12 lays it down: 'Anyone who presumes to disobey . . . that person shall die.'

The sin of ignorance is pardonable; the sin of presumption is not. Nevertheless, we must note that by the sin of ignorance the Jews meant more than simply lack of knowledge. They included the sins committed when someone was carried away in a moment of impulse or anger or passion or was overcome by some irresistible temptation, and the sins were followed by repentance. By the sin of presumption, they meant the cold, calculated sin for which the perpetrator was not in the least sorry, the open-eyed disobedience of God. So, the priest existed to open for sinners the way back to God – as long as they wanted to come back.

(2) Priests must be at one with others. They must have gone through the same experiences and must be in full sympathy with others. At this point, the writer to the Hebrews stops to point out – he will later show that this is one of the ways in which Jesus Christ is superior to any earthly priest – that earthly priests are so at one with other people that they have an obligation to offer sacrifice for their own sin before they offer sacrifice for the sins of others. Priests must be bound up with other men and women in all that life brings. In connection with this, the writer used a very difficult but wonderful word – *metriopathein* – which can be translated it as *to feel gently*.

The Greeks defined a virtue as the mid-point between two extremes. On either hand, there was an extreme into which people might fall; in between, there was the right way. So, the Greeks defined *metriopatheia* (the corresponding noun) as the mid-point between extravagant grief and utter indifference. It was feeling about others in the right way. W. M. Macgregor, Principal of Trinity College, Glasgow, defined it as 'the mid-course between explosions of anger and lazy indulgence'. The Greek philosopher and historian Plutarch spoke of that *patience* which was the child of *metriopatheia*. He spoke of it as that sympathetic feeling which enabled people to lift up and to save, to spare and to hear. Another Greek blames a man for having no *metriopatheia* and for therefore *refusing to be reconciled* with someone who had differed from him. It is a wonderful word. It means the ability to put up with people without getting irritated; it means the ability not to lose one's temper with people when they are foolish and will not learn and do the same thing over and over again. It describes the attitude which does not get angry at the faults of others and which does not condone them, but which to the end of the day devotes itself to offering gentle yet powerful sympathy which by its very patience directs people back to the right way. We can never deal with others unless we have this strong and patient, God-given *metriopatheia*.

(3) The third essential characteristic of a priest is this: people do not appoint themselves to the priesthood; their appointment is from God. The priesthood is not an office which is taken; it is a privilege and a glory to which people are called. The ministry of God is neither a job nor a career but a calling. Those who are called to the priesthood ought to be able to look back and say not: 'I chose this work' but rather: 'God chose me and gave me this work to do.'

(For discussion of the last section of this passage, see The Fifth Sunday of Lent, pp. 101–104.)

Mark 10:35–45

The action of James and John will have aroused deep resentment among the other ten disciples. It seemed to them that they had tried to steal a march and to take an unfair advantage. Immediately the controversy about who was to be greatest began to rage again.

This was a serious situation. The fellowship of the apostolic band might well have been wrecked, had Jesus not taken immediate action. He called them to him, and made quite clear the different standards of greatness in his kingdom and in the kingdoms of the world. In the kingdoms of the world the standard of greatness was power. The test was: how many people does a man control? How great an army of servants has he at his beck and call? On how many people can he impose his will? In the kingdom of Jesus the standard was that of service. Greatness consisted not in reducing others to one's service, but in reducing oneself to their service. The test was not what service can I extract?, but, what service can I give?

We tend to think of this as an ideal state of affairs, but, in point of fact, it is the soundest common sense. It is in fact the first principle of ordinary everyday business life. It has been pointed out that the basis on which some motor companies will claim the patronage of prospective customers is that they will crawl under your car oftener and get themselves dirtier than any of their competitors. They are in other words prepared to give more service. It is also pointed out that although the ordinary office worker may go home at 5.30 pm, the light will be seen burning in the office of the chief executive long into the night. It is that willingness to give the extra service that marks out the head of the company.

The basic trouble is that it is human nature to want to do as little as possible and to get as much as possible. It is only when we are filled with the desire to put into life more than we take out that life for ourselves and for others will be happy and prosperous. The world needs people whose ideal is service – that is to say it needs people who have realized what sound sense Jesus spoke.

To clinch his words Jesus pointed to his own example. With such powers as he had, he could have arranged life entirely to suit himself, but he had spent himself and all his powers in the service of others. He had come, he said, *to give his life a ransom for many*. This is one of the great phrases of the gospel, and yet it has been sadly mishandled and maltreated. People have tried to erect a theory of the atonement on what is a saying of love.

It was not long before people were asking to whom this ransom of the life of Christ had been paid. In the third century Origen asked the question, 'To whom did he give his life a ransom for many? It was not to God. Was it not then to the evil one? For the devil was holding us fast until the ransom should be given to him, even the life of Jesus, for he was deceived with the idea that he could have dominion over it and did not see that he could not bear the torture involved in retaining it.' It is an odd conception that the life of Jesus was paid as a ransom to the devil so that he should release human beings from the bondage in which he held them, but that the devil found that in demanding and accepting that ransom, he had, so to speak, bitten off more than he could chew.

In the fourth century, Gregory of Nyssa saw the flaw in that theory, namely that it really puts the devil on an equality with God. It allows him to make a bargain with God on equal terms. So Gregory conceived of the extraordinary idea of *a trick* played by God. The devil was tricked by the seeming weakness of the incarnation. He mistook Jesus for a mere man. He tried to exert his authority over him and, by trying to do so, lost it. Again it is an odd idea – that God should conquer the devil by a trick.

Another 200 years passed and Gregory the Great took up the idea. He used a fantastic metaphor. The incarnation was a divine stratagem to catch the great leviathan. The deity of Christ was the hook, his flesh was the bait. When the bait was dangled before Leviathan, the devil, he swallowed it, and tried to swallow the hook, too, and so was overcome forever.

Finally, in the twelfth century, Peter the Lombard brings this idea to its most grotesque and repulsive. 'The cross', he said, 'was a mousetrap to catch the devil, baited with the blood of Christ.' All this simply shows what happens when a lovely and precious picture is taken and attempts are made to make a cold theology out of it.

Suppose we say, 'Sorrow is the *price of love*,' we mean that love cannot exist without the possibility of sorrow, but we never even think of trying to explain to whom that *price* is paid. Suppose we say that freedom can be obtained only at the *price* of blood, toil, tears and sweat, we never think of investigating to whom that *price* is paid. This saying of Jesus is a simple and pictorial way of saying that it cost the life of Jesus to bring men and women back from their sin into the love of God. The cost of our salvation was the cross of Christ. Beyond that we cannot go, and beyond that we do not need to go. We know only that something happened on the cross which opened for us the way to God.

The Sunday between 23 and 29 October
The High Priest We Need *and* A Miracle by the Wayside

Hebrews 7:23–28

The writer to the Hebrews says that the priesthood of Jesus is one *that will never pass away*. It is something which can never be taken from him, something that no one else can ever possess, something that is as lasting as the laws which hold the universe together. Jesus is and will always remain the only way to God.

He also says of Jesus that *he remains forever*. In that phrase there is wrapped up the amazing idea that *Jesus is forever at the service of men and women*. In eternity as he was in time, Jesus exists to be of service to all people. That is why he is the complete Saviour. On earth, he served men and women and gave his life for them; in heaven, he still exists to make intercession for them. He is the priest forever, the one who is forever opening the door to the friendship of God and is forever the great servant of all.

The writer to the Hebrews is filled with the thought of Jesus as high priest. He continues by using a series of great words and phrases to describe him.

(1) He says that Jesus is *holy* (*hosios*). This word is used of Jesus in Acts 2:27 and 13:35; it is used of the Lord in Revelation 15:4 and 16:5; it is used of the Christian bishop in Titus 1:8; it is used of the hands that must be presented to God in prayer in 1 Timothy 2:8. Behind it, there is always one special idea. It always describes those who faithfully do their duty to God. It

describes people not so much as they appear before others but as they appear before God. *Hosios* has in it the greatest of all goodnesses, the goodness which is pure in the sight of God.

(2) He says that Jesus *never hurt anyone* (*akakos*). *Kakia* is the Greek word for evil; and *akakos* describes someone who is so cleansed of evil that only good remains. It describes the effect an individual has upon other people. Individuals who are described as *akakos* are so cleansed that their presence is like an antiseptic, and in their hearts there is nothing but the loving kindness of God.

(3) He says that Jesus is *stainless* (*amiantos*). *Amiantos* describes someone who is absolutely free from any of the blemishes which might make it impossible to draw near to God. The blemished victim cannot be offered to God; the defiled individual cannot approach him; but the one who is *amiantos* is fit to enter into God's presence.

(4) He says that Jesus is *different from sinners*. This phrase does not mean that Jesus was not really fully human. He was different from sinners in that, although he underwent every temptation, he conquered them all and emerged without sin. The difference between him and other men and women lies not in the fact that he was not fully human, but in the fact that he was the highest and best of all humanity.

(5) He says that Jesus *was made higher than the heavens*. In this phrase, he is thinking of the exaltation of Jesus. If the last phrase stresses the perfection of his humanity, this one stresses the perfection of his godhead. He who was truly one with us is also exalted to the right hand of God.

The writer to the Hebrews now introduces another aspect in which the priesthood of Jesus is far superior to the Levitical priesthood. Before the high priest could offer sacrifice for the sins of the people, he had first to offer sacrifice *for his own sins*, for he was a sinful man.

The writer is thinking particularly of the Day of Atonement. This was the great day when atonement was made for all the sins of the people, the day on which the high priest personally performed his supreme function. The very first item in the ritual of that day was a sacrifice for the sins of the high priest himself. He washed his hands and his feet; he put aside his gorgeous robes; he clothed himself in spotless white linen. A bullock that he had purchased with his own money was brought to him. He laid both hands on the bullock's head to transfer his sin to it; and he made confession. The greatest of all the Levitical sacrifices began with a sacrifice for the sins of the high priest. That was a sacrifice Jesus never needed to make, for he was without sin. The Levitical high priest was a sinful man offering animal sacrifices for sinful people; Jesus was the sinless Son of God offering himself for the sin of all. Because he was what he was, the sinless Son of God, he was equipped for his office as no human high priest could ever be.

Now the writer to the Hebrews puts down a marker to indicate the direction he is going to take. He says of Jesus that *he offered himself*. Two things were necessary in a sacrifice. There was the priest and there was the sacrifice. With long and intricate argument, the writer has proved that Jesus was the perfect high priest; now he moves on to another thought. Not only was Jesus the perfect high priest; *he was also the perfect offering*. Jesus alone could open the way to God because he was the perfect high priest and he offered the one perfect sacrifice – himself.

There is much in this argument which is difficult because it speaks and thinks in terms of ritual and ceremony long since forgotten; but one eternal thing remains. Men and women seek the presence of God; their sin has put up a barrier between them and God, but they are restless until they rest in God; and Jesus alone is the priest who can bring the offering that can open the way back to God.

Mark 10:46–52

For Jesus the end of the road was not far away. Jericho was only about fifteen miles from Jerusalem. We must try to visualize the scene. The main road ran right through Jericho. Jesus was on his way to the Passover. When a distinguished Rabbi or teacher was on such a journey it was the custom that he was surrounded by a crowd of people, disciples and learners, who listened to him as he discoursed while he walked. That was one of the commonest ways of teaching.

It was the law that every male Jew over twelve years of age who lived within fifteen miles of Jerusalem must attend the Passover. It was clearly impossible that such a law should be fulfilled and that everyone should go. Those who were unable to go were in the habit of lining the streets of towns and villages through which groups of Passover pilgrims must pass to bid them godspeed on their way. So then the streets of Jericho would be lined with people, and there would be even more than usual, for there would be many eager and curious to catch a glimpse of this audacious young Galilaean who had pitted himself against the assembled might of orthodoxy.

Jericho had one special characteristic. There were attached to the Temple over 20,000 priests and as many Levites. Obviously they could not all serve at the one time. They were therefore divided into twenty-six courses which served in rotation. Very many of these priests and Levites resided in Jericho when they were not on actual temple duty. There must have been many of them in the crowd that day. At the Passover all were on duty for all were needed. It was one of the rare occasions when all did serve. But many would not have started yet. They would be doubly eager to see this rebel who was about to invade Jerusalem. There would be many cold and bleak and hostile eyes in the crowd that day, because it was clear that if Jesus was right, the whole Temple worship was one vast irrelevance.

At the northern gate sat a beggar, Bartimaeus by name. He heard the tramp of feet. He asked what was happening and who was passing. He was told that it was Jesus. There and then he set up an uproar to attract Jesus' attention to him. To those listening to Jesus' teaching as he walked, the uproar was an offence. They tried to silence Bartimaeus, but no one was going to take from him his chance to escape from his world of darkness, and he cried with such violence and persistence that the procession stopped, and he was brought to Jesus.

This is a most illuminating story. In it we can see many of the things which we might call the conditions of miracle.

(1) There is the sheer persistence of Bartimaeus. Nothing would stop his clamour to come face to face with Jesus. He was utterly determined to meet the one person whom he longed to confront with his trouble. In the mind of Bartimaeus there was not just a vague, wistful, sentimental wish to see Jesus. It was a desperate desire, and it is that desperate desire that gets things done.

(2) His response to the call of Jesus was immediate and eager, so eager that he cast off his hindering cloak to run to Jesus the more quickly. Many people hear the call of Jesus, but say in effect, 'Wait until I have done this,' or 'Wait until I have finished that.' Bartimaeus came like a shot when Jesus called. Certain chances happen only once. Bartimaeus instinctively knew that. Sometimes we have a wave of longing to abandon some habit, to purify life of some wrong thing, to give ourselves more completely to Jesus. So very often we do not seize the moment to act on it – and the chance is gone, perhaps never to come back.

(3) He knew precisely what he wanted – his sight. Too often our admiration for Jesus is a vague attraction. When we go to the doctor it is to have something specific dealt with. When we go to the dentist we do not ask to have *any* tooth extracted, but the one that is diseased. It should be so with us and Jesus. And that involves the one thing that so few people wish to face – *self-examination*. When we go to Jesus, if we are as desperately definite as Bartimaeus, things will happen.

(4) Bartimaeus had a quite inadequate conception of Jesus. *Son of David*, he insisted on calling him. Now that was a messianic title,

but it has in it all the thought of a conquering Messiah, a king of David's line who would lead Israel to national greatness. That was a very inadequate idea of Jesus. But, in spite of that, Bartimaeus had *faith*, and faith made up a hundredfold for the inadequacy of his theology. The demand is not that we should fully understand Jesus. That, in any event, we can never do. The demand is for *faith*. A wise writer has said, 'We must ask people to think, but we should not expect them to become theologians before they are Christians.' Christianity begins with a personal reaction to Jesus, a reaction of love, feeling that here is the one person who can meet our need. Even if we are never able to think things out theologically, that response of the human heart is enough.

(5) In the end there is a precious touch. Bartimaeus may have been a beggar by the wayside but he was a man of gratitude. Having received his sight, he followed Jesus. He did not selfishly go on his way when his need was met. He began with need, went on to gratitude, and finished with loyalty – and that is a perfect summary of the stages of discipleship.

The Last Sunday after Trinity (Bible Sunday)

Foolish Listeners *and*
The Witness of God

2 Timothy 3:14–4:5

As Paul comes to the end of his letter, he wants to encourage and to challenge Timothy to his task. To do so, he reminds him of three things concerning Jesus.

(1) Jesus is the judge of the living and the dead. Some day, Timothy's work will be tested, and that by none other than Jesus himself. Christians must do every task in such a way that they can offer it to Christ. They are not concerned with either the criticism or the verdict of others. The one thing they long for is the 'Well done!' of Jesus Christ. If we all did our work in that spirit, the difference would be incalculable. It would save us from being so touchy that we are offended by criticism; it would save us from the self-importance which is concerned with personal rights and personal prestige; it would save us from being self-centred and demanding thanks and praise for everything we do; it would even save us from being hurt by people's ingratitude.

(2) Jesus is the returning conqueror. 'I charge you', says Paul, 'by his *appearing*.' The word is *epiphaneia*. *Epiphaneia* was used in two special ways. It was used for the clear intervention of some god, and it was especially used in connection with the Roman emperor. His accession to the throne was his *epiphaneia*, and in particular – and this is the background of Paul's thought here – it was used of his visit to any province or town. Obviously, when the emperor was due to visit any place, everything was put in perfect order. The streets

were swept and decorated, and all work was brought up to date so that the town might be fit for *epiphaneia*. So, Paul says to Timothy: 'You know what happens when any town is expecting the *epiphaneia* of the emperor; *you* are expecting the *epiphaneia* of Jesus Christ. Do your work in such a way that all things will be ready whenever he appears.' Christians should order their lives in such a way that at any moment they are ready for the coming of Christ.

(3) Jesus is king. Paul urges Timothy to action by the remembrance of the kingdom of Jesus Christ. The day comes when the kingdoms of the world will be the kingdom of the Lord; and so Paul says to Timothy: 'So live and work that you will have an honourable place on the roll of its citizens when the kingdom comes.'

Our work must be such that it will stand the scrutiny of Christ. Our lives must be such that they will welcome the appearance of the King. Our service must be such that it will demonstrate the reality of our citizenship of the kingdom of God.

Paul goes on to warn Timothy that the day is coming when people will refuse to listen to sound teaching and will surround themselves with teachers who will satisfy their desire with precisely the easy-going, comfortable things they want to hear.

In Timothy's day, it was tragically easy to find such teachers. They were called *sophists* and wandered from city to city, offering to teach anything in return for money. Isocrates, the Athenian orator, said of them: 'They try to attract pupils by low fees and big promises.' They were prepared to teach the whole of virtue for a modest fee. They would teach people to argue subtly and to use words cleverly until they could make 'the worse appear the better reason'. Plato described them savagely: 'Hunters after young men of wealth and position, with sham education as their bait, and a fee for their object, making money by a scientific use of quibbles in private conversation, while quite aware that what they are teaching is wrong.'

In the days of Timothy, people were surrounded by false teachers offering their sham knowledge. Their deliberate policy was to find arguments whereby people could justify anything they wanted to. Any teacher, even today, whose teaching tends to make people think less of sin is a menace to Christianity and to society as a whole.

In complete contrast to that, certain duties are to be laid on Timothy.

He is to be *steady in all things*. The word (*nēphein*) means that he is to be sober and self-disciplined, like an athlete who has all passions, appetites and nerves well under control. The biblical scholar F. J. A. Hort says that the word describes 'a mental state free from all perturbations or stupefactions . . . every faculty at full command, to look all facts and all considerations deliberately in the face'. Christians are not to be the victims of crazes; in an unbalanced and often insane world, they are to stand out for their stability.

He is to *accept whatever suffering comes upon him*. Christianity will cost something, and Christians are to pay the price of it without grumbling and without regret. He is to do the work of an evangelist. In spite of the demand for conviction and rebuke, Christians are essentially the bringers of good news. If they insist on discipline and self-denial, it is because an even greater happiness may be attained than common and easily bought pleasures can bring.

He is to leave *no act of service unfulfilled*. Christians should have only one ambition – to be of use to the Church of which they are a part and the society in which they live. The opportunity not to be missed is not that of a cheap profit but that of being of service to God, to the Church and to other people.

John 5:36b–47

The early part of this section may be taken in two ways.

(1) It may be that it refers to the unseen witness of God in the heart of every individual. In his First Letter, John writes: 'Those

who believe in the Son of God have the testimony [of God] in their hearts' (1 John 5:10). A Jew would have insisted that no one can ever see God. Even in the giving of the Ten Commandments, 'You heard the sound of words but saw no form; there was only a voice' (Deuteronomy 4:12). So this may mean: 'It is true that God is invisible; and so is his witness, for it is the response which rises in the human heart when anyone is confronted with me.' When we are confronted with Christ, we see in him the altogether lovely and the altogether wise; that conviction is the witness of God in our hearts. The Stoics held that the highest kind of knowledge comes not by thought but by what they called 'arresting impressions' – being seized by a conviction like someone laying an arresting hand on the shoulder. It may be that Jesus here means that the conviction in our hearts of his supremacy is the witness of God within.

(2) It may be that John is really meaning that God's witness to Christ is to be found in the Scriptures. To Jews, the Scriptures were all in all. 'He who has acquired the words of the law has acquired eternal life.' 'He who has the law has a cord of grace drawn around him in this world and in the world to come.' 'He who says that Moses wrote even one verse of the law in his own knowledge is a despiser of God.' 'She is the book of the commandments of God, the law that endures forever. All who hold her fast will live and those who forsake her shall die' (Baruch 4:1–2). 'If food, which is your life but for an hour, requires a blessing before and after it be eaten, how much more does the law, in which lies the world that is to be, require a blessing?' The Jews searched the law and yet failed to recognize Christ when he came. What was wrong? The best Bible students in the world, people who meticulously and continuously read Scripture, rejected Jesus. How could that happen?

One thing is clear – they read Scripture in the wrong way.

(1) They read it with a shut mind. They read it not to search for God but to find arguments to support their own positions. They did not really love God; they loved their own ideas about him.

Water has as much chance of getting into concrete as the word of God had of getting into their minds. They did not humbly learn a theology from Scripture; they used Scripture to defend a theology which they themselves had produced. There is still danger that we should use the Bible to prove our beliefs and not to test them.

(2) They made a still bigger mistake – they regarded God as having given a written revelation. The revelation of God is a revelation in history. It is not God speaking, but God acting. The Bible itself is not his revelation; it is *the record of* his revelation. But they worshipped the Bible's words. There is only one proper way to read the Bible – to read it as all pointing to Jesus Christ. Then many of the things which puzzle us, and sometimes distress us, are clearly seen as stages on the way, a pointing forward to Jesus Christ, who is the supreme revelation and by whose light all other revelation is to be tested. The Jews worshipped a God who wrote rather than a God who acted, and therefore when Christ came they did not recognize him. The function of the Scriptures is not to give life but to point to him who can.

Jesus finishes with a charge that would strike home. The Jews believed the books which they believed Moses had given them to be the very word of God. Jesus said: 'If you had read these books aright, you would have seen that they all pointed to me.' He went on: 'You think that because you have Moses to be your mediator you are safe; but Moses is the very one who will condemn you. Maybe you could not be expected to listen to me, but you are bound to listen to the words of Moses to which you attach such value – and they all spoke of me.'

Here is the great and threatening truth. What had been the greatest privilege of the Jews had become their greatest condemnation. No one could condemn anyone who had never had a chance. But knowledge had been given to the Jews; and the knowledge they had failed to use had become their condemnation. Responsibility is always the other side of privilege.

The Fourth Sunday before Advent

The Sacrifice Which Opens the Way to God *and* Love for God and Love for Neighbour

Hebrews 9:11–14

In considering this passage, we must remember three things which are basic to the thought of the writer to the Hebrews. (1) Religion is access to God. Its function is to bring people into God's presence. (2) This is a world of pale shadows and imperfect copies; beyond is the world of realities. The function of all worship is to bring people into contact with the eternal realities. That was what the worship of the tabernacle was meant to do; but the earthly tabernacle and its worship are pale copies of the real tabernacle and its worship; and only the real tabernacle and the real worship can give access to reality. (3) There can be no religion without sacrifice. Purity is a costly thing; access to God demands purity; somehow human sin must be atoned for and uncleanness cleansed. With these ideas in his mind, the writer to the Hebrews shows that Jesus is the only high priest who brings a sacrifice that can open the way to God, and that that sacrifice is himself.

To begin with, he refers to certain of the great sacrifices which the Jews were in the habit of making under the old covenant with God.

(1) There was the sacrifice of *bullocks* and of *goats*. In this, he is referring to two of the great sacrifices on the Day of Atonement – of the bullock which the high priest offered for his own sins, and of the scapegoat which was led away to the wilderness bearing the

sins of the people (Leviticus 16:15, 21–2). (2) There was the sacrifice of the *red heifer*. This strange ritual is described in Numbers 19. Under Jewish ceremonial law, if someone touched a dead body, that person was unclean. Such people were barred from the worship of God, and everything and everyone they touched also became unclean. To deal with this, there was a prescribed method of cleansing. A red heifer was slaughtered outside the camp. The priest sprinkled the blood of the heifer in front of the tabernacle seven times. The body of the beast was then burned, together with cedar and hyssop and a piece of red cloth. The resulting ashes were placed outside the camp in a clean place and constituted a purification for sin.

The writer to the Hebrews tells of these sacrifices and then declares that the sacrifice that Jesus brings is far greater and far more effective. The worship of the ancient tabernacle was designed to bring people into the presence of God, but only in the most shadowy and imperfect way. The coming of Jesus really brought men and women into the presence of God, because in him God entered this world of space and time in a human form, and to see Jesus is to see what God is like.

The great superiority of the sacrifice Jesus brought lay in three things.

(1) The ancient sacrifices cleansed the body from ceremonial uncleanness; the sacrifice of Jesus cleansed the soul. An individual's body might be clean ceremonially, and yet the heart of that person might be torn with remorse. A person might feel able to enter the tabernacle and yet at the same time be far away from the presence of God. The sacrifice of Jesus takes the load of guilt from people's *consciences*. The animal sacrifices of the old covenant might well leave them estranged from God; the sacrifice of Jesus shows us a God whose arms are always outstretched and in whose heart is only love.

(2) The sacrifice of Jesus brought eternal redemption. The idea was that human beings were under the dominion of sin;

and, just as the purchase price had to be paid to free individuals from slavery, so the purchase price had to be paid to free us from sin.

(3) In his sacrifice Jesus not only won forgiveness for past sin, he enabled men and women in the future to live godly lives. His sacrifice was not only the paying of a debt; it was the giving of a victory. What Jesus did puts us right with God, and what he does enables us to stay right with God. The act of the cross brings the love of God to us in a way that takes our terror of him away; the presence of the living Christ brings the power of God to us so that we can win a daily victory over sin.

The New Testament scholar B. F. Westcott outlines four ways in which Jesus' sacrifice of himself differs from the animal sacrifices of the old covenant.

(1) The sacrifice of Jesus was *voluntary*. The animal's life was taken from it; Jesus gave his life. He willingly laid it down for his friends.

(2) The sacrifice of Jesus was *spontaneous*. Animal sacrifice was entirely *the product of law*; the sacrifice of Jesus was entirely *the product of love*. We pay our debts in business dealings because we have to; we give gifts to our loved ones because we want to. It was not law but love that lay behind the sacrifice of Christ.

(3) The sacrifice of Jesus was *rational*. The animal victim did not know what was happening; Jesus all the time knew what he was doing. He died, not as an ignorant victim caught up in circumstances over which he had no control and did not understand, but with eyes wide open.

(4) The sacrifice of Jesus was *moral*. Animal sacrifice was mechanical; but Jesus' sacrifice was made through *the eternal Spirit*. What happened on Calvary was not a matter of prescribed ritual, mechanically carried out; it was a matter of Jesus obeying the will of God for the sake of men and women. Behind it, there was not the mechanism of law but the choice of love.

Mark 12:28–34

The scribe came to Jesus with a question which was often a matter of debate in the Rabbinic schools. In Judaism there was a kind of double tendency. There was the tendency to expand the law limitlessly into hundreds and thousands of rules and regulations. But there was also the tendency to try to gather up the law into one sentence, one general statement which would be a compendium of its whole message. Rabbi Hillel was once asked by a proselyte, a convert to Judaism, to instruct him in the whole law while he stood on one leg. Hillel's answer was, 'What thou hatest for thyself, do not to thy neighbour. This is the whole law, the rest is commentary. Go and learn.' Rabbi Akiba had already said, '"Thou shalt love thy neighbour as thyself" – this is the greatest general principle in the law.'

Rabbinic ingenuity did try to contract as well as to expand the law. There were really two schools of thought. There were those who believed that there were lighter and weightier matters of the law, that there were great principles which were all important to grasp. As Augustine later said, 'Love God – and do what you like.' But there were others who were much against this, who held that every smallest principle was equally binding and that to try to distinguish between their relative importance was highly dangerous. The expert who asked Jesus this question was asking about something which was a living issue in Jewish thought and discussion.

For answer Jesus took two great commandments and put them together.

(1) 'Hear, O Israel: The Lord is our God, the Lord alone.' That single sentence is the real creed of Judaism (Deuteronomy 6:4). It had three uses. It is called *the Shema*. *Shema* is the imperative of the Hebrew verb to *hear*, and it is so called from the first word in the sentence.

(a) It was the sentence with which the service of the synagogue always began and still begins. The full Shema is Deuteronomy 6:4–9, 11:13–21; Numbers 15:37–41. It is the declaration that God is the only God, the foundation of Jewish monotheism.

(b) The three passages of the Shema were contained in the *phylacteries* (Matthew 23:5), little leather boxes which devout Jews wore on their foreheads and on their wrists when they were at prayer. As they prayed they reminded themselves of their creed. The warrant for wearing *phylacteries* is found in Deuteronomy 6:8.

(c) The Shema was contained in a little cylindrical box called the *Mezuzah*, which was and still is affixed to the door of every Jewish house and the door of every room within it, to remind Jewish families of God as they went out and as they came in.

When Jesus quoted this sentence as the first commandment, every devout Jew would agree with him.

(2) 'You shall love your neighbour as yourself.' That is a quotation from Leviticus 19:18. Jesus did one thing with it. In its original context it has to do only with *fellow Jews*. It would not have included the Gentiles, whom it was quite permissible to hate. But Jesus quoted it without qualification and without limiting boundaries. He took an old law and filled it with a new meaning.

The new thing that Jesus did was to put these two commandments together. No Rabbi had ever done that before. There is only one suggestion of connection previously. Round about 100 BC there was composed a series of tractates called The Testaments of the Twelve Patriarchs, in which an unknown writer put into the mouths of the patriarchs some very fine teaching. In the Testament of Issachar (5:2), we read:

Love the Lord and love your neighbour,
Have compassion on the poor and weak.

In the same testament (7:6), we read:

I loved the Lord,
Likewise also every man with my whole heart.

In the Testament of Dan (5:3), we read:

Love the Lord through all your life,
And one another with a true heart.

But no one until Jesus put the two commandments together and made them one. Religion to him was loving God and loving one another. He would have said that the only way to prove love for God is by showing love for others. The scribe willingly accepted this, and went on to say that such a love was better than all sacrifices. In that, he was in line with the highest thought of his people. Long, long ago Samuel had said, 'Has the Lord as great delight in burnt offerings and sacrifices, as in obedience to the voice of the Lord? Surely, to obey is better than sacrifice, and to heed than the fat of rams' (1 Samuel 15:22). Hosea had heard God say, 'I desire steadfast love and not sacrifice' (Hosea 6:6).

But it is always easy to let ritual take the place of love. It is always easy to let worship become a matter of the church building instead of a matter of the whole life. The priest and the Levite could pass by the wounded traveller (see Luke 10:25–37) because they were eager to get on with the ritual of the Temple. This scribe had risen beyond his contemporaries, and that is why he found himself in sympathy with Jesus.

There must have been a look of love in Jesus' eyes, and a look of appeal as he said to him, 'You have gone so far. Will you not come further and accept my way of things? Then you will be a true citizen of the kingdom.'

The Third Sunday before Advent
The Perfect Purification *and*
The Message of the Good News

Hebrews 9:24–28

Here the writer to the Hebrews stresses the way in which the work and the sacrifice of Christ are supreme.

(1) Christ did not enter a holy place that had been specially created for worship; he entered into the presence of God. We are to think of Christianity not in terms of church membership but in terms of intimate fellowship with God.

(2) Christ entered into the presence of God not only for his own sake but also for ours. It was to open the way for us and to plead our cause. In Christ, there is the greatest paradox in the world, the paradox of the greatest glory and the greatest service, the paradox of one for whom the world exists and who exists for the world, the paradox of the eternal king and the eternal servant.

(3) The sacrifice of Christ never needs to be made again. Year after year, the ritual of the Day of Atonement had to go on, and the things that blocked the road to God had to be atoned for; but, through Christ's sacrifice, the road to God is always open. Men and women were always sinners and always will be, but that does not mean that Christ must go on offering himself again and again. The road is open once and for all. We can draw a faint analogy of that. For a long time, a particular surgical operation may be impossible. Then some surgeon finds a way round the difficulties. From that day, that same road is open to all surgeons. We may put it this way: nothing need ever be added to what Jesus Christ has done to keep open the way to God's love for sinning humanity.

Finally, the writer to the Hebrews draws a parallel between human life and the life of Christ.

(1) Human beings die, and then comes the judgement. That itself was a shock to the Greeks, for they tended to believe that death was final. It was a belief expressed in the writings of the greatest Greek poets and dramatists. 'When earth once drinks the blood of a man,' said Aeschylus, 'there is death once and for all and there is no resurrection.' Euripides said: 'It cannot be the dead to light shall come.' 'For the one loss is this that never mortal maketh good again the life of man – though wealth may be re-won.' Homer makes Achilles say when he reaches the realm of the dead: 'Rather would I live upon the soil as the hireling of another, with a land-less man whose livelihood was small, than bear sway among all the dead who are no more.' The Greek poet Mimnermus writes with a kind of despair:

O Golden love, what life, what joy but thine?
Come death, when thou art gone, and make an end!

There is a simple Greek epitaph:

Farewell, tomb of Melitē; the best of women lies here, who loved her loving husband, Onesimus; you were most excellent, wherefore he longs for you after your death, for you were the best of wives. Farewell you too, dearest husband, only love my children.

As G. Lowes Dickinson, who wrote about the life of the ancient Greeks, points out, in the Greek, the first and the last word of that epitaph is 'Farewell!' Death was the end. When Tacitus wrote the tribute of biography to the great Agricola, all he could finish with was an 'if '. If there be any habitation for the spirits of just men, if, as the sages will have it, great souls perish not with the body, may you rest in peace.

'If' is the only word. Marcus Aurelius can say that when a person dies and the individual spark goes back to be lost in God, all that is left is 'dust, ashes, bones and stench'. The significant thing about this passage from Hebrews is its basic assumption that people will rise again. That is part of the certainty of the Christian creed; and the basic warning is that they rise to judgement.

(2) With Christ, it is different – he dies and rises and comes again, and he comes not to be judged but to judge. The early Church never forgot the hope of the second coming. That hope throbbed through their belief. But, for the unbeliever, that coming day was a day of terror. As the Book of Enoch describes the day of the Lord, before Christ came: 'For all you who are sinners there is no salvation, but upon you all will come destruction and a curse' (1 Enoch 5:6). In some way, the consummation must come. If in that day Christ comes as a friend, it can be only a day of glory; if he comes as a stranger or as one whom we have regarded as an enemy, it can be only a day of judgement. We may look to the end of things with joyous expectation or with shuddering terror. What makes the difference is how our hearts are with Christ.

Mark 1:14–20

In the summary of the message of Jesus found at the beginning of this passage there are three great, dominant words of the Christian faith.

(1) There is *the good news*. It was pre-eminently good news that Jesus came to bring to all. If we follow the word *evangelion, good news, gospel* through the New Testament, we can see at least something of its content.

(a) It is good news of *truth* (Galatians 2:5; Colossians 1:5). Until Jesus came, it was possible only to guess and grope after God. 'O that I knew where I might find him,' cried Job (Job 23:3). Marcus Aurelius said that the soul can see but dimly, and the word he uses is the Greek word for seeing things through water. But with the coming of Jesus we see clearly what God is like. No longer do we need to guess and grope; we know.

(b) It is good news of *hope* (Colossians 1:23). The ancient world was a pessimistic world. Seneca talked of 'our helplessness in necessary things'. In the struggle for goodness, humanity was defeated. The coming of Jesus brings hope to the hopeless heart.

(c) It is good news of *peace* (Ephesians 6:15). The penalty of being human is to have a split personality. In human nature, the beast and the angel are strangely intermingled. It is told that once Schopenhauer, the gloomy philosopher, was found wandering. He was asked, 'Who are you?' 'I wish you could tell me,' he answered. Robert Burns said of himself, 'My life reminded me of a ruined temple. What strength, what proportion in some parts! What unsightly gaps, what prostrate ruins in others!' The human predicament has always been that we are haunted both by sin and by goodness. The coming of Jesus unifies that disintegrated personality into one. We find victory over our warring selves by being conquered by Jesus Christ.

(d) It is good news of God's *promise* (Ephesians 3:6). It is true that the tendency has been to think of a God of threats rather than a God of promises. Non-Christian religions think of a demanding God; only Christianity tells of a God who is more ready to give than we are to ask.

(e) It is good news of *immortality* (2 Timothy 1:10). To the pagan, life was the road to death; but Jesus came with the good news that we are on the way to life rather than death.

(f) It is good news of *salvation* (Ephesians 1:13). That salvation is not merely a negative thing; it is also positive. It is not simply liberation from penalty and escape from past sin; it is the power to live life victoriously and to conquer sin. The message of Jesus is good news indeed.

(2) There is the word *repent*. Now repentance is not so easy as sometimes we think. The Greek word *metanoia* literally means *a change of mind*. We are very apt to confuse two things – sorrow for the consequences of sin and sorrow for sin. Many people become desperately sorry because of the mess that sin has got them into, but they know very well that, if they could be reasonably sure that they could escape the consequences, they would do the same thing again. It is not the sin that they hate; it is its consequences. Real repentance means coming not only to be sorry for the consequences of sin but to hate sin itself. Long ago, that wise old writer, Montaigne, wrote in his autobiography, 'Children should be taught to hate vice for its own texture, so that they will not only avoid it in action, but abominate it in their hearts – that the very thought of it may disgust them whatever form it takes.' Repentance means that anyone who was in love with sin comes to hate sin because of its exceeding sinfulness.

(3) There is the word *believe*. 'Believe', says Jesus, 'in the good news.' To believe in the good news simply means to take Jesus at his word, to believe that God is the kind of God that Jesus has told us about, to believe that God so loves the world that he will make any sacrifice to bring us back to himself, to believe that what sounds too good to be true is really true.

The Second Sunday before Advent
The Meaning of Christ for Us *and* His Coming Again

Hebrews 10:11–14, 19–25

In the second section of this passage the writer to the Hebrews comes to the practical implication of all that he has been saying. From theology, he turns to practical exhortation.

He begins by saying three things about Jesus.

(1) *Jesus is the living way to the presence of God.* We enter into the presence of God by means of the veil, that is, by the flesh of Jesus. What he means is this. In front of the Holy of Holies in the tabernacle, there hung the veil to screen off the presence of God. For anyone to enter into that presence, the veil would have to be torn apart. Jesus' flesh is what veiled his godhead. Charles Wesley, in his great hymn 'Hark the herald angels sing', made this appeal:

Veiled in flesh the godhead see.

It was when the flesh of Christ was torn upon the cross that people really saw God. As the tearing of the tabernacle veil opened the way to the presence of God, so the tearing of the flesh of Christ revealed the full greatness of his love and opened up the way to him.

(2) *Jesus is the high priest over God's house in the heavens.* The function of the priest was to build a bridge between the people and God. This means that Jesus not only shows us the way to God but also, when we get there, introduces us to his very presence.

(3) *Jesus is the one person who can really cleanse.* In the priestly ritual, the holy things were cleansed by being sprinkled with the blood

of the sacrifices. The high priest bathed himself in the brass basin of clear water. But these things were ineffective to remove the real pollution of sin. Only Jesus can really cleanse people. His is no external purification; by his presence and his Spirit, he cleanses their innermost thoughts and desires until they are really clean.

From this, the writer to the Hebrews goes on to urge three things.

(1) *Let us approach the presence of God.* That is to say, let us never forget the duty of worship. It is given to everyone to live in two worlds – this world of space and time, and the world of eternal things. Our danger is that we become so involved in this world that we forget the other. As the day begins, as the day ends and repeatedly throughout the day's activities, we should turn aside, if only for a moment, and enter God's presence. We all carry with us our own secret shrine, but so many of us forget to enter it.

(2) *Let us hold fast to our creed.* That is to say, let us never lose our grip of what we believe. The cynical voices may try to take our faith away; the materialists and their arguments may try to make us forget God; the events of life may conspire to shake our faith, but we must have a grip on the faith that nothing can loosen.

(3) *Let us put our minds to the task of taking thought for others.* That is to say, let us remember that we are Christians not only for our own sake but also for the sake of others. No one ever achieved personal salvation by devoting all time and energy to that purpose; but many have saved their souls by being so concerned for others that they forgot that they had their own souls to save. It is easy to drift into a kind of selfish Christianity; but a selfish Christianity is a contradiction in terms.

But the writer to the Hebrews goes on to outline our duty to others in the most practical way. He sees that duty extend in three directions.

(1) *We must encourage one another to noble living.* We can do that best by setting a good example. We can do it by reminding others of their traditions, their privileges and their responsibilities when they

are likely to forget them. It has been said that a saint is someone in whom Christ stands revealed; we can seek always to encourage others to goodness by showing them Christ.

(2) *We must worship together*. There were some among those to whom the writer of the Hebrews was writing who had abandoned the habit of meeting together. It is still possible for some to think that they are Christians and yet abandon the habit of worshipping with God's people in God's house on God's day. It would be a good thing if we remembered that, apart from anything else, to go to church is to demonstrate where our loyalty lies. Even if the sermon is poor and the worship uninspiring, the church service still gives us the chance to show to others what side we are on.

(3) *We must encourage one another*. One of the highest of human duties is that of encouragement. It is easy to laugh at people's ideals, to pour cold water on their enthusiasm, to discourage them. The world is full of discouragers; we have a Christian duty to encourage one another. So many times, words of praise or thanks or appreciation or cheer have kept people on their feet. Blessed are those who speak such words.

Finally, the writer says that our Christian duty to each other is all the more pressing because the time is short. The day is approaching. He is thinking of the second coming of Christ when things as we know them will be ended. The early Church lived in that expectation. Whether or not we still do, we must realize that none of us knows when the summons to rise and go will come to us also. In the time we have, it is our duty to do all the good we can to all the people we can in all the ways we can.

Mark 13:1–8

This passage begins with the prophecy of Jesus which foretold the doom of Jerusalem. The Temple which Herod built was one of the wonders of the world. It was begun in 20–19 BC and in the time of Jesus was not yet completely finished. It was built on the top of Mount Moriah. Instead of levelling off the summit of the mountain, a kind of vast platform was formed by raising up walls of massive masonry and enclosing the whole area. On these walls a platform was laid, strengthened by piers which distributed the weight of the superstructure. The Jewish historian Josephus tells us that some of these stones were 40 feet long by 12 feet high by 18 feet wide. It would be some of these vast stones that moved the Galilaean disciples to such wondering amazement.

The most magnificent entrance to the Temple was at the southwest angle. Here between the city and the Temple hill there stretched the Tyropoeon Valley. A marvellous bridge spanned the valley. Each arch was 41.5 feet and there were stones used in the building of it which measured 24 feet long. The Tyropoeon valley was no less than 225 feet below. The breadth of the cleft that the bridge spanned was 354 feet, and the bridge itself was 50 feet in breadth. The bridge led straight into the Royal Porch. The porch consisted of a double row of Corinthian pillars all 37.5 feet high and each one cut out of one solid block of marble.

Of the actual Temple building itself, the holy place, Josephus writes, 'Now the outward face of the Temple in its front wanted nothing that was likely to surprise men's minds or their eyes, for it was covered all over with plates of gold of great weight, and, at the first rising of the sun, reflected back a very fiery splendour, and made those who forced themselves to look upon it to turn their eyes away, just as they would have done at the sun's own rays. But this Temple appeared to strangers, when they were at a distance, like a mountain covered with snow, for, as to those parts of it which were not gilt, they were exceeding white . . . Of its stones, some of them were forty-five cubits in length, five in height and six in breadth.' (A cubit was eighteen inches.)

It was all this splendour that so impressed the disciples. The Temple seemed the summit of human art and achievement, and seemed so vast and solid that it would stand forever. But Jesus made the astonishing statement that the day was coming when not one of these stones would stand upon another. In less than fifty years his prophecy came tragically true. As Robert Bridges wrote so eloquently in that great hymn, 'All my hope on God is founded':

> Pride of man and earthly glory,
> Sword and crown betray his trust;
> What with care and toil he buildeth,
> Tower and temple, fall to dust.
> But God's power,
> Hour by hour,
> Is my temple and my tower.

In verses 7–8 Jesus unmistakably speaks of his coming again. But he clothes the idea in pictures which are part and parcel of the apparatus connected with the day of the Lord. The day of the Lord was to be preceded by a time of wars. Fourth Ezra [2 Esdras] declares that before the day of the Lord there will be

> Earthquakes
> Tumult of peoples,
> Intrigues of nations,
> Wavering of leaders,
> Confusion of princes. (9:3)

The Sibylline Oracles foresee that

> King captures king and takes his land, and nations
> ravage nations and potentates people, and rulers all flee

to another land, and the land is changed in men and a
barbarian empire ravages Hellas and drains the rich land
of its wealth, and men come face to face in strife.
(3:635–41)

So it is abundantly clear that when Jesus spoke of wars and
rumours of wars he was using pictures which were part and parcel
of Jewish dreams of the future.

When we read these pictorial words of Jesus about the second
coming, we must remember that he is giving us neither a map of
eternity nor a timetable to the future, but that he is simply using
the language and the pictures that many Jews knew and used for
centuries before him.

But it is extremely interesting to note that the things Jesus
prophesied were in fact happening. He prophesied wars, and the
dreaded Parthians were in fact pressing in on the Roman frontiers.
He prophesied earthquakes, and within forty years the Roman
world was aghast at the earthquake which devastated Laodicaea
and at the eruption of Vesuvius, which buried Pompeii in lava. He
prophesied famines, and there was famine in Rome in the days of
Claudius. It was in fact such a time of terror in the near future that
when Tacitus began his histories he said that everything happening seemed to prove that the gods were seeking not salvation but
vengeance on the Roman Empire.

In this passage, the one thing that we must retain is the fact that
Jesus did foretell that he would come again. The imagery we can
disregard.

The Sunday next before Advent
The Titles of Jesus and the Coming Glory *and* Jesus and Pilate

Revelation 1:4b–8

In this passage, three great titles are given to Jesus Christ.

(1) He is the witness on whom we can rely. It is a favourite idea of the Fourth Gospel that Jesus is a witness of the truth of God. Jesus said to Nicodemus: 'Very truly, I tell you, we speak of what we know and testify to what we have seen' (John 3:11). Jesus said to Pilate: 'For this I came into the world, to testify to the truth' (John 18:37). A witness is essentially a person who speaks from first-hand knowledge. That is why Jesus is God's witness. He is uniquely the person with first-hand knowledge about God.

(2) He is the first-born of the dead. The word for *firstborn* is *prōtotokos*. It can have two meanings. (a) It can mean literally *first-born*. If it is used in this sense, the reference must be to the resurrection. Through his resurrection, Jesus gained a victory over death, which all who believe in him may share. (b) Since the first-born was the son who inherited his father's honour and power, *prōtotokos* comes to mean *one with power and honour, one who occupies the first place*. When Paul speaks of Jesus as the first-born of all creation (Colossians 1:15), he means that the first place of honour and glory belongs to him. If we take the word in this sense – and probably we should – it means that Jesus is Lord of the dead as he is Lord of the living. There is no part of the universe, in this world or in the world to come, and nothing in life or in death of which Jesus Christ is not Lord.

(3) He is the ruler of kings on earth. There are two things to note here. (a) This is a reminiscence of Psalm 89:27: 'I will make him the firstborn, the highest of the kings of the earth.' That was always taken by Jewish scholars to be a description of the coming Messiah; and, therefore, to say that Jesus is the ruler of kings on earth is to claim that he is the Messiah. (b) In *The Apocalypse of St John*, H. B. Swete very beautifully points out the connection between this title of Jesus and the temptation story. In that story, the devil took Jesus up into a high mountain and showed him all the kingdoms of the earth and their glory and said: 'All these I will give you, if you will fall down and worship me' (Matthew 4:9; Luke 4:6–7).

It was the devil's claim that the kingdoms of the earth were delivered into his power (Luke 4:6); and it was his suggestion that, if Jesus would strike a bargain with him, he would give him a share in them. The amazing thing is that what the devil promised Jesus – and could never have given him – Jesus won for himself by the suffering of the cross and the power of the resurrection. Not compromise with evil but the unswerving loyalty and the unfailing love which accepted the cross brought Jesus his universal lordship.

In the final verses, John sets down the motto and the text of his whole book, his confidence in the triumphant return of Christ, which would rescue Christians in distress from the cruelty of their enemies.

(1) To Christians, the return of Christ is a *promise on which to feed the soul*. John takes as his picture of that return Daniel's vision: 'As I watched in the night visions, I saw one like a [son of man] coming with the clouds of heaven. And he came to the Ancient One and was presented before him. To him was given dominion and glory and kingship, that all peoples, nations and languages should serve him' (Daniel 7:13–14). It is from that passage in Daniel that there emerges the ever-recurring picture of the Son of Man coming on the clouds (Mark 13:26, 14:62; Matthew 24:30, 26:64). When we strip away the purely temporary imagery – we, for instance, no

longer think of heaven as a localized place above the sky – we are left with the unchanging truth that the day will come when Jesus Christ will be Lord of all. In that hope, there has always been the source of strength and the comfort of Christians for whom life was difficult and for whom faith meant death.

(2) To the enemies of Christ, *the return of Christ is a threat*. To make this point, John again quotes the Old Testament, from Zechariah 12:10, which contains the words: 'When they look on the one whom they have pierced, they shall mourn for him, as one mourns for an only child, and weep bitterly over him, as one weeps over a firstborn.' The story behind the Zechariah saying is this. God gave his people a good shepherd; but the people in their disobedient folly killed him and took to themselves evil and self-seeking shepherds. But the day will come when in the grace of God they will bitterly repent, and in that day they will look on the good shepherd whom they pierced and will sorrowfully lament for him and for what they have done. John takes that picture and applies it to Jesus. The day will come when all people, even those who crucified him, will look on him again; and, this time, he will be not a broken figure on a cross but a regal figure to whom universal dominion has been given. The first reference of these words is to the Jews and the Romans who actually crucified Jesus. But, in every age, all who sin crucify him again. The day will come when those who disregarded and those who opposed Jesus Christ will find him the Lord of the universe and the judge of their souls.

John 18:33–37

John's account of the trial of Jesus is the most dramatic in the New Testament, and the drama of this passage lies in the clash and interplay of personalities. Let us consider Pilate.

(1) There is a hint of Pilate's ingrained attitude of contempt. He asked Jesus if he was a king. Jesus asked whether he asked this

on the basis of what he himself had discovered, or on the basis of information indirectly received. Pilate's answer was: 'Am I a Jew? How do you expect me to know anything about Jewish affairs?' He was too proud to involve himself in what he regarded as Jewish squabbles and superstitions. And that pride was exactly what made him a bad governor. No one can govern a people without making an attempt to understand them and to enter into their thoughts and minds.

(2) There is a kind of superstitious curiosity about Pilate. He wished to know where Jesus came from – and it was more than Jesus' native place that he was thinking of. When he heard that Jesus had claimed to be the Son of God, he was still more disturbed. Pilate was superstitious rather than religious, fearing that there might be something in it. He was afraid to come to a decision in Jesus' favour because of the Jews; he was equally afraid to come to a decision against him, because he had the lurking suspicion that God might be in this.

(3) At the heart of Pilate was a wistful longing. When Jesus said that he had come to witness to the truth, Pilate's answer was: 'What is truth?' There are many ways in which that question might be asked. It might be asked in cynical and sardonic humour. The philosopher Francis Bacon immortalized Pilate's answer, when he wrote: 'What is truth? said jesting Pilate; and would not stay for an answer.' But it was not in cynical humour that Pilate asked this question; nor was it the question of a man who did not care. Here was the chink in his armour. He asked the question wistfully and wearily.

Pilate by this world's standards was a successful man. He had come almost to the top of the Roman civil service; he was governor-general of a Roman province; but there was something missing. Here in the presence of this simple, disturbing, hated Galilaean, Pilate felt that for him the truth was still a mystery – and that now he had got himself into a situation where there was no chance to learn it. It may be he jested, but it was the jest of despair. The historian Philip Gibbs tells of listening to a debate between his fellow historian Margaret Irwin, the poets T. S. Eliot, and C. Day Lewis and other distinguished people on the subject, 'Is this life worth living?' 'True, they jested,' he said, 'but they jested like jesters knocking at the door of death.'

Pilate was like that. Into his life there came Jesus, and suddenly he saw what he had missed. That day he might have found all that he had missed; but he had not the courage to defy the world in spite of his past, and to take his stand with Christ and a future which was glorious.

Jesus speaks with utter directness to us of his kingdom; it is not, he says, of this earth. The atmosphere in Jerusalem was always explosive; during the Passover it was sheer dynamite. The Romans were well aware of that, and during the Passover time they always drafted extra troops into Jerusalem. But Pilate never at any time had more than 3,000 men under his command. Some would be in Caesarea, his headquarters; some would be on garrison duty in Samaria; there cannot really have been more than a few hundred on duty in Jerusalem. If Jesus had wished to raise the standard of rebellion and to fight it out, he could have done it easily enough. But he makes it quite clear that he claims to be a king and equally clear that his kingdom is not based on force but is a kingdom in the hearts of men and women. He would never deny that he aimed at conquest; but it was the conquest of love.

Jesus tells us why he came into the world. He came to witness to the truth; he came to tell people the truth about God, the truth about themselves, and the truth about life. As the American poet Ralph Waldo Emerson put it in these lines from his poem 'Give All to Love':

When half-gods go,
The gods arrive.

The days of guessings and gropings and half-truths were gone. He came to tell men and women the truth. That is one of the great reasons why we must either accept or refuse Christ. There is no half-way house about the truth. We either accept it or reject it; and Christ is the truth.

Lightning Source UK Ltd.
Milton Keynes UK
UKHW02f2043260418
321710UK00005B/249/P

9 780861 537976